HARVARD HISTORICAL STUDIES

Published under the direction of the Department of History
from the income of the
Henry Warren Torrey Fund

Volume LXXXII

LEONARDO BRUNI
Tomb, Santa Croce, Florence
(Courtesy of Anne Markham Schulz)

The Development of Florentine Humanist

Historiography in the Fifteenth Century

Donald J. Wilcox

HARVARD UNIVERSITY PRESS

Cambridge, Massachusetts

1969

To My Parents

Acknowledgments

In the five years I have devoted to this study, debts have accumulated which are too profound to assess and too numerous to list. Most difficult of all to acknowledge are those to people, including the professors of my earliest years in college, who first introduced me to intellectual life and helped in formulating those questions which I have been trying to refine and answer ever since.

Several scholars, in reading sections of the manuscript and making important criticisms, have lent aid which is easier to identify though no less crucial to this study. In particular, Professor Hannah Holborn Gray of the University of Chicago spent many an hour pointing out the hazy places in my reasoning with a sympathy undeserved but highly appreciated. Research on the topic was facilitated by a fellowship from Harvard University for study in Florence during the academic year 1963–1964 and by a fellowship from the Newberry Library where a most pleasant and rewarding year was spent.

Two people must be singled out for providing both precise assistance with this study and a more general effect on my personal and intellectual development. Professor Myron Gilmore, through his humane scholarship, through his tolerance for new ideas in their formative stages, and in his creative and analytical approach to historical writing, has, since my entry into graduate school, set an example which has been a continual source of inspiration and support. My intellectual debt to the work of Professor Hans Baron is so clear in the following pages that I hardly need expatiate upon it. During my stay at the Newberry Library he showed that intense and genuine interest in the work of a young scholar which is such an abiding characteristic of Professor Baron. Unbending in both criticism and encouragement, he deepened my appreciation of his immense contribution to the field and gave me confidence in the significance of my own work. These two scholars have provided not only many of the analytical tools to be found in this book but also many of the values and commitments which underlie it. I sincerely hope that it does not wholly disappoint their trust.

Finally, Doctor David Walters of the Biology department of Harvard University read the manuscript with the critical eye of one outside the field of history and pointed out numerous instances where needlessly professional language had been used. He must be given credit for much of whatever interest this book may afford the nonspecialist.

Donald J. Wilcox

Cambridge, Massachusetts
June 1968

Contents

The Development of Florentine Humanist
Historiography in the Fifteenth Century

Chapter One

The Historical Perspective

Only with difficulty can the modern historian appreciate the full extent to which his art was honored in Renaissance Florence. The tomb of Leonardo Bruni, erected by the Florentines in the church of Santa Croce as a measure of their regard for the great chancellor, affords visible testimony to this reverence for historical writing. Graphically illustrating a passion for history which Bruni himself had once likened to Orpheus' love for Euridice,[1] the marble figure of the humanist clasps to its breast the history of Florence on which he had lavished care and effort during the last thirty years of his life.[2]

[1] "Equidem fateor non tam cupide Orpheum . . . Eurydicis amore infernas adiisse sedes, quam ego si spes modo aliqua offeratur antiquos illos praestantes viros intuendi, ad ultimas penetrarim terras. Quos quia oculis intueri non licet, quod secundum est: mente et cogitatione libens complector, resque ab illis gestas, in quibus huius soli decus et gloria continetur, omnibus esse cognitas quam maxime opto." (L. Bruni, "Prooemium in commentaria primi belli Punici," in H. Baron, *Leonardo Bruni Aretino: Humanistisch-Philosophische Schriften* [Leipzig, 1928], p. 122.) This passage refers explicitly to the ancients, but Bruni's regard for history in general is clear not only from the energy he devoted to the Florentine history but also from his direct statements on its value. See, for instance, his letter to the King of Spain (*Leonardo Bruni Arretini: Epistolarum libri VIII*, ed. L. Mehus [Florence, 1741], book VII, ep. 6), in which he says, "Historia quoque magistra vitae, quantum affere regenti fructum potest." (This work is cited hereafter as Bruni, *Epistolae*.)

[2] See Naldo Naldi, *Vita Janotii Manetti*, in vol. XX of *Rerum Italicarum scriptores* (hereafter *RR.II.SS.*), ed. L. Muratori (Milan, 1731), col. 544: "Supra pectus eius apposito libro in quo ille Historiam populi fiorentini magna sua cum laude prosequutus fuisset." Vespasiano da Bisticci, whom Naldi has largely copied in writing his own life of Manetti, does not mention this, though he does describe other parts of the funeral ceremony. Naldi, however, was nine years old when Bruni died and could have secured the information on his own. Even if Naldi's attribution is no more than probable, as E. Panofsky suggests in *Tomb Sculpture* (New York,

Buried next to Bruni in Santa Croce is another Florentine who served the city with both his political genius and intellectual talents. The simple inscription "Tanto nomini nullum par elogium" appears on Machiavelli's eighteenth-century tomb, suggesting that a more recent age did not presume to identify his most significant achievement. But Machiavelli's own contemporaries were not so modest. In the gallery Doria-Pamphili in Rome stands a portrait executed by an unknown sixteenth-century Florentine. Here the author of the *Prince* and the *Discourses*, the self-proclaimed expert on military affairs, the experienced diplomat and one of the finest dramatists of his age, is characterized by the simple phrase "Nicholaus Machiavellus Historiarum Scriptor."

Between Bruni's appointment in 1427 [3] and the expulsion of the Medici in 1494, which opened the way to Machiavelli's political career, five humanists held the post of first chancellor for the republic.[4] Of these five only Carlo Marsuppini, chancellor from 1444 to 1453 and Bruni's successor in that office, failed to produce a work of history. Of the four historians only Benedetto Accolti, chancellor from 1458 to 1464, did not write a history of Florence. It is to the Florentine histories of the three remaining chancellors that these chapters are devoted.

Leonardo Bruni, an Aretine by birth who had come to Florence while still an adolescent, directed the Florentine chancery from 1427 until his death in 1444.[5] Well before his appointment, how-

1964), p. 74, the statement shows the belief among fifteenth-century Florentines that the book was the Florentine history.

[3] This was Bruni's second appointment. He had served briefly in 1410.

[4] The standard work on the Florentine chancery is still D. Marzi, *La cancelleria della repubblica fiorentina* (San Casciano, 1910). For an interpretive study of the role of the chancery, see E. Garin, "I cancellieri umanisti della repubblica fiorentina da Coluccio Salutati a Bartolommeo Scala," *Rivista storica italiana*, 71 (1959), 185–208. Garin suggests that from Salutati to Scala there was a decline both in the personal stature of the chancellors and in the extent of their political influence. The temptation to see this decline manifested in the histories of Bruni, Poggio, and Scala must, however, be resisted. As chancellors the historians had access to state documents and other archival materials, an access of which Bruni at least took considerable advantage (see the beginning of chap. iv), but any attempt to relate Bruni's historical approach to concrete aspects of his practical experience would involve profitless speculation beyond the available evidence. It would be still more tenuous to suggest a precise relationship between the experience and ideas of Poggio and Scala.

[5] For the details of Bruni's life see L. Martines, *The Social World of Florentine Humanists: 1390–1460* (Princeton, 1963), especially pp. 117–123; and G. Mancini, "Aggiunte e correzioni alla vita di Leonardo Bruni," in *Istoria fiorentina di L. Aretino tradotta in volgare da D. Acciaiuoli*, ed. G. Mancini et al. (3 vols.; Florence: Le Monnier, 1855–1860). F. Beck, *Studien zu Leonardo Bruni* (Berlin, 1912), is less reliable.

ever, he had already begun work on his *Historiae Florentini populi*, for in 1415 he wrote to Poggio Bracciolini, who would one day succeed him both as chancellor and as Florentine historian, describing the difficulties encountered in gathering material for the first book.[6] In fact, by 1429 the first six books were completed and published,[7] and in 1439 the first nine books were formally presented to the Florentine *signoria* (governing council).[8]

In spite of the formal presentation, there is no positive evidence that Bruni wrote the *Historiae* either as part of his official duties in the chancery or under a commission from the republic.[9] The lack of such evidence should not, however, obscure the peculiarly close

[6] Bruni, *Epistolae*, book IV, p. 4.

[7] The oldest dated manuscript is of June 1429. See E. Santini, *Leonardo Bruni Aretino e i suoi "Historiarum florentini populi libri xii"* (Pisa, 1910), pp 125–127. H. Baron, *The Crisis of the Early Italian Renaissance* (Princeton, 1955), p. 611, n. 14, and p. 618, no. 4, has devoted much attention to dating individual books of this first section. (The second edition of *Crisis* [Princeton, 1966] is revised and enlarged, but since the notes of the first edition are more complete, all references here are to the first edition unless otherwise stated.) Book II, Baron says, was written during the first half of 1419; Book III in 1420; Book IV in 1421; Books V and VI, between the autumn of 1426 and the end of 1428. Baron has marshaled a great deal of evidence, both internal and external, in support of his dating, and no attempt has been made here to improve upon it.

[8] See Archivio di Stato di Firenze, *Provvisioni Registri*, 129, c. 277–278, printed in Santini, *Leonardo*, pp. 139–141.

[9] Several registers of archival documents covering the period from 1416 to 1444 were consulted while seeking this sort of evidence, including the formal *Provvisioni registri*, the *Consulte e pratiche*, the *Deliberazione di signore e collegi*, and the *Uscite* of both the *scrivano di camera* and the *notario di camera*. Since the commission for Machiavelli's history of Florence appears in the *Uscita di studiolo*, that source was also investigated. In addition to the basic archival sources of the republic, other collections were examined, including the available *spogli* of the Strozzi archives, which summarize various archival documents that are no longer available.

None of these sources contained any indication either that Bruni had been commissioned by the republic or that he had ever been paid by the commune specifically for the *Historiae*. A further search in the archives of the more important guilds, as well as those of the Parte Guelfa, was similarly fruitless, virtually ruling out the possibility that he had been commissioned by one of the semipublic institutions of Florence. (E. H. Gombrich, "The Early Medici as Patrons of Art," in *Italian Renaissance Studies*, ed. E. F. Jacob [London, 1960], pp. 279–311, has shown that such institutions were an important instrument of patronage in this period.)

Yet the gaps in the sources are sufficiently large that the possibility of such a commission cannot be completely excluded. The principal *Uscite*, which record disbursements from the treasury, are missing for the periods August 1416–April 1417, April 1428–1431, and from March 1436 on. Other series of treasury documents contain even larger gaps. There is, for instance, no record of disbursements of any kind to Bruni, even for his salary as chancellor, though he was certainly paid. Furthermore, there are records of other chancellors being paid (see *Uscita del scrivano di camera*, Serie Piccolo, May 14, 1416, c. 9: "Ser Pagliolo di Ser Lando Fortini, chancelliere del commune di Firenze a detto ufficio detto per anno comminciato a die 9 Aprile, 1415 – 70 Florini").

relationship between Bruni and the Florentine state, a relationship which lends a quasi-official tone to the work. In the first place, Bruni obtained and used a rare exemption from direct taxes.[10] The attention to Bruni's personal well-being suggested by this exemption was matched by a concern for a wider dissemination of the *Historiae* than could be afforded by the original Latin text. In 1442 the signoria empowered Bruni to choose a translator for the work and pay him from the funds of the commune.[11] The Florentines were rewarded for their expense with Donato Acciaiuoli's translation of the history, completed by 1473.[12]

[10] The grants of this exemption coincide, whether by happenstance or not, with significant dates in the writing of the *Historiae*, the first grant being awarded in 1416 and the second in 1439 (see documents in Santini, *Leonardo*, pp. 133–141). L. Martines, *The Social World*, p. 168, n. 115, finds only six other persons who, in making their declarations for the *catasto* of 1427, claim this sort of exemption. The two for whom the document granting the exemption can be found claim it on highly specific grounds. For example, Francesco Nerli is exempted for a period of twenty years to lighten the burden on the Nerli family while a brother pursues a business career in France (*Provvisioni registri*, 108, c. 4, April 14, 1418). The most common ground for a general tax reduction, as opposed to an exemption, is poverty, and application for this must be made each year (see *Provvisioni registri*, 111, c. 131, concerning an exemption for Biagio di Guasconi because of a debt of 110 florins). Of the six instances Martines has found, only Francesco Nerli and Bruni were still claiming an exemption in 1427.

That Bruni used his exemption on a permanent basis is clearly seen from his two identical pronouncements in 1427 (*Portata al catasto*, 29, c. 406–416) and 1433 (*Portata al catasto*, 477, c. 653): "Protesto per questo raporto io non intendo ne consento in alcuno modo partirmi dalle conventioni le quali io ho col comune di Firenze expresse nel privilegio mio, il quale privilegio intendo usare et adomando che mi sia osservato con ogni immunità et beneficio che in esso si contiene, ne intendo ne aconsento che mie sustantie siano messe o scripte ne catasto ma questo raporto faccio per vostro commandamento a questo fine che possiate distinguere le sustantie mie da quelle degli altri cittadini."

[11] The deliberations of the *Signori e collegi* for September 1442 (*Deliberazione*, 58, c. 36v) permit a translator to be chosen "a nobili viro domino Leonardi Francesci Bruni dignissimo cancellaris communis Fiorentinis," to be paid as much as sixty florins "pro translatandi laudabile opus factum et compositum per dictum dominum Leonardum." The relevant *Uscite*, which would record the actual disbursement of the sum, are unfortunately not available.

[12] In the *Proèmio* to his translation Acciaiuoli clearly states that he is doing the work at the behest of the signoria. Dedicated to the "Excellentissimi signori priori di libertà e gonfaloniere di justizia del popolo florentine," the Proèmio begins, "Molto sono le cagioni eccellentissimi Signori che mi hanno indotto a tradurre di latino in volgare la Istoria di Firenze elegantissimamente composta da Leonardo Aretino. La prima e principale si è per ubbidire alla vostra eccelsa signoria e quanto porta la facoltà del mio ingegno satisfare a vostri giusti ed onesti desideri." The Proèmio suggests, however, that Leonardo did not live to carry out his duty of choosing a translator, nor did he supervise the first part of the translation.

The date for the completion of the translation is taken from the *Istoria fiorentina* (Venice, 1476). On the final page of the text we find, "Fine del duodecimo et ultimo libro della historia del popolo Fiorentino composta da messer Leonardo Are-

The formal presentation of 1439 was not repeated, however, and Bruni finished only three more books, leaving the *Historiae* uncompleted at his death.[13] In these twelve books Bruni, after a short introduction treating the city from its origins as a Roman colony to its emergence as an independent commune in the middle of the thirteenth century, presents a detailed account of Florentine history from 1250 to the death of Giangaleazzo of Milan in 1402.

Poggio Bracciolini, the second of the fifteenth-century chancellors to write the history of the republic, entered the service of Florence in 1453 after a distinguished career in the Roman curia and with a long-established reputation as a humanist and man of letters.[14] Already a septuagenarian at the time of his appointment, Poggio soon found his duties as chancellor excessive and moved to the country in semiretirement. Despite the declining energies suggested by his departure from the chancery, Poggio between 1455 and 1459 composed eight books of a history of Florence, leaving the work (like Bruni's) unfinished at his death.[15]

---

tino in latino et tradocta in lingua tosca da Donato Acciaiuoli, a di XXVII d'agosto, MCCCCLXXIII."

The commune's continued interest in the work is attested by the fact that copies of it were paid for out of the treasury. A *spoglio* of various fiscal documents made by Carlo Strozzi in 1670 contains the following entry: "Joanni Pieri Ser Picciardi scriptori storie fio. pro parte eis laboris, 4 Florini August 9, 1470" (*Strozziana* II, 52, c. 251; the original document is lost). The small sum definitely indicates a scribe, and the proximity of the date to Acciaiuoli's translation suggests that this is the work in question.

A tentative connection between the scribe and Acciaiuoli can be suggested. There was no Picciardi family in Florence but there was a family of Piccardi, and it is to this family that the document doubtless refers. On May 23, 1471, three brothers of the family, Francesco, Ugolino, and Giovanni, sold some property of their late father's (Archivio Diplomatico Fiorentino, *Spoglio delle carte di S. M. Nuova*; noted in the *Poligrafo* of Gargagni, 1546). If this was indeed the Giovanni who copied out the *Istoria fiorentina* for the commune, then the family had further dealings with Donato, for Giovanni's brother Francesco transcribed the Italian translation of Acciaiuoli's Latin oration to Sixtus IV, delivered October 3, 1471 (National Library at Florence, S. II, VI, 17).

13 Baron has also refined the traditional dating of the last four books, placing the composition of Book IX in 1437–38 and Books X, XI, and XII between mid-1441 and early 1444 (see *Crisis*, p. 630, n. 37). For evidence that contemporaries of Bruni did not consider the *Historiae* to be a completed work, see Poggio's funeral oration in Bruni's *Epistolae* (I, cxii), "Non autem quod proposuerat ad extremum deduxit."

14 The best work on Poggio's life is still E. Walser, *Poggius Florentinus: Leben und Werke* (Berlin, 1914). See also D. Bacci, *Poggio Bracciolini nella luce dei suoi tempi* (Florence, 1959), and *Cenni biografici e religiosi di Poggio Bracciolini* (Florence, 1963).

15 See Appendix A.

Poggio's *Historia fiorentina*, researched and written in far less time than Bruni had spent on the *Historiae Florentini populi*, is smaller both in scope and in size. It provides detailed coverage of the century of Florentine history between the first war with Giovanni Visconti of Milan in 1350 and the conclusion of the Holy League under the leadership of Nicholas V in 1455. Within this period Poggio concentrates on the theme of Florence's wars, particularly those fought with the Visconti of Milan.

The last of the chancellor-historians of Florence in this century was Bartolommeo della Scala. Chancellor for over thirty years, Scala held the office even longer than had Coluccio Salutati, the first of the great humanist chancellors, who had so ably guided Florence's foreign relations during the critical period between the War of Eight Saints and the death of Giangaleazzo Visconti in 1402.[16] In spite of his long service to Florence, Scala's history of the city is the shortest of the three. Of a projected twenty books, Scala had finished only four when he died in 1497.[17] These four, however, show that Scala's intended scope is greater than either Bruni's or Poggio's, for he planned to write a detailed history of Florence from its legendary beginnings to his own day, and the first four books cover only the period down to the battle of Tagliacozzo in 1267.

These three men and their histories are similar in several ways. The historians were all chancellors and the histories all of Florence. None of the men was a native Florentine, Bruni being an Aretine, Poggio a native of Terranuova Bracciolini, and Scala of Colle di Val d'Elsa. All were born of obscure parentage.[18] All three began writing their histories late in life, and all were interrupted in their labors by death. More important is the chronological relationship among the histories. Taken together, they were composed over a broad section of the fifteenth century, from 1415, when Bruni started work on the first book of the *Historiae*, to the death of Scala in 1497. Moreover, the subject matter of the books, while unified by the common theme of Florentine history, avoids monotony and

16 Scala entered the chancery by 1465, and, though he was briefly discharged in 1494, he was still first chancellor at his death in 1497 (see Marzi, *La cancelleria*, p. 236). Garin ("I cancellieri") has suggested that, in spite of his long tenure, Scala was not deeply involved in the political life of the republic and served a more or less ornamental function. The letters of Scala, preserved in the Archivio di Stato, seem, however, to indicate that he was close to Lorenzo and served as liaison between Lorenzo and the members of the signoria, particularly while Lorenzo was in Naples.

17 See Appendix B.

18 Scala, in particular, boasts of having risen from the ranks of the underprivileged.

repetition because of the different periods of time which each historian treats. The only significant overlap is the period between 1350 and 1400, which is discussed by both Bruni and Poggio.

The histories, however, are bound together by similarities beyond these common topics and external resemblances. They betray similar historical presuppositions, analytical tools, and narrative techniques. In fact, as one of its chief tasks the present study seeks to expose the internal connections among the three histories as an illustration of the general coherence of the humanist historical art in fifteenth-century Florence.

Subsequent chapters will analyze the internal structure and content of the histories in order to illustrate their basic coherence. This chapter will fix upon the historical context which gives meaning to such an approach. It is of crucial importance to understand how the critical appreciation of humanist historiography develops, particularly in the last quarter of the fifteenth century and the early years of the sixteenth.

The years from 1480 to 1525 boast of two achievements in the understanding of humanist historiography; though both are important, they have had contradictory effects. First of all, there was a growing appreciation of the basic goals of the humanist historians together with an attempt to judge their success in achieving these goals. But this positive criticism was accompanied by an equally strong tendency to undermine the goals of humanist historians and suggest new ones more proper for an historian to pursue. It is the second aspect of fifteenth- and early sixteenth-century criticism which has most influenced later critics, especially those of the nineteenth century, and which makes a balanced judgment on Bruni, Poggio, and Scala so difficult in the twentieth.

Enthusiasm for humanist history slightly but perceptibly diminished during the course of the fifteenth century, a process which cannot wholly be explained by the obvious fact that the works themselves decline in importance and stature during this period. The *Historiae Florentini populi* of Leonardo Bruni, received by his humanist circle with praise and wonder and considered the masterpiece of the author, were heralded as a work which would introduce an age of historical writing to rival that of Livy himself. The official attention which the Florentine signoria paid to both Bruni and his history has already been noted. Nor did the work go unnoticed by other Italians. In a letter to two secretaries of the Visconti at Milan, the Archbishop of that city, Bartolommeo della Capra, writing from Genoa, mentions Bruni's achievement with evident admiration.[19] The signoria, perhaps because of the attention the history commanded outside Florence, but more probably because of the Florentines' own eagerness to consult it, carefully controlled the use of its copy. Of the documents which record the lending of the work only a scrap has survived, but this shows that it was lent five times between 1446 and 1450, when at least the first half of the work had been published for over twenty years.[20]

The full extent of contemporary admiration for the *Historiae* becomes evident only after Bruni's death. Poggio Bracciolini, who would eventually succeed Bruni both as chancellor and as historian of Florence, composed a funeral oration for Bruni in which the *Historiae* are singled out among Bruni's achievements: "But what must receive the highest praise from all ages is the history of Florentine affairs which he wrote in twelve books . . . In this splendidly written work by an author of highest superiority the fame and name of Florence will certainly come down to posterity and even into eternity." [21] A contemporary anonymous *laudatio* of Bruni also notes his achievement with respect. "Having undertaken to write of Florentine affairs, he embellished a history in twelve books by which he kept alive the memory of many things done by Florence which were already being forgotten." [22]

[19] "Florentini nuper in scriptis sua gesta fecerunt sex libris distincta." The letter, dated April 9, 1429, and found in the Biblioteca Ambrosiana at Milan, was first published by R. Sabbadini in the *Archivio storico Lombardo*, 43 (1916), 27. Since the first six books of the *Historiae* could not have been published much before the end of 1428, the speed with which news of their composition, and presumably a copy of the books themselves, spread through a territory with which Florence had been at war until 1428 is truly remarkable. It indicates the high regard in which Bruni in particular and the writing of history in general were held by Italians of the fifteenth century.

[20] *Carte di Corredo*, 39, c. 192. Of the five lendings, two are of only the first volume, suggesting that it was not simply the novelty of the recently finished last three books which created the interest, and furthermore, that in an earlier period requests to borrow the book had been even more frequent. Many persons, moreover, must have studied the books without removing them from the palace.

[21] "Sed quod sibi summam etiam laudem omnibus afferet seculis historia est de rebus Florentinorum duodecim libris scripta . . . Opus certe luculentum et quo fama nomenque Florentiae urbis in aeternum ad posteros certo et maximae auctoritatis scriptore damanabitur" (Bruni, *Epistolae*, cviii). Mehus includes in the epistolary, in addition to the text of Poggio's oration, the one delivered by Manetti on the same occasion. The contemporary sources which describe the service mention only Manetti's oration (see Santini, *Leonardo*, p. 8). Manetti concentrates less on Leonardo than on the general state of learning at Leonardo's death.

[22] "Hinc res gestas florentini populi scribere adorsus, supra quantum memoria haberi potuit florentiae civitatis historiam, quae eam obliterata poene remanserat

Considering the brief period of time which Poggio devoted to the composition of his *Historia fiorentina* at the very end of his life, one need hardly be surprised at the lack of direct comment on the work during his lifetime or in the years immediately following his death. Marsilio Ficino, in a letter to Poggio's son, Jacopo, seeks to encourage him in his own historical writing.[23] The letter does not mention Jacopo's translation of his father's history, but it is conceivable that this was among the historical works Ficino praised. Muratori, however, seems to be correct in asserting that the Latin version was largely unknown to contemporaries.[24]

Scala's *Historia Florentinorum*, though less complete than Poggio's history, was written over a period of more than ten years, when the author was actively engaged in the chancellorship, in the composition of several other works in prose and poetry, and in his longstanding feud with Poliziano. Yet the work seems to have attracted little attention outside the circle of humanists working together in the Florence of Lorenzo dei Medici. Erasmus, who was well acquainted with the arguments between Poliziano and Scala, does not even mention it. Other humanists either do not know about the history Scala is working on or do not think it worthy to be set beside his achievements as an orator. Both Cristoforo Landino and Naldo Naldi, along with Ficino, praise Scala's merits as an orator and poet without mentioning his history of Florence.[25]

Stranger still than the relative silence among his close friends is the tenor of those contemporary observations on Scala's history which are available. The unrestrained praise which greeted Bruni's work gives way to an appraisal which, while never openly critical, dwells less on the specific merits of Scala's *Historia Florentinorum* than on the value of history in general or the difficulties of its composition. Ugolino Verino in a eulogy of the famous men of Florence notes simply that Scala wrote histories in addition to other works.[26]

---

duodecim libris illustravit" (quoted in Santini, *Leonardo*, p. 152, from a manuscript entitled *Laudatio Leonardi historici et oratoris* in the Biblioteca Laurenziana, Plutarch LXXXX, sup. cod., c. 817–884).

[23] "Sed antequam finem faciam rogo te me Bacciolini ut ab incepto componendarum historiarum studio non desistas, nam stylum orationis tuae historici laudant" (M. Ficino, "Epistolarum," in *Opera* [Basel, n.d.], p. 658).

[24] See the introduction to Muratori's edtiion (1731) of the *Historia in RR.II.SS.*, vol. XX, col. 159.

[25] See Cristoforo Landino, *Carmina omnia*, ed. A. Perosa (Florence, 1939), pp. 24–25; Naldo Naldi, *Elogiarum*, book I (MS), quoted by Oligero in his introduction to Scala's *Historia*.

[26] "Scala quoque Historias . . . explicat" (Ugolino Verino, *De illustratione urbis Florentiae* [Paris, 1583], book I, p. 13).

Poliziano, from whom even the faintest of praise for Scala is hardly damning, credits him with at least making a sincere effort at a difficult task.[27] Fontius, congratulating Scala for putting his time to good use, says, "For your soul is vexed with the cares of the *patria*, and, however trifling your leisure from these may be, you either try to understand the causes of things, write pleasant verse, or work on the Florentine history. How better could you pass your time?" [28]

This failure among Scala's friends to laud his achievements along with his good intentions is particularly striking in the light of the humanists' capacity for exuberant and virtually uncritical praise on almost all occasions. Of all Scala's associates only Alessandro Braccessi has a kind word to say of his virtues as an historian, and this consists of a single epigram describing him in complimentary but hardly effusive terms.[29]

In the twentieth century, when Scala is considered one of the lesser representatives of Italian humanism, lacking the stature of either Poggio or Bruni, such lukewarm appreciation does not create astonishment. But his minor intellectual powers do not explain the hesitation of his contemporaries, for they did not share our opinion of Scala. His position as chancellor of Florence, Lorenzo's close and unceasing support and patronage, and the many eulogies to be found among the writings of his colleagues all suggest the high regard in which Scala's abilities as a humanist were held.[30] When the fact that his historical writing alone was singled out for indifferent praise is added to these considerations, the possibility arises that the problem lies less in Scala than in the discipline of writing history. Perhaps towards the end of the century a new and more critical understanding of humanist history was emerging.

This possibility may be considered by analyzing in a closer and

[27] "Sed historiam componis certe longum opinor et arduum" (A. Poliziano, *Angeli Politiani et aliorum virorum illustrium epistolarum libri XII* [Hanover, 1612], book V, p. 162).

[28] "Publica nam patrae vexant tua pectora cura,
  cum tamen oblata est quantulacumque quies
  vel fingis causas vel condis amabile carmen
  vel Florentinae consulis Historiae.
  Qua melius posses in re consumere Tempus"
(B. Fontius, *Carmina*, ed. I. Fogel and L. Juhász [Leipzig, 1932], p. 6).

[29] From a manuscript in the Biblioteca Laurenziana, Plutarch XCI, sup. cod. 40, c. 28, quoted by A. Lazzari, *Ugolino e Michele Verino* (Turin, 1897), p. 49.

[30] On this point see F. Gilbert, *Machiavelli and Guicciardini* (Princeton, 1965), p. 320.

more discriminating fashion the terms in which an earlier gen-
eration had eulogized Bruni. Their praise had emphasized both
the accuracy and the elegance of his history. Not only did Leonardo
record for posterity important events which would otherwise have
been lost, but he narrated them in fine Latin periods worthy of his
classical models.[31] Such a twin emphasis is perfectly consistent with
the theory of historical writing as it was conceived in the fifteenth
century.[32] This consistency is not, however, an indication that
Bruni's contemporaries analyzed the *Historiae* as a concrete example of humanist historical theory. On the contrary, without considering any of the specific problems Bruni faced in implementing
this ideal of historical writing, all commentators seem content simply to state that the work in general manifests the characteristics
of elegance and accuracy.

The generalized and uncritical nature of the contemporary appraisal of Bruni suggested by these comments is reflected most
clearly in the fact that Bruni's successors, while praising his accuracy and elegance, frequently failed to use his scholarship in those
specific areas where the *Historiae* are indeed more accurate or more
elegant than previous histories of Florence.

For instance, Bruni's desire to get at the precise truth of Florence's past led him to reassess the legendary role of Charlemagne in
early Florentine history. Until the fifteenth century the sack and
destruction of Florence by Totila and its subsequent reconstruction
by Charlemagne had been considered key events in the origin of
Florence. In fact, this idea of Florentine fall and rebirth reveals
certain important aspects of Florentine political theory during the
thirteenth and fourteenth centuries.[33] In Book I of the *Historiae*,
Bruni criticizes on basically practical grounds the traditional reading

---

[31] See B. Accolti, *De praestantia virorum sui aevi*, in P. Villani, *Liber de civitatis Florentiae famosis civibus* (Florence, 1847), p. 112: "Sed ut alios omittam et de Latinis loquar, vel qui inter Latinos sunt versati, legisti tu aliquando libros a Leonardo Arretino prisca eloquentia conscriptis? In quibus dum Florentini populi res prosequitur memoria dignos omnem Italiae historiam annorum plurimum describit in qua tam multa sunt memoratu digna ut quicumque libros illos diligenter legerit . . . Quae omnia se Leonardus non fuisset, iacerint in obscuro et omnino apud hominum memoriam deperissent."

[32] The most complete treatment of the theory of humanist history, and especially of the place of rhetoric in this theory, is to be found in an unpublished doctoral thesis by Hannah Gray entitled "History and Rhetoric in Quattrocento Humanism" (unpub. diss. Harvard University, 1956). An excellent summary of this theory is found in Gilbert, *Machiavelli*, pp. 203–235.

[33] See N. Rubinstein, "The Beginnings of Political Thought in Florence," *Journal of the Warburg and Courtauld Institute*, 5 (1942), 198–227.

of the period. How inconceivable it is, says Bruni, that Florence should have lain deserted and desolate for the three hundred years between Totila and Charlemagne, to be recolonized by descendants of the very people who had been driven out by the Goths! [34] It is far more likely that Florence, though indeed it suffered heavily under Totila, was not totally destroyed. Charlemagne had only to repair some of the walls and bring in additional settlers from the countryside to strengthen those already inhabiting the city.

Bruni's concern with the origin of Florence can be seen as part of the early fifteenth-century attempt to credit republican Rome rather than the empire with the founding of Florence.[35] The specific question of Charlemagne's role involves a more subtle — even tangential — attack, lessening the consequences of an event which clearly happened while leaving the basic chronological outline intact. The two reinterpretations are, however, similar in reducing the debt Florence owes to representatives of the imperial tradition, and each one is sufficiently important to come to the mind of those who praise Bruni's history for its accuracy and thoroughness in criticizing accepted facts.

Not only do contemporary eulogies fail to note Bruni's comments on Totila and Charlemagne, but his new interpretation is ignored in subsequent Quattrocento historiography.[36] The anonymous writer of the previously mentioned *laudatio* [37] does credit Bruni with establishing that the city of Florence was founded under Sulla, but he includes this fact only as an aside in a period describing the chronological scope of the work. Poggio, who knew about Bruni's concern for accuracy from personal correspondence,[38] not only failed to mention this concern in his funeral oration but reverted in his own history of Florence to the traditional interpretation of Charlemagne's contribution, ignoring all of Bruni's arguments for a reinterpretation.[39]

---

[34] L. Bruni, *Historiarum Florentini populi libri XII* (vol. XIX, part 3, of RR.II.SS., ed. E. Santini, n.s. [Città di Castello, 1934]), vol. I, book i, p. 146. (Hereafter cited as Bruni, *Historiae*.)

[35] Though Bruni has often received credit for this, Baron shows that a sophisticated defense of the thesis originated with Salutati (see *Crisis*, 2nd ed., pp. 75–76).

[36] Both Baron, *Crisis*, p. 478, n. 13, and Santini, *Leonardo*, p. 38, comment on this.

[37] See note 22.

[38] See Bruni, *Epistolae*, book IV, ep. 4, written in January 1416: "Sed tantus est labor in quaerendis investigandisque rebus, ut jam plane me poeniteat incoepisse."

[39] Poggio, *Historia*, col. 3: "A quo [Totila] sexcentesimo fere post eam con-

The matter-of-fact tone in which Poggio narrates the traditional interpretation suggests not that he rejected Leonardo's criticisms but that he simply neglected to consider them. While such neglect cannot be positively established in Poggio's case, it is quite clear that Scala does not understand that Bruni has challenged tradition. Mentioning the *Historiae* as a source for his narrative of the period including Totila and Charlemagne, Scala states Bruni's position accurately enough [40] but then proceeds to narrate at great length the version as it stood in the centuries before Bruni, even rendering orations that the scattered descendants of the former inhabitants of Florence delivered to Charlemagne.

Other Florentine historians seem equally oblivious of Bruni's contributions. Only a few years after Poggio wrote the *Historia*, Donato Acciaiuoli composed a life of Charlemagne in which, without specifically refuting Bruni's thesis, he seems to ignore the difference between Bruni and tradition.[41] Finally, Machiavelli, who considers the histories of both Bruni and Poggio to be "diligentissimi," [42] adopts Poggio's version of the events without any apparent suspicion that it might be in disagreement with Leonardo's.[43]

The astounding failure of these historians to accept Bruni's thesis can be explained by sound political factors. Bruni wrote at a period in which French influence had reached its nadir. Beginning his history in the year of Agincourt, he published the first six books,

---

ditam anno captam et eversam tradunt trecentos deinde circiter annos deserta cultoribus demum a Carolo Magno post adeptum imperium restituta civibus variis in locis a fortuna dispersis receptaculum fuit."

[40] "Leonardus certe Aretinus gravissimus auctor disiecta magna ex parte a Totila edificia a Carlo reparata esse putat" (Scala, *Historia Florentinorum*, p. 43).

[41] The *Vita Caroli Magni*, written in 1461, is found in a manuscript in the National Library at Florence, col. naz. II, II, 10. The passage directly concerned with Charlemagne is quoted by E. Garin in a review of F. Simone's *La coscenza della Rinascita negli umanisti francesi*, in *Rinascimento*, 1 (1950), 93-94: "Fede deinde vastantibus Italiam barbarus . . . imperium trecentis et triginta annis cessavit . . . Carolus . . . Romanorum imperator . . . cum . . . per Etruriam facerit, in memoriam dignitatis accepte, Florentiam urbem quam olim magna ex parte deliverant gothi, in pristinum statum cum summa celeritate restituit." Acciaiuoli not only was familiar with Bruni, but in all probability he had begun translating the first book by 1461; yet he fails to see the significance of Bruni's reconsideration of Charlemagne's act.

[42] N. Machiavelli, *Istorie fiorentine*, in *Opere*, ed. F. Flora and C. Cordié (2 vols.; Milan: Mondadori, 1960), II, Proèmio.

[43] "E quando quello imperio fu da barbari afflitto fu ancora Florentia da Totila re degli Ostrogoti disfatta e dopo 250 anni dipoi da Carlo Magno riedificata" (Machiavelli, *Istorie fiorentine*, book II, chap. 1). Guicciardini, however, adopts Bruni's view, referring to the story as an ancient but untrue legend (see *Storia d'Italia*, book I, chap. 6).

containing the reassessment of Charlemagne's role in Florentine history, in the year of Orleans, when the long campaign which was eventually to drive the English back across the Channel was just beginning. Poggio, on the other hand, entered the chancery in the year the English were finally compelled to abandon Bordeaux, at a time when amicable relations between Florence and France were rapidly becoming a constant factor in Italian affairs.[44] To re-emphasize the importance of Charlemagne is under the circumstances fully understandable, and since the stress lies on Charlemagne's national character rather than his imperial title, it does not constitute a betrayal of Bruni's republican, anti-imperial bias. Scala's acceptance of the legend can be explained less by his affection for the French than by his concern for the problems facing Florence in his own day. He pointedly holds up the beneficial character of the first French intervention in Italian affairs as a contrast to the catastrophic invasion by Charles VIII in 1494.[45]

It is not, then, surprising that Bruni was ignored in this particular instance. What causes astonishment is the fact that neither Poggio nor Scala seems to see his own return to the traditional idea as a repudiation of Bruni's oft-noted accuracy. The fifteenth century considered Bruni accurate not because he had cogently refuted the traditional misconceptions and falsehoods about the course of Florentine history but because accuracy is a virtue of ideal humanist history. Praise of Bruni as an historian proceeds as a deduction from the assumption that he has written a model history and not as an induction from the *Historiae* themselves.[46]

Nor do Bruni's successors seem to make critical use of his reputation for a fine Latin style. While it was generally agreed that humanist historians must be elegant, there was less consensus on

[44] Acciaiuoli's *Vita Caroli Magni* is dedicated to Louis XI; the most consistent reference to Charlemagne's resurrection of Florence is found in the orations which embellished the more practical diplomatic interchanges between the two powers (see Baron, *Crisis*, p. 478, n. 13).

[45] Scala, *Historia Florentinorum*, pp. 39–40.

[46] The evidence Santini has marshaled to prove that Bruni's history was studied basically as a source of facts ("La fortuna della storia fiorentina di Leonardo Bruni nel Rinascimento," in *Studi storici*, 20 [1911]) is taken, with but one exception, either from chancery documents, which would of course support the theses of the chancellor, or from the Cinquecento, which, in fact, was highly critical of Bruni's accuracy on quite specific grounds. The exception is Gianozzo Manetti, who accepted Bruni's redating of the Ordinances of Justice. That many people of the early Quattrocento used Bruni as a source can hardly be doubted, though this does not alter the fact that there was no serious historiographical criticism of Bruni until well after his death.

the exact nature of elegance. In fact, the business of establishing criteria for stylistic excellence was a common source of those heated disputes among humanists which characterized the period. The question was most often posed in the following form: Should one perfect a style by the closest possible imitation of Cicero, or should the perspective be broadened to include, and even emphasize, Quintilian's rules of stylistic composition?

Around 1430 an argument of particular fury was begun in these terms by Lorenzo Valla, when at the age of twenty-three he wrote the *De Comparatione Ciceronis Quintilianique*.[47] This debate formed a prelude to the full-fledged and embittered dispute which characterized the 1450's. Bruni, of course, did not live to become involved in the more heated stages of the dispute, when Valla, attempting to illustrate the barbarisms and inadequacy of Poggio's style, subjected several of his works to the most minute scrutiny.[48] Even Poggio's epistolary is attacked. Valla in turn is severely censured for criticizing the styles of others without himself possessing an elegant mode of writing.[49] His own history, the *Historiae Ferdinandi Regis Aragonae*, is assaulted by his Neapolitan rival Fazio for errors of vocabulary, construction, and general style.

No argument from silence is conclusive, but in view of the general failure to use Bruni's researches the fact that his history stands untouched in a dispute of such magnitude is certainly suggestive. Noted for the elegance of its Latin by the Florentine signoria during his lifetime and at his death by Poggio himself, his work does not serve as a concrete example of style for either side, nor is it subject to the devastating analysis inflicted upon some of the works of Poggio and Valla.[50] In praising Bruni's elegance contemporaries seem to have in mind less the precise elements of the *Historiae* than certain basic assumptions about the nature of ideal history.

Fifteenth-century scholars seem no more eager to criticize the accepted theoretical basis of humanist history than they seem in-

[47] See R. Sabbadini, *Storia del ciceronianismo* (Turin, 1885), p. 25. Valla's work has since been lost.

[48] L. Valla, *In Poggium Florentinem antidoti libri quatuor* (Cologne, 1527). This and the following references to the dispute are noted by Sabbadini in *Storia*.

[49] P. Cortesi, *De hominibus doctis*, in P. Villani, *Liber*, p. 229.

[50] This is even more striking in the light of Valla's esteem for Bruni, shown in the following comment: "Latine scibendo ingenium excitavit meum" (Valla, *Opera* [Basel, 1543], p. 42). Sabbadini, in *Studi sul Panormita e sul Valla* (Florence, 1891), p. 53, says that this would refer to Valla's meeting Bruni at Rome in 1426. Bruni, in his turn, praises Valla's style in a letter dated 1433, quoted by Sabbadini in the same work (p. 66).

terested in Bruni's concrete implementation of the theory. There is, for example, some evidence to show that, at least outside humanist circles, Bruni's history was valued as an illustration of how liberty is to be achieved and maintained. Santini has discovered an anonymous tract in the Riccardiana which finds valuable maxims in the work.[51] How does the presence of this element in the *Historiae* affect Bruni's merits as an historian? Are the histories greater for embracing in the narrative the ideals of Florentine society? Both Poggio and Accolti, accepting accuracy and elegance as implicit standards of good historical writing, fail to face these questions. A meaningful criticism of the achievements of specific historians is obviously impossible while the principles of humanist historiography remain unquestioned.

It is the equivocal evaluation of Scala's *Historia Florentinorum* in the 1490's which has prompted a closer analysis of earlier comments on humanist historians, leading to the discovery of those areas in which analysis is deficient. It is from the same decade that the first evidence of a more critical perspective on humanist history clearly appears in Paolo Cortesi's *De hominibus doctis*.[52] Written in 1490 and dedicated to Lorenzo dei Medici, this work has not received sufficient attention from scholars.[53] Cortesi, within the basic structure of a conversation among three people, discusses the learned men who have embodied the revival of culture in Italy. The account begins with Chrysoloras and the study of Greek, though from this point Cortesi searches back in time to consider the contributions of Dante, Petrarch, and their fourteenth-century successors. Such a study of illustrious or learned men is part of a large body of Renaissance literature of which perhaps the most famous example is Vespasiano da Bisticci's *Vite di uomini illustri.*

[51] "Come si conserva la libertà se ne potra dare moltissima autorità . . . ma piglieremo la più breve del dottissimo huomo nostro ciptadino et chancelliere messer Leonardo Bruni nelle storie fiorentine ove dice, 'libertas populi duabus rebus continetur'" (Santini, "La fortuna," p. 183, taken from a manuscript in the Biblioteca Riccardiana, Cod. Ricc., 1396, c. 83). Santini does not attempt to date the document, but it was probably written before Acciaiuoli's translation was available, and possibly during Bruni's lifetime.

[52] Naples seems to be ahead of Florence in the realm of historical criticism, if not in that of historical writing, for Fazio's criticism of Valla antedates Cortesi by forty years. Not until the sixteenth century, however, does Pontano, in the *Actius*, apply the moral and spiritual significance of rhetoric to problems of historical writing.

[53] For example, Rossi, *Il Quattrocento*, p. 384, simply mentions it as Cortesi's chief work and describes it as a compilation of humanists from Dante to Cortesi's contemporaries; Sabbadini, *Storia*, p. 33, sees some of its significance when he calls it "il primo libro di vera critica letteraria e stilistica nel periodo del risorgimento."

Cortesi's importance lies not in his quite conventional selection of men for discussion but in the digressions which rise naturally out of the dialogue form and deal with general matters of style, learning, and culture. The dialogue structure of the *De hominibus* puts these general observations in a different context from those comments on the ideal method of writing to be found in more conventional treatises. Since the general ideals in Cortesi grow out of questions on specific authors, they have an immediacy and applicability transcending the dry and often sterile recitation of classical maxims which characterizes so many theoretical works of the period.

The departure from conventional platitudes is most evident in his treatment of historical writing, which he takes up in discussing Bruni. Introducing Bruni as an orator of considerable repute, Cortesi goes on to indicate that his historical works are even more widely esteemed.[54] When he turns to a consideration of the *Historiae*, the late-century humanist fills the traditional ideals of accuracy and elegance with a content relevant to the precise work being examined. "He [Bruni] wrote a truly accurate history; the deliberations in council are serious, both the events of war and the stratagems used in conducting wars are clearly explained; the style is rather of Livy than of Cicero." [55]

Though Cortesi has not departed from classical maxims here, he has nevertheless introduced a new dimension into the Quattrocento's appreciation of humanist history. He praises Bruni specifically for his re-creation of deliberative councils, his analysis of stratagems and maneuvers, and his penetration into the origins and issues of wars. Similarly, Bruni's style is analyzed in terms of specific models for imitation.

Cortesi soon expands his discourse to include more general considerations. Directly after these comments, which suggest Cortesi's sensitivity to the need for specific criticism, he says, "But though of all things history is most difficult, Bruni attained in it such diligence of imitation and goodness of character that in my opinion he easily stands before all who came after him." [56] This judgment con-

[54] "Historiam complexus est animo aliquanto maiore; nam orationes eius quae extant non aeque ac historiae probantur" (Cortesi, *De hominibus*, p. 224).

[55] "Historiam vero scripsit accurate; conciones aliquot sunt graves; consilia et bellorum initia atque eventus explicantur valde prudenter. Consectatur in historia quiddam livianum non ausim dicere ciceronianum." (Cortesi, *De hominibus*, p. 225).

[56] "Sed cum historia sit rerum omnium difficillima tantum ea imitandi industria

tains several elements which had by then become commonplace in the humanist *ars historica*. The superiority of Bruni to his successors, the importance of good character to historical writing, and even the emphasis on the difficulty of writing history, which is a corollary to the high esteem in which history was held, were all familiar themes by 1490.[57]

Cortesi, however, means something more than the traditional commonplaces when he notes the difficulties of writing history. Leaving the subject of history for the moment, he narrates in the dialogue the achievements of other early fifteenth-century humanists. Then, reaching Poggio Bracciolini and the *Historia fiorentina*, he makes an observation strikingly similar to the previously noted appraisals of Scala's *Historia Florentinorum*. "Poggio also wrote a history, but as I said before, history is a great task and the most difficult of all things." [58] This is said without specific attention either to the factual element in the *Historia* or to Poggio's style, certainly more acceptable than Bruni's by Cortesi's standards.

The great representative of mid-century humanism cannot, however, be dismissed with a brief observation on the difficulty of his task. Wherein exactly does this difficulty lie? First of all, says Cortesi, it stems from the fact that, although the ancients must have known the principles of good writing, none of these principles can be extrapolated from ancient histories. "Since history embraces such a great variety of things, I often wonder why no precepts have come down in the arts of the ancients to teach how it should be written and what should be preserved in it. Some disciplines use

---

et bonitate quadam naturae consequutus est ut omnibus mea sententia qui post eum fuerunt facile praestiterit" (Cortesi, *De hominibus*, p. 225).

[57] Mrs. Gray in her doctoral thesis (see note 32 above), on the basis of these comments on Bruni, places the *De hominibus* in the tradition of theoretical works on history and rhetoric which includes Trapezuntius' *Rhetoricorum libri cinque*, Giorgio Valla's *Rhetorica*, Guarino of Verona's *De historia conscribendae forma*, and Poliziano's *Praefatio in Suetonii expositionem*. It has already been seen that Cortesi approaches the problem from an essentially different perspective. It will presently emerge that his conceptual understanding of the *ars historica* is more penetrating and questioning than, for instance, his contemporary, Poliziano, who contents himself with a collection of classical maxims, fails utterly to refer to contemporary histories, and reveals the total irrelevance of his conception of history to any specific work by saying of Suetonius, "Nulla in his libris suspicio est gratiae, nulla simulatatis, nihil studio dictum, nihil suppressum metu rebus ipsis data omnia veritati in primis servitum est (Poliziano, *Praefatio*, in *Opera*, p. 503).

[58] "Scripsit etiam historiam, sed est magnum munus historia et, ut paulo ante dixi omnium rerum difficillimum." This and the citations in the following two paragraphs of text (and their notes) are taken from Cortesi, *De hominibus*, p. 228.

rules of line, others of measure. In both sculpture and painting it is known that nothing can be done without a certain order of art. I never cease to marvel that history, being of such difficulty and ardor, should lack its own rules." [59] Cortesi maintains that the lively contemporary disagreements over the nature of the ideal history arise from the ancients' strange silence on the subject. Some fifteenth-century theorists say that history should be written "sine ullis ornamentis oratoriis," with a single end of truth in mind. Cortesi himself insists on the value of "delectationem" and "utilitatem," which can only be assured by a clear and well-expressed arrangement of the great variety of events that a history must include in its narrative.

Not only has the lack of rules given rise to conflicting theories concerning the ideal history, says Cortesi, but it has had a pernicious effect on the actual histories written. "For I know very well that those ancient historians possessed rules for the art. This much is clear from their histories. Our own historians, however, lack all of these tools, and without them nothing, especially in this kind of writing, can emerge worthy of praise except by chance or accident." [60]

Paolo certainly does not mean that a theory of history cannot be reconstructed from classical writings. Late-century humanists were quite familiar with the basic writings of Cicero and Quintilian on the subject, as the most cursory glance at Poliziano's *Praefatio* will reveal.[61] He means instead that the ideas on writing history to be found in the theoretical works of the classical rhetoricians do not adequately explain the qualities of classical histories. Though the excellence of these histories presupposes, according to Cortesi's assumptions about human knowledge, a sophisticated set of rules, the body of these rules has not yet been discovered, and consequently humanist writers are unable to rival their classical models except by chance. Since the dialogue form of the *De hominibus* precludes

[59] "Ego vero saepe soleo mirari, quid sit, quod cum historia tot, tantarumque rerum dissimilitudinem complectatur, nulla praecepta in priscorum artibus tradantur, quae quomodo scribendum quid servandum sit in historia doceant . . . Alii in lineis alii in mensuris alii ad fingendum, alii ad pingendum certis praeceptis utuntur ex quo intelligitur nihil magnum fieri posse sine quadam artis ratione; historiam autem, tam arduum, tam difficile opus nihil habere praeceptorum non desino hercle satis mirari."

[60] "Nam priscos illos ut ex eorum historiis apparet praeclare intelligebam huius artis praecepta tenuisse. Nostros autem his instrumentis scribendi genere nihil admodum laudis consequi posse nisi quando temere aut casu."

[61] Mrs. Gray deals with this cognizance at some length.

a thoroughgoing examination of the problem, the issues remain unclear as Cortesi leaves the subject and proceeds to a eulogy of Pius II.

Brief and even desultory in its treatment, the *De hominibus
doctis* nevertheless introduces the critical study of humanist histories. In the first place, the dialogue considers the problem of how
and to what extent humanists answered the questions they themselves asked of history. Though Cortesi does not attempt to find
specific lapses of style and accuracy in Bruni, he leads the way to
the sixteenth-century attack on humanists' accuracy by posing the
problem in its most general terms. At the same time, however, Cortesi questions the adequacy of these traditional means of approach,
suggesting the necessity for a more complete statement of principles which will raise historical writing to its former pinnacle.
The real difficulty in writing history does not lie in the mere per-
fection of one's narrative style and the search for new and higher
standards of accuracy. These are only means to an end. The true
goal is the creation of a vital historical form by a new synthesis of
these and other elements to be found in the works of Livy, Tacitus,
Sallust, and other classical historians. It is in this larger context
that the restrained quality of the commentary on Scala in the 1490's
is most readily understood.

The appearance in the late Quattrocento of a questioning stance
toward humanist historians has had no direct impact on modern
scholarship. The questions of Cortesi and his contemporaries do,
however, serve as a background to Machiavelli's remarks, which in
turn provide the framework within which historians of several
centuries have approached the humanists. Because of the long-
range effects which Machiavelli's brief comments on his humanist
predecessors have had, his appraisal of the humanist achievement
in the field of historical writing must be carefully evaluated.

On the one occasion when Machiavelli explicitly discusses the
merits of the humanists as historians, in the introduction to his
Istorie fiorentine, he notes first of all his respect for Poggio and
Bruni. Not only does he call them "duoi excellentissimi istorici,"
but he specifies the ways in which he has found their works useful.
"I read their writings diligently to see with what method and order
they wrote, so that our own history, by imitating theirs, would be
better approved by its readers . . ." [62] Machiavelli goes on, how-

[62] "Avendo io dipoi diligentemente letto gli scritti loro per vedere con quali
ordini e modi nello scrivere procedevono, acciò che imitando quelli la istoria nostra
fusse meglio dai leggenti approvata" (*Istorie fiorentine*, Proèmio).

ever, to criticize the content of both histories of Florence, noting that Poggio and Bruni tend to neglect domestic affairs in their accounts of the wars and foreign relations of the city.[63]

Machiavelli's determination to imitate the formal elegance rather than the factual accuracy of his predecessors cannot be wholly explained by his preference for vernacular sources. His own reputation for accuracy has suffered both because of his supposed willingness to distort the facts to fit a preconceived theory and because of his failure to use his sources critically.[64] Machiavelli's general lack of interest in critical scholarship, as well as his attitude toward humanist historians, takes on larger significance in the light of a passage in Book II of the *Discorsi*, where he condemns those who always praise former ages above their own. These people are mistaken for a number of reasons. "The first, I think, is that we do not understand the whole truth about classical times; more often than not anything which would bring infamy to those times is hidden, and anything which would be a source of glory is magnified and emphasized." [65] From this passage as well as from others in the *Discorsi*,[66] it can be seen that Machiavelli, conscious of the inevitable distortion which passions and partisanship introduce into the sources, understood the difficulty of obtaining an accurate record of the past.

Unlike modern historians who share this understanding, however, he did not try to separate events from prejudices by using the tools of critical scholarship and analysis of sources.[67] Instead he

---

[63] "Ma delle civili discordie e delle intrinseche inimicizie e degli effetti che da quelle sono nati, averne una parte al tutto taciuta e quell'altra in modo brevemente descritta che ai leggenti non puote arrecare utile o piacere alcuno" (*Istorie fiorentine*, Proèmio).

[64] This criticism is particularly directed against his *Vita di Castruccio Castracani*, where he is usually accused of having constructed a complete fable. P. Villari, *Niccolò Machiavelli and his Times*, trans. L. Villari (London, 1883), IV, 90, and O. Tommasini, *La vita e gli scritti di Niccolò Machiavelli* (Rome, 1911), II, 429, both comment disfavorably on the *Vita*. J. H. Whitfield in "Machiavelli and Castruccio," *Italian Studies*, 8 (1953), 1–28, has pointed out the dangers of such a simplistic approach to the work. The *Istorie fiorentine*, while not attacked on this basis, are judged harshly for uncritical use of the sources (see F. Gilbert's introduction to the Torchbook edition of the English translation of the *Istorie* [New York, 1960], p. xiv).

[65] "E la prima credo sia, che delle cose antiche non s'intenda al tutto la verità, e che di quelle il più delle volte si nasconda quelle cose che recherebbono a quelli tempi infamia, e quelle altre che possano partorire loro gloria si rendino magnifiche ed amplissime" (Machiavelli, *Discorsi sopra la prima deca di Tito Livio* [in *Opere*, vol. I], book II, Proèmio).

[66] See book I, chap. 10, where he talks about how historians have come to know Julius Caesar.

[67] He did, however, on occasion attempt to solve the problem by including all

frankly employed the events of history to express his own biases and preconceptions about reality, seeking to arrive at a true understanding of history by refining these biases and preconceptions. He intended that in reading of historical events his audience should "savor that taste which the events have in themselves" [68] instead of being simply amused by the "variety of particulars." [69] In pursuing this intention he found help from humanist histories. The humanist concern for elegance, which the fifteenth century tended to see as a narrow problem of style, appeared to Machiavelli a broader one of form and order.[70] Though he found weaknesses in the scope of humanist histories, he recognized a value in the narrative tools they had placed in his hands.

Machiavelli saw not only the larger implications of the concern for elegance but the depth of the humanists' commitment to the historical realities with which they dealt. Explaining their lack of interest in domestic matters, he says, "I think that they did this either because these matters seemed so insignificant that they did not consider them worthy to be written up or because they feared offending the descendants of those who would be attacked in narrating these things." [71] The first of these reasons suggests that Machiavelli saw, as subsequent generations of historians often have not seen, that the humanists had a deep sense of the significance of their undertaking. They selected their themes not with a view to mere pleasure and delight in telling but with a desire to perpetuate in letters only those things worthy of honor, excluding those that were not considered worthy.

By his appreciation of the broader contributions of humanist historical style in providing an ordered and well-structured narrative and by his clear perception of the concern for significance implicit in the histories, Machiavelli achieved a critical insight into humanist historiography that was at once profound and useful to

---

possible renditions of the facts. Consider, for instance, his narrative of the founding of Florence. In the *Istorie*, to be sure, he accepts the theory, established by 1525, of foundation under Sulla (book II, chap. 2); in the *Discorsi*, however, he refuses to decide between Sulla, Fiesole, and the Empire (book I, chap. 1).

[68] "Gustare di loro quel sapore che le hanno in se."

[69] "Varietà degli accidenti che in essi si contengono."

[70] This broader perspective does not, in fact, appear suddenly with Machiavelli; its development will be traced through the fifteenth century in later chapters.

[71] "Il che credo facessero, o perchè parvono loro quelle azione si deboli che le giudicorono indegne di essere mandate alla memoria delle lettere o perchè temessino di non offendere i discesi di coloro i quali per quelle narrazioni avessero a calumniare" (*Istorie*, Proèmio).

his own ends. In a limited sense he suggested answers to the questions of Cortesi and his contemporaries by showing that these histories could be approached in terms of both general values and specific points for imitation. Unfortunately, the implications which have just been drawn from Machiavelli's brief remarks in the *Istorie fiorentine* have seldom been seen by scholars. Instead of penetrating to the essence of Machiavelli's attitude toward his predecessors, most scholars have concentrated on his single censure of the humanists — the statement that they neglected domestic affairs. Because of this emphasis, criticism after the sixteenth century has concentrated more on the questions which humanists did not seek to answer than on those historical problems which they sought to solve, and few if any critics have achieved an understanding of humanist histories as broadly conceived and as probing as that intimated by Machiavelli. The following discussion of modern critics of humanist historiography will trace the effects of this mistaken application of Machiavelli's insights. A full grasp of the contributions of the humanist historians remained impossible until new general interpretations of the Renaissance, appearing in the twentieth century, opened up fresh avenues of specific inquiry.

Machiavelli's immediate successors among practicing historians tended either to ignore the humanists completely or to attack them for factual inaccuracy.[72] Nor did the writers of *artes historicae* rely

---

[72] Guicciardini, for instance, does not acknowledge a debt to Bruni either in his youthful *Storie fiorentine* nor in the later *Storia d'Italia*, though Bruni's history covers at least part of the period included in Guicciardini's history of Florence. Paolo Giovio, although he viciously denounces Machiavelli for being a dishonest historian, does not mention the humanists either in the *Elogi* or in the *Historiarum sui temporis*. In the latter work he explicitly acknowledges his models to be the classical historians and not those of the Quattrocento (see *Historiarum sui temporis* [Rome, 1957], p. 6). Volterranus finds Bruni's theories of the founding of Rome unacceptable: "Hanc Arretinus a Sillanis conditam fuisse quod omnino esse falsum liber colonarum nuper inventus manifesto demostrat" (quoted by Santini, "La fortuna," p. 186).

Sannazaro takes Poggio to task for distorting history to his own purposes: "Dum patriam laudat, damnat dum Poggio hostem,/ nec malus est civis nec bonus historicus" (J. Sannazaro, *Epigrammaton*, book I, p. 20, in *Opera omnia* [Frankfurt, 1709], p. 132). Vicenzo Borghini in his *Discorsi* discusses at great length, without mentioning Bruni, both the foundation of Florence and the question of whether or not it was sacked by Totila and rebuilt by Charlemagne (see V. Borghini, *Discorsi* [4 vols.; Milan, 1808–1809], I, 3–97). This, in spite of the fact that he seems to place a certain value on at least Scala's history: "Scrisse latinamente Istoria nostra, la quale non so perchè non sia data fuora" (quoted in Oligero's edition of Scala's history, from a manuscript of Borghini).

The only historian who seems to use the humanists as sources is Filippo Nerli. Listing his sources for the *Commentari dei fatti civili occorsi dentro la città di Firenze*

on the humanists to help them provide a broad, sound, and productive theoretical basis for historical writing.[73] Only at the end of the century did an historian explicitly appraise the humanists as historians. Scipio Ammirato, in the *Proèmio* to his *Istorie fiorentine*, notes the clarity and gravity of Bruni's narrative, claiming that he cannot hope to imitate Bruni in this area.[74]

The two centuries following Ammirato were devoted to the compilation of information on the humanists and the publication of the printed texts of their histories.[75] The pattern for collecting data on the humanists as historians was set by Gerhard Vossius when he published the *De historicis latinis* in 1651.[76] In this work Vossius, avoiding any expression of his own opinions, assembled all the past comments he could find on Latin historians. Prominent in his sections on Bruni and Poggio is Machiavelli's complaint that these men have left domestic affairs out of their narrative. Between Vossius' writing and the publication of Domenico Moreni's *Bibliografia storico-ragionata della Toscana* in 1805, several scholars worked in the field, all drawing on Vossius in both form and content, and none offering any fresh critical insights into humanist historiography.[77]

---

dall'anno 1215 al 1537 (Trieste, 1859), Nerli mentions in the Proèmio that, for the early part of the work, facts will be taken "dal Villani, dall'Istorie fiorentine e da molte altre memorie scritte da vari scrittori delle cose di Firenze." That Nerli includes Bruni among these various writers is clear from a reference to the events of 1343, which, he says (p. 35), are "tanto particularmente scritta nella crònica del Villano e nell'Istorie dell'Aretino e del Machiavello." Neither Poggio nor Scala is mentioned by Nerli, however.

[73] Typifying these productions in Italy are the *Dialoghi* of Sperone Speroni (Venice, 1548); the *De historia laudibus* of Giovan Michele Bruto (Cracow, 1589); and, above all, Francesco Patrizzi's *Della historia diece dialoghi* (Venice, 1560). See F. Lamprecht, *Zur Theorie der humanistischen Geschichtschreibung* (Zurich, 1950), for a discussion of these works, with particular emphasis on Patrizzi. Among writers of the productions north of the Alps are Jean Bodin and Louis le Roy. See J. L. Brown's monograph, *The 'Methodus ad facilem historiarum cognitionem' of Jean Bodin* (Washington, 1939), and W. Gundesheimer's "The Opportunistic Humanism of Louis le Roy," *Journal of the History of Ideas*, 8 (1964), 324–339.

[74] Scipio Ammirato, *Istorie fiorentine* (11 vols.; Florence, 1846–1849), I, 13–15. Ammirato, who worked on the history until his death in 1601 (although his son did not complete the work for publication until 1647), complains like Machiavelli that the humanists leave much material out of their accounts.

[75] Bruni's was printed first, at Strasbourg in 1610; then Scala's at Rome in 1677; and finally Poggio's, at Venice in 1715.

[76] *De historicis latinis* (Lyons, 1651), pp. 549 and 558. For the date of composition of the *De historicis*, see J. Niceron, *Memoires pour servir à l'histoire des hommes illustres* (42 vols.; Paris, 1729–1745), vol. XIII.

[77] See, for instance, Niceron's *Memoires*, vol. XX on Scala and Poggio, and vol. XXV on Bruni; Zeno, *Dissertazione Vossiane*, which is intended to be a supplement to Vossius; G. Mazzuchelli, *Gli scrittori d'Italia* (2 vols.; Brescia, 1753–1763); P.

Ironically, the first full-length critical appraisal of Florentine historians came from the pen of one who not only questioned the importance of a good Latin style in an historian but who believed that in pursuing elegance the humanists had sacrificed accuracy and attention to detail. George Gervinus, writing in 1833, proposes to deal with all Florentine historical writing down to the sixteenth century, but Machiavelli is his hero and two thirds of the book is devoted to the *Istorie fiorentine*.[78] Vossius and his successors simply quoted Machiavelli's complaints about the absence of domestic affairs from humanist histories; Gervinus develops these complaints into a full-fledged attack on the form of the histories. Disagreeing with the long tradition of esteem in which the humanists have been held, he offers excuses "if I pass over [the humanists' histories] quickly or dare explicitly to lay a hand on the halo which the centuries have placed on their heads." [79]

No one had considered Scala's history to be the best example of humanist historiography, but Gervinus chose the *Historia Florentinorum* to illustrate the weaknesses of the humanists' manner of writing history. In Scala "it is readily obvious how soon this Latin history must live beyond its usefulness in a land where there is a strong desire for history and political instruction." [80] As if it were not enough that Scala is insensitive to the more vital and significant aspects of Florentine culture, he does not succeed even in pursuing his own narrow and useless ends. His style is replete with barbarisms.[81]

Gervinus, aware that Machiavelli had used and respected Bruni, reserves a separate judgment for him, but even here a derogatory note prevails. Gervinus has no use for Bruni's classicism: Bruni omits the anecdotes and color, so full of insight and charm, which had characterized the fourteenth-century chronicles, while he imitates the style of Livy's wars, a pursuit worthless to a student of Bruni's epoch.[82] Poggio is even worse; he consciously and delib-

---

Negri, *Istoria degli scrittori fiorentini* (Ferrara, 1722); and D. Manni, *Metodo per istudiare la storia di Firenze* (Florence, 1755).

[78] G. Gervinus, *Geschichte der Florentinischer Historiografie bis zum sechzehnten Jahrhundert* (Frankfurt, 1833).

[79] Gervinus, *Geschichte*, p. 55. The sense that he is attacking an entrenched position lends to the book an acid and polemical tone, which sets it apart from its predecessors even before the novelty of Gervinus' approach is grasped.

[80] Gervinus, *Geschichte*, p. 56.

[81] Gervinus, *Geschichte*, p. 57.

[82] Gervinus, *Geschichte*, p. 59.

erately ignores events which do not redound to the glory of Florence. Here dishonesty is added to irrelevance and tedium.

It is clear that, however much Gervinus admired Machiavelli in his capacity as an historian, he did not respect his views on other historians. Not only is Gervinus more extreme in his condemnation, but he also ignores the principal aspect of Machiavelli's judgment: admiration for the clarity and order which Bruni gave to history and for the very involvement in Florentine culture which Gervinus finds so lacking. Machiavelli's attack on the humanists for failing to answer questions which they never posed, but which he, Machiavelli, thought relevant, forms only a minor part of his total evaluation. In Gervinus this standard of criticism is central. At precisely the point where humanist historians come to be analyzed within the scope of an explicitly historiographical study, all attempt at constructive criticism is abandoned in favor of judgment in terms of a conception of history foreign to them. Gervinus' interest in the humanists falls away when he discovers that they do not share his own historical presuppositions.

Gervinus' importance lies in his influence on the three great nineteenth-century general historians of the Renaissance, Voigt, Burckhardt, and Symonds, all of whom shared in some measure his general approach to humanist historians.[83] Symonds, harshest of the three, says, "Their admiration for Livy and the pedantic properties of a laboured Latinism made them pay more attention to rhetoric than to the substance of their work. We meet with frigid imitations and bombastic generalities, where concise details and graphic touches would have been acceptable. In short, these works are rather studies of style in an age when the greatest stylists were but bunglers and beginners, than valuable histories." [84] Not only were the humanists mistaken in their intentions but they failed to do well even the little which they attempted. Harsher criticism could hardly be given.

The nineteenth-century understanding of humanist historiography was unsatisfactory indeed. Unsympathetic to, and often unaware of, the stated goals of the humanists, first Gervinus and then the great synthesizers of Renaissance culture could find little to

[83] See G. Voigt, *Il risorgimento dell'antichità classica*, trans. D. Valbusa (Florence, 1888–1890), II, 478; J. Burckhardt, *The Civilization of the Renaissance in Italy*, trans. S. Middlemore (London, 1960), p. 145; and J. A. Symonds, *The Renaissance in Italy*, vol. I, *The Age of Despots* (New York, 1960), p. 217.

[84] Symonds, *Renaissance in Italy*, I, 217.

praise in their histories. The fact that the humanists did not provide answers to the questions that the nineteenth-century historians
raised was decisive. That the men of the fifteenth century might have
faced other problems and solved them did not occur to the critics,
and consequently the direct study of humanist history languished
in an atmosphere of scorn and invective. Gervinus, in spite of the
fact that he was the first to study Florentine historiography as such,
added no insights. Nor did Burckhardt, Voigt, and Symonds, despite
their admittedly superior feeling for the period as a whole.

A more balanced understanding of the humanists emerged only
in the early years of the twentieth century in what has become a
classic work on historiography: Eduard Fueter's *Geschichte der
neueren Historiographie.*[85] Fueter points out the humanists' secu-
larism and independence from authority, their use of history to
embellish cultural ideals, their superior narrative and stylistic techniques, and, finally, the extent to which they made critical use of
sources.[86] In spite of these positive features which Fueter finds in
the humanist histories, his analysis still betrays a strong tendency to
criticize the historians of the Quattrocento for failing to answer
questions which only later historians thought relevant. He suggests
that imitation of the classics robbed the humanists of considerable
value [87] and that neither the extent of their research nor the accuracy of their reporting is above reproach.[88] Perhaps the most obvious example of this tendency is Fueter's suggestion that Bruni
should have dealt more fully with the economic affairs of Florence.[89]

Fueter, in attacking Bruni for omitting economic facts from his
narrative, is strikingly reminiscent of Machiavelli and his complaint
that Bruni and Poggio do not devote sufficient attention to domestic
affairs. In each case the humanists are criticized for not answering
questions in which they are not interested. Machiavelli's comment,
however, is a mere aside to be understood in the context of his

[85] E. Fueter, *Geschichte der neueren Historiographie* (Munich and Berlin,
1911).

[86] Fueter, *Geschichte*, pp. 1–14.

[87] "Bruni und seine nachfolger hatten wohl historiche Werke von grosserem
werte geschaffen, wenn sie die Anregungen der antiken Historiker hatten ignorieren
und eine neue ihnen selbst und ihrer zeitgemasse Form hatten schaffen durfen"
(Fueter, *Geschichte*, p. 11). See also pp. 22–23, where he criticizes Poggio's excessive concern with style at the expense of true history.

[88] See Fueter, *Geschichte*, p. 3, where he deals with some of Petrarch's inaccu-
racies.

[89] Fueter, *Geschichte*, p. 21.

fundamental appreciation of the humanists' ability to deal with their own questions. Both Fueter and Gervinus seem unable to look beyond their historical presuppositions in order to judge the humanists in fifteenth-century terms.[90]

In the fifteenth century the basic goals of the humanist historians came to be appreciated only at a time when these goals were being undermined by the process of elaborating general principles of historical writing. At the beginning of the twentieth century, scholars had not yet succeeded in disentangling their own historical ideals from their judgments of the humanists. This century has produced little in the way of direct insight into humanist historiography,[91] but two important developments in the general intellectual history of the Renaissance have provided new perspectives for understanding the field.

The first development is associated with the work of Paul Oscar Kristeller. In an address delivered at Brown University in 1944, Kristeller sought to refine the accepted definitions of humanism and to stress the essential place of rhetoric as a humanist concern.[92] "I am inclined to consider the humanists not as philosophers with a curious lack of philosophical ideas and a curious fancy for classical studies, but rather as professional rhetoricians with a new, classicist ideal of culture, who tried to assert the importance of their field of learning and to impose their standards upon other fields of learning and of science, including philosophy." [93] Kristeller does not follow the implications of his insights into the field of historiography,[94] but by stressing the central place of rhetoric in all the activities of the humanists he opens the way to a serious consideration of the implications of a rhetorical conception of historical

[90] Fueter's general approach to the problem is found in most twentieth-century surveys of historical writing. See, for example, H. E. Barnes, *A History of Historical Writing* (Norman, Okla., 1937), pp. 101–107. Santini, who has written the most thorough monograph on Bruni, takes a similar stance, seeking to prove that Bruni is adequate when judged by positivistic standards.

[91] Perhaps the best essay concerned explicitly with humanist historiography is B. Ullman's "Leonardo Bruni and Humanist Historiography," in *Medievalia et Humanistica*, 4 (1946), 45–61.

[92] This address has been printed, along with several other essays written both earlier than 1944 and later, in *Studies in Renaissance Thought and Letters* (Rome, 1956). He also discusses the problem in *The Classics and Renaissance Thought* (Cambridge, Mass., 1955).

[93] Kristeller, *Studies in Renaissance Thought*, p. 563.

[94] In fact, he tends to stress the similarity between humanist and medieval historians: "The link betwen history and rhetoric that seems to be so typical of the Renaissance was apparently a medieval heritage" (*Studies in Renaissance Thought*, p. 567).

writing. Hannah Gray and Felix Gilbert have been prominent in giving this sort of consideration to humanist historical theory, for both emphasize its moral and didactic element.[95]

If a sympathetic analysis of the historical theory of the humanists has shown that they sought by eloquence to teach men virtue and to stimulate them to right conduct, a second development — the investigation of the specific character of Florentine humanism — has had even more important consequences for the study of Bruni, Poggio, and Scala. This investigation has been largely the work of Hans Baron, who has tried to show that the political and social situation of Florence at the very beginning of the Quattrocento, coupled with the threat of imminent invasions by the Duke of Milan, served to mobilize a new set of attitudes and concerns among Florentine intellectuals. Furthermore, Baron sees these new attitudes and concerns most clearly in the work and life of Leonardo Bruni.[96]

[95] Gilbert, for instance, says, "The humanists regarded history . . . as an instrument by which the accepted doctrines of moral philosophy would be presented in such a persuasive manner that people would act according to the tenets of moral philosophy" (*Machiavelli*, p. 217).

[96] Baron's clearest statement of this thesis is, of course, in the *Crisis*, especially in the Epilogue to the second edition, but the thesis can be seen in development in a series of articles, beginning shortly after his publication of Bruni's humanistic philosophical writings in 1928 (*Leonardo Bruni Aretino: Humanistisch-Philosophische Schriften*). Some of the more important of his early articles are "Das Erwachen des Historischen Denkens in Humanismus des Quattrocento," *Historische Zeitschrift*, 147 (1932), 5–21, where he stresses the importance of Bruni's concern for Etruscan history as an indication of his republican sentiments; "La rinascita statale romana nell'umanesimo fiorentino del Quattrocento," *Civiltà Moderna*, 7 (1935), 21–49, where he underlines and locates in the period of Salutati the growth in popularity of Cicero's *De officiis* and others of his more politically involved works. The growing appreciation of this element in Cicero during the early Quattrocento is also the subject of Baron's "Cicero and the Roman Civic Spirit in the Middle Ages and the Early Renaissance," *Bulletin of the John Rylands Library*, 22 (1938), 73–97. Baron applies this thesis specifically to Bruni and the *Historiae* in "Lo sfondo storico del Rinascimento fiorentino," *La Rinascita*, 1 (1938), 50–73. For a critical but sympathetic appreciation of Baron's work see Wallace Ferguson, "Interpretation of Italian Humanism: The Contribution of Hans Baron," *Journal of the History of Ideas*, 19 (1958), 14–25, and Baron's reply in the same issue, pp. 26–34.

Jerrold Seigel, " 'Civic Humanism' or Ciceronian Rhetoric? The Culture of Petrarch and Bruni," *Past and Present*, 34 (1966), 3–48, has sought to show that Bruni is basically a rhetorician with no deep political commitments. Baron has ably replied to this attack in "Leonardo Bruni: 'Professional Rhetorician' or 'Civic Humanist'?" *Past and Present*, 36 (1967), 21–37. In addition to defending the particular datings by which he has assigned the birth of civic humanism to the period of the Giangaleazzo wars, Baron makes the telling point that the larger phenomenon of civic humanism, as a particular sort of political analysis and the attitudes associated with it, was unquestionably prevalent among Florentine intellectuals during the first half of the Quattrocento.

Bruni and his colleagues were, according to Baron, civic humanists. Their basic commitments were formed less by acquaintance with the classics than by their political experience as Florentines. The classics were used as instruments for extolling Florentine liberty and attacking the imperialism of the city's enemies. By using the classics in defense of the city, the intellectuals of the early Quattrocento in Florence achieved an impressive synthesis between rhetorical training and a vital interest in specific contemporary issues.

The last decades, then, have opened new paths of inquiry into humanist historiography and have suggested new analytical tools for a study of the field. On the one hand, recent scholarship has stressed the moral and didactic elements of the rhetorical theory of history; on the other, Baron has suggested certain concrete ideals and values which Florentine humanists in particular were interested in teaching. Neither Baron, Gray, nor Gilbert, however, has tried to deal directly with the development of the humanist historical tradition in Florence. The historical theory which Gray and Gilbert cite is elaborated only at the end of the fifteenth century. Although Baron does explicitly discuss Bruni's *Historiae*, he is mainly interested in the political significance of the work, and he hardly mentions Poggio or Scala.

In tracing the development of the art of historical writing among Florentine humanists in the Quattrocento, the present study remains an *explication de texte* in its fundamental approach, however much the insights derived from this extrapolation may depend on the secondary material just described. In the chapters to follow, the texts will be approached in terms of three basic questions.

The first concerns the nature of the reality the historian is recounting. What interests and engages the writer? What is the substance of his narrative? This is a complex question which can be approached partly through explicit statements contained mainly in the prefaces of his work and partly in a more indirect manner through an analysis of his use of the basic historical tools of selection and reconstruction. What does he choose from his sources to include in the narrative and what does he ignore? Even more important, what does he interpolate into the account by drawing on his own understanding of the nature of history?

The second question deals with the broad spectrum of attitudes the historian brings to the substance of his narrative: his moral judgments, his analysis of specific situations, the extent to which he illumines historical problems by means of his basic understanding of the reality of the historical process. At the same time, and especially in Bruni's case, consideration is given to his ability to grasp his own contemporary problems in terms of values related to his historical conceptions.

Finally, the historian's narrative techniques are analyzed in an attempt to identify the difficulties involved in expressing his historical ideas in narrative form, as well as the means the historian developed for overcoming those difficulties. This is the aspect of humanist historiography to which previous scholars have paid least attention, in spite of the oft-repeated observation that the humanist's chief interest lay in the elaboration of an elegant and refined narrative style.

These are, of course, not the only relevant questions one could pose in analyzing the works of the fifteenth-century humanists, nor do they wholly comprehend the dimensions of the present inquiry. The value of these questions cannot, in fact, be established so clearly by reference to an abstract philosophy of history as by the fruitfulness with which they may be applied to the specific historical works under study. It is hoped that in the context of the following chapters they will take on meaning.

Chapter Two
The Substance of Bruni's Narrative

The scope of the *Historiae Florentini populi* [1] is plainly stated in the author's preface when he says, "I intend to write down the deeds of the Florentine people, their weighty struggles at home and abroad, their renowned deeds in peace and in war." [2] This explicit and forthright statement of intention stands in marked contrast not only to the previous tradition of Florentine historiography, including Bruni's basic sources,[3] but also to the vernacular histories contemporary with the *Historiae*. The chronicle of Giovanni Villani,

[1] The page references are to the Le Monnier edition, *Istoria fiorentina di L. Aretino tradotta in volgare da D. Acciaiuoli*. The critical edition which Santini prepared for the new series of the *RR.II.SS.*, *Historiarum Florentini populi libri XII*, has been consulted throughout. Santini includes Le Monnier's pagination, which has been retained here for convenience. This work alone will be considered in dealing with Bruni's historical preconceptions. Though his other historical writings and translations could be drawn upon to support specific points, the *Historiae* represent the most mature expression of his ideas and, being composed over a substantial period of his life, show the development of important ideas and techniques of historical writing.

[2] "Res gestas Florentini populi, forisque et domi contentiones habitas et vel pace vel bello inclita facta mandare literis aggrederer" (*Historiae*, vol. I, Proèmio, p. 50).

[3] The principal sources Bruni uses in writing the *Historiae* are outlined by Santini in his monograph on Bruni and also in his edition of the work prepared for the *RR.II.SS.* The first book, in its broad summary of Florentine and Italian history down to the time of Frederick II, makes use of a wide variety of standard works, including the *Ab urbe condita* of Livy, the *Adversus Paganos* of Paulus Orosius, the *Historia Romanorum* and the *Historia Langobardorum* of Paulus Diaconus, and the *Bellum Gothicum* of Procopius. From the last section of Book I to the middle section of Book VIII the basic source is the Villani chronicle, supplemented by occasional facts drawn from the *Crònica* of Dino Compagni, the anonymous *Storie Pistoresi*, and the *Crònica fiorentina* of the Marchionne di Stefani. For the period of the Ciompi revolt, Di Stefani's work seems to form the basic source of information. For the last three books it is impossible to find a principal source. Bruni seems to have used the *Crònica* of Buonacorso Pitti and certainly relied on Gregorio Dati's *Istoria*, though neither Baron nor Santini can find undoubted evidence of borrowing (see *Crisis*, p. 506, n. 7). For a discussion of the way in which Bruni criticizes and draws upon these sources see chap. iv.

which was Bruni's principal source, begins with a confused sentence in which the author suggests why the early history of Florence is obscure, explains his motivations in composing the work, and promises to recount "the origin and early history of such a famous city together with the various changes, happy and unfortunate, it has endured and its past deeds." [4]

Other Florentine chronicles are introduced with expressions of purpose equally confused and as broadly and unselectively conceived. Matteo Villani, continuing his brother's chronicle, attempts to list all the subjects he will cover.[5] Dino Compagni, after explaining his motives, promises to write of the "dangerous events" which have occurred in the course of the city's history.[6] The Marchionne di Stefani begins his chronicle by stating his intention to write of the "building and growth of Florence, the mode of life of its citizens, and the rules of the city." [7] The *Istoria fiorentina* of Malespini, written before the Villani chronicles, contains no statement

---

[4] "Con ciò sia cosa che per gli nostri antichi Fiorentini poche e non ordinate memorie si trovino di fatti passati della nostra città di Firenze o per difetto della loro negligenzia o per cagione che al tempo che Totile Flagellum Dei la distrusse si perdessono scritture; io Giovanni cittadino di Firenze, considerando la nobiltà e grandezza della nostra città a nostri presenti tempi mi pare che si convenga di raccontare e fare memoria dell'origine e cominciamento di così famosa città, e delle mutazioni avverse, felici, e fatti passati di quella" (G. Villani, *Cronica* [4 vols.; Florence, 1846], book I, chap. 1). The most satisfactory work on the Villani chronicles is R. Morghen, *La storiografia fiorentina del Trecento*, in *Libera Cattedra di Storia della Civiltà Fiorentina* (Florence, 1958), which stresses the political passions of Villani in contrast to the previous tradition. E. Mehl, in *Die Weltanschauung des Giovanni Villani* (Leipzig, 1927), attempts to extrapolate from the *Cronica* a coherent set of general attitudes. F. Chabod, "La concezione del mondo di Giovanni Villani," *Nuova rivista storica*, 13 (1929), 336–390, is a bit unfair to Mehl in pointing out that Villani does not always use particular words in the sense in which Mehl says he does. No man is perfectly consistent in his use of words, even key words, and Villani's inconsistency has not kept Mehl from finding the basic concept the chronicler sought to express by certain words. Mehl's failure in this book springs, I think, from trying to draw from Villani's historical writings implications which pertain to his general thought without relating these directly to his historiography. Mehl does not seem to understand the limits of this sort of textual extrapolation.

[5] "Inquietazioni di guerra, movimenti di battaglie, furore di popoli, mutamenti di reami, occupazioni di tiranni, pestilenzie, mortalità e fame, diluvi, incendi, naufragi, e altre gravi cose" (Matteo Villani, *Cronica* [2 vols.; Florence, 1846], book I, chap. 1).

[6] "Le ricordanze dell'antiche istorie lungamente anno stimolata la mente mia di scrivere i pericolosi advenimenti non prosperevoli i quali ha sostenuti la nobile città figliuola di Roma, molti anni, e spezialmente nel tempo del giubileo dell'anno MCCC" (D. Compagni, *Cronica*, vol. IX, part 2, of *RR.II.SS.*, ed. I del Lungo [Città di Castello, 1913], p. 3). Compagni is treated by Morghen, *La storiografia*.

[7] "Pensando quanto è a grado agli uomini trovare cosa che riduca a memoria le cose antiche e spezialmente i principi e le origini della vita de'cittadini e i reggimenti della città" (Marchionne di Coppo Stefani, *Cronica fiorentina*, vol. XXX, part 1, of *RR.II.SS.*, ed. N. Rodolico [Città di Castello, 1903], p. 1).

of theme but only a promise of accuracy.[8] The anonymous *Storie Pistoresi* has no preface, beginning with an account of an earthquake.[9] Among histories contemporary with the *Historiae*, Domenico Buoninsegna's *Historia fiorentina* has no introduction at all.[10] Giovanni Cavalcanti credits his imprisonment with inspiring his work,[11] and the domestic *ricordi* of Pitti and Morelli simply state that they hope to perpetuate the memory of the families they describe.[12]

Bruni's statement of theme differs from the opening sections of all these chronicles and vernacular histories in two major respects. First, in no case do the chroniclers present a clear statment of the scope of their subject. Any indications of the substance of the narrative to follow are buried in a confused sentence seeking mainly to show why the author chose to write history at all. The attempt to justify his efforts dominates the chronicler's preface, if indeed there is one. Bruni's clear introduction is an excellent example of one of his improvements upon the traditional narrative style of Florentine historiography, improvements which will be considered at length in Chapter Four. The second difference between the preface of Bruni and those of the chroniclers illustrates even more plainly his departure from tradition. The chroniclers' statements of scope are not only confused but basically nonselective, including everything in any way connected with the general topic of their work, whether that is a city or a family. The rigor with which Bruni applies his principle of selectivity separates him strikingly from the group of vernacular historians.

It is clear from the body of the *Historiae* as well as from the introductory sentence that Bruni is not writing a world history or even a general history of Florence. He is presenting a political history in which he asks how decisions are made in both foreign and domestic spheres, who makes them, how and to what extent they are effective. He is dealing, in short, with the instruments and workings of power. The political nature of Bruni's work becomes

---

[8] R. Malespini, *Istoria fiorentina* (Florence, 1718), pp. 1–2.

[9] *Storie Pistoresi*, vol. XI, part 15, of *RR.II.SS.*, ed. S. Barbi (Città di Castello, 1907).

[10] He begins immediately, narrating from Noah (D. Buoninsegna, *Historia fiorentina* [Florence, 1581], p. 1).

[11] G. Cavalcanti, *Istorie fiorentine* (Florence, 1838), p. 2. Cavalcanti's history, together with the domestic *ricordi* of Pitti and Morelli, has been studied most recently by C. Varese, *Storia e politica nella prosa del Quattrocento* (Turin, 1961).

[12] B. Pitti, *Crònica* (Florence, 1720), p. 1; and G. Morelli, *Ricordi*, ed. V. Branca (Florence, 1955), p. 82.

increasingly apparent as one penetrates the narrative,[13] but the political scope of the *Historiae* is unmistakably suggested in the opening sentence by the use of the phrase "res gestas florentini populi," since Bruni usually endows the word *populus* with strong political connotations.[14]

That Bruni should elect to write this particular type of history and that he should state the subject of his work with such clarity and precision are facts not to be explained by reference to previous Florentine historiography. Nor can they be directly credited to the influence of those classical historians who captured Bruni's most intense interest. Livy, whose *Ab urbe condita* provides the model for most of the formal elements in the *Historiae*,[15] is not writing explicitly political history, even though he uses the alternation between domestic and foreign affairs as a basic organizational device. Moreover, he fails to introduce his work with an explicit description of its subject matter. Livy talks instead about the difficulty and value of the task, justifying his labors in a manner better suited to be a model for the vernacular chroniclers than for Bruni. After this Livy does say that he will treat the specific theme of Roman moral decline, but this passage should not be compared with Bruni's introduction, which is not only more succinctly stated but also abstracted from any specific theme.

Sallust adopts the practice of a succinct statement of theme, but he only writes of particular wars. Though the political dimension of the *Bellum Jugurthinum* is strong, Sallust's statement of theme does not refer explicitly to the work's political aspect, and in introducing the *Bellum Catilinae* he only promises to talk of the conspiracy.[16] Both of these histories differ from Bruni's in their monographic scope. The best model for Bruni among the Roman historians is Tacitus, who was only beginning to attract the attention of humanists in the first part of the Quattrocento.[17] Tacitus

---

[13] Bruni's specific concerns in this field will be studied more closely in chap. iii.
[14] See Appendix C.
[15] See chap. iv.
[16] In neither case does Sallust begin the work with a statement of theme. The *Bellum Catilinae* promises, "Igitur de Catilinae conjuratione quam verissime potero paucis absolvam" (IV, 3); and the *Bellum Jugurthinum* says, "Bellum scripturus sum quod populus Romanus cum Jugurtha rege Numidarum gessit" (V, 1).
[17] G. Toffanin, in *Machiavelli e il tacitismo* (Padua, 1921), chap. 1, attributes the displacement of Livy by Tacitus as an historical model to the period of the Counter Reform. But Boccaccio had found Books XI–XVI of the *Annales* and Books I–V of the *Historiae* in Monte Cassino and had brought the MS to Florence, where it eventually came into the possession of Bruni's friend Niccolò Niccoli (see R.

describes his task in the *Historiae* in these terms: "The history I have begun is that of a period rich in disasters, terrible with battles, torn by civil strife, horrible even in peace." [18] This is, of course, specifically a description of the period and only indirectly a delineation of scope. Thus, though Bruni could have gained from the Roman historians an appreciation for the virtues of a succinct prefatory description of his theme, it was not in their works that he discovered a model for his own statement of the political scope of the *Historiae*.

If Bruni's statement of scope is indeed to be traced to a classical model, it is to the tradition of Greek historiography and particularly to the Hellenistic historian Polybius that one must look. Bruni was fond of Polybius and translated the early sections of his history of the rise of Rome, although this task was not undertaken until 1418 or 1419, after work on the *Historiae* had already started.[19]

Sabbadini, *Le Scoperte dei codici latini e greci ne'secoli XIV e XV*, I [Florence, 1905], 29–30, and II [Florence, 1914], 254). Bruni's acquaintance with Tacitus can be definitely established from the reference in Book I to the decline of letters under the emperors (I, 100), an interpretation taken from the first book of Tacitus' *Historiae* (see Baron, *Crisis*, pp. 47–48).

[18] "Opus adgredior opimum casibus, atrox praeliis, discors seditionibus, ipsa etiam pace saevum" (Tacitus, *Historiarum libri*, trans. C. Moore [2 vols.; London, 1925], vol. I, book i, chap. 2; hereafter *Historiae*).

[19] Baron (*Crisis*, p. 612, n. 16) dates the *De primo bello punico* thus on the basis of a letter of Ambrogio Traversini's. The earlier dating for the work had been 1421. Within the scope of this study it is neither expedient nor necessary to draw out at great length the similarities between Bruni and Polybius. The important elements found in Polybius which also appear in Bruni's *Historiae* should, however, be noted here. The most significant of these is the existence in both works of a coherent concept of history in terms of which the specific details of the narrative are interpreted. Though Bruni's interest in his concept remains implicit and will be extrapolated in this chapter, Polybius states his outright: "The historian should bring before his readers under one synoptical view the operations by which she [Fortune] has accomplished her general purpose" (Polybius, *The Histories*, trans. W. Paton [6 vols.; London, 1922–1927] vol. I, book i, chap. 4). Polybius goes on to state that the historian, starting from this view, should study the interconnections of all the particulars of history. Indeed, Polybius himself frequently reconstructs past events and criticizes his sources from just such a coherent view (see book I, chap. 15). The political dimensions of Polybius' historical understanding are also clear (I shall deal with them in the text).

There are, of course, important differences between Bruni and Polybius. The Florentine historian is not really interested in universal history, but then his theme is not that of a world empire. More weighty is Polybius' emphasis on the power and importance of Fortune, which finds small echo in Bruni. Nor does Bruni conceptualize the rise and fall of states in the manner of the Greek historian. (It must be kept in mind, of course, that the sixth book of Polybius, which contains his cyclical view of history, was not familiar to Italian humanists of Bruni's time; see J. H. Hexter, "Seyssel, Machiavelli, and Polybius VI: the Mystery of the Missing Translation," *Studies in the Renaissance*, 3 [1956], 75–96.) In spite of these differences, the fact that both historians base their works on a political conceptualization of history,

He had begun to study Greek under Chrysoloras early in the century, however, and his acquaintance with Polybius before 1415 can be assumed.[20]

Polybius, lacking the narrative gifts of either his Greek forerunners or his Roman successors, prefaces his work with a confused paragraph justifying history in general and his own study of the rise of Rome in particular. He works out this justification, however, in terms which forcefully indicate the political nature of his historical studies, stressing the usefulness of the study of history for a life of active politics and promising to interpret the rise of Rome as a function of its political institutions. The work which follows this preface is, like Bruni's *Historiae*, political in scope and analysis. Though the Roman historians were uppermost in suggesting to Bruni the means of expressing his ideas, it is Polybius, among all the classical historians, who best prefigures Bruni's historical scope, in the prefatory section as well as in the body of his work.

It is a mistake, however, to search for Bruni's inspiration solely among classical historians. He was, after all, as Hans Baron has shown, a leading figure in the movement of civic humanism, a movement whose basic dimensions were established by the great crisis of the war between Florence and Giangaleazzo of Milan.[21] Bruni's concern for political history sprang as surely from his own historical environment, which posed questions in this form, as from any intellectual sources which might have suggested answers. When his modes of expression and narrative style are studied in Chapter Four, the problem of intellectual sources will become clearer and quite specific influences will be suggested, but for the moment a simple outline of the principal factors involved will suffice.

Bruni, in choosing the political history of Florence from all the possible subjects open to him, was engaging in a process of selection quite different from that of modern historians. Here in this

---

taken together with Bruni's long interest in Polybius, bespeaks a strong if problematic influence on Bruni by the Greek.

[20] See L. Bruni, *Suo tempore in Italia gestarum commentarius* (Lyons, 1539), p. 14, which talks of his studies under Chrysoloras. In this work, written late in life (1440–41), Bruni records the great impression the Greek classics had made on him, stressing in addition to the pleasures involved the utility of the study: "Quanta igitur vel ad cognitionem utilitas, vel ad famam accessio, vel ad voluptatem cumulatio tibi ex linguae huius cognitione proveniet" (p. 15).

[21] See chap. i, n. 96.

book, for example, I am concerned with the historiographical tradition of Florence in the Quattrocento. In selecting this subject matter, however, I mean to imply not that the economic, political, or artistic history of Florence is unimportant but simply that the subject I have chosen is worth investigating on its own terms. Having inherited from such nineteenth-century historians as Ranke a concept of universal history which defines all historical events as significant, the modern historian understands the impossibility of comprehending all significant facts in one definition of scope and chooses to divide up the field into manageable proportions, suspending his judgment on the relative importance of the various factors.

This particular concept of universal history was not a commonplace of the fifteenth century, and its absence from Bruni's historical ideas can be noticed in his historical method, his approach to the subject, and the very substance of his narrative. In choosing political history Bruni did not mean to select one out of many significant historical factors. Instead he meant to choose the one significant factor which he considered the key to understanding all important historical events and human activities. The importance Bruni attached to the political factor is shown most clearly by his presentation of the relationship between foreign and domestic affairs. The division of the *Historiae* into foreign and domestic themes was obviously of great importance to Bruni, for he states it in two different ways in the one sentence delineating the subject matter: "contentions at home and abroad" and "deeds in war and in peace." Livy, of course, had organized his history in this dual fashion, but Bruni had grounds beyond pure classical imitation for including both aspects in his work.

The relationship between foreign and domestic affairs is crucial to an understanding of the basic themes of the *Historiae*, but Bruni allows this relationship to develop only with great care and deliberation. Not until Book IV does he explicitly refer to the meaning of the introductory link between the two elements. There he simply states that they are related to each other like members of the same body.[22] Having indicated that the decision to narrate the

---

[22] "Nam cum duae sint historiae partes et quasi membra, foris gesta et domi, non minoris sane putandum fuerit domesticos status quam externa bella cognoscere" (I, iv, 418). The classical historian who most clearly states the close relationship between foreign and domestic affairs is Sallust. Stating his reasons for writing the *Bellum Jugurthinum*, he mentions its relevance to the ensuing civil strife: "Quae

two is not arbitrary, the historian passes on to suggest, but not to explicate, a basis for their relationship. He observes that, at the end of the Pisan war in 1291, the people were able to turn their energies towards establishing liberty at home,[23] which could imply that war and domestic politics use the energies of the state in much the same way. The justice of that implication is shortly revealed when, in an oration of Giano della Bella's, Bruni says that those cities which are competent in war ought, for that very reason, to be able to manage their affairs at home.[24]

By the sixth book Bruni has shown that foreign and domestic affairs concern similar problems and reflect similar historical realities. In this book he begins to investigate the inner workings of the relationship. To explain the rise to power of the Duke of Athens he points to the domestic unrest and discontent which followed an unsuccessful war with Lucca, showing that one of the factors connecting foreign and domestic matters is psychological. A more tangible factor uniting these two dimensions of history is found in the exiles. They clearly constitute a domestic element, since they are created by the factional discord that is the single most pressing domestic problem. However, by combining with foreign enemies they pose a military threat, and Bruni often deals with them as a foreign problem.[25]

That the categories into which Bruni divides his narrative should be seen as elements of a single reality is not a coincidence, for he understands the fundamental attribute of the substance of this narrative to be the interconnection of all significant historical events. In fact, this very relatedness, and not a moralizing presentation of values received either from his own tradition or from his

----

contentio divina et humana cuncta permiscuit eoque vecordiae processit, ut studiis civilibus bellum atque vastitas Italiae finem faceret" (V, 1). See R. Syme, *Sallust* (Berkeley, 1964), pp. 138–177, where he deals with the importance of this connection to Sallust. If Bruni is indebted to any classical historian for this dimension of his historical vision, it is to the author of the *Bellum Jugurthinum* and the *Bellum Catilinae*.

23 I, iv, 430.

24 I, iv, 442. The problem of interpreting the orations in general will be taken up in chap. iv. One of the most important functions of the orations in the *Historiae* is to underline and clarify some of the themes implied in the narrative. This is not their only purpose, however, and no major point can be established solely from comments to be found in speeches. Here, as elsewhere in the book, evidence from orations is used only to support points already suggested by the narrative itself.

25 See, for instance, III, ix, 16: "Altero dehinc anno foris omnia, praeterquam ab exulum metu."

encounter with the classics, underlies the moral element of Bruni's history.

It is a commonplace in humanist historical theory that an historian should be guided by moral considerations in writing history. Pontano says in the *Actius*, "By preserving these things [past deeds] the worthy expositor of deeds shows himself to be one who not only praises noble achievements and outstanding acts but also denounces shameful and degrading ones; indeed, he makes himself a protector of virtue itself, a guardian of wisdom and almost a teacher, since history itself is a teacher of life, of men, and of human affairs." [26] Bruni's preface contains an explicit concern with the moral value of history,[27] and on several occasions in the narrative he obviously wishes an event to serve a didactic function. Justifying the space he devotes to Walter of Brienne, he says, "For the affair is worth setting down in writing either to admonish citizens or to castigate rulers." [28] He is similarly frank about the lessons to be learned from his narrative of the Ciompi revolt.[29] In addition, there are many examples of people who learn from history.[30] Finally, implicit lessons can be found within the narrative itself.[31]

Bruni's purpose is thus clearly moral: he intends the *Historiae* to be didactic and carries out his intention in the narrative. In spite of its moral purpose, however, the work does not apply received moral categories to individual and group actions. Explicit judgments based on such categories are rare. In one of the few remarks of this kind, Bruni reproaches Bernarbo of Milan with

[26] "His itaque servandis non laudatorem modo se nobilium nunc facinorum praeclarissimarumque actionum nunc reprehensorem turpium abiectorumque ostendet egregius rerum gestarum expositor, verum etiam virtutis ipsius patronum admonitoremque sapientiae prae se feret et quasi magistrum quando historia ipsa vitae est hominum ac rerum humanarum magistra" (G. Pontano, *I dialoghi*, ed. C. Previtera [Florence, 1943], p. 227). This element in humanist historical theory has been stressed by modern scholars, including Felix Gilbert and Hanna Gray (see Chap. i at note 95).

[27] "Nam cum provecti aetate homines eo sapientiores habeantur, quo plura viderunt in vita, quanto magis historia novis, si accurate legerimus hanc praestare poterit sapientiam, in qua multarum aetatum facta consiliaque cernuntur, ut et quid sequare et quid vites faciliter sumas excellentiumque virorum gloria ad virtutem excitere" (I, Proèmio, 50).

[28] "Res enim digna est quae literis annotetur vel pro admonitu civium, vel pro castigatione regnantium" (II, vi, 290).

[29] III, ix, 8.

[30] The original settlers of Florence learn the dangers of overindulgence (I, i, 64), and the Florentines learn new military tactics (II, v, 46).

[31] For instance, the sack and destruction of Arezzo carry lessons for the internal government of cities (III, ix, 42). See chap. iii for a discussion of this particular incident.

ingratitude but points out immediately the practical significance of his ungrateful actions.[32] On another occasion, when he explains Gambacurta's downfall and death as the result of his excessive goodness, he even suggests that history teaches us the dangers of moral rectitude.[33] He makes every attempt, in fact, to suppress the personal dimensions of morality. In the section describing the horrible fate of Ugolino of Pisa and his nephews and sons, who are locked in a tower to die of starvation, Bruni relies for his source material on the chronicle of Giovanni Villani. Villani's narrative is full of moral indignation, saying that Ugolino deserved his fate because of his past crimes and that the Pisans in their turn were punished for the outrage.[34] Bruni will have none of this, concluding his account of the incident by placing it in the context of political problems and ignoring the issues of personal morality.[35]

Thus the moral element in Bruni's history must be very carefully defined. It is not sufficient to say that Bruni is writing history to teach the moral and spiritual values of his age, for he is not conspicuously moralistic. He is certainly less so than the Villani, whose power to suspend moral judgment on the characters in their chronicles is weak. He is even less so than Livy, whose anecdotes frequently contain judgments from received moral principles.[36] History for Bruni is didactic not because it can be used to uphold traditional morality but because historical events are interrelated in such a way that no moral decision can be made without reference to all significant historical factors and ultimately to the substantial reality of history itself. In this understanding of history all actions become morally significant, not simply those to which accepted canons of behavior can be applied.

There is no place in Bruni's approach for uncritical moral categories, and the manner in which he weaves moral considerations into the narrative reveals an increasing sophistication in the anal-

---

[32] II, viii, 500.

[33] III, x, 188.

[34] G. Villani, *Crònica*, VII, 128.

[35] The Pisans are "ad eam immanitatem nihil ob aliud quam ob studia partium impulsi" (I, iii, 398). In the same vein Bruni frequently encounters faithlessness and dishonesty without any explicit judgment or recognition that moral values are being violated (see II, vi, 222, and II, vii, 406).

[36] W. S. Anderson, "Livy and Machiavelli," *Classical Journal*, 53 (1957-58), 232-235, brings out this element in Livy by studying his account of Manlius Torquatus' execution of his son in 340 B.C. Anderson is led to an unsound judgment of the difference between Livy and Machiavelli precisely by failing to distinguish between morality and moralism.

ysis of these categories. The work opens with an incident charged with moral significance. Drawing his material from the second Catilinarian,[37] Bruni describes the implication of the early Florentines in the conspiracy of Catiline. He explains their involvement in terms of their mode of life, presenting with strong moral overtones their high living, luxurious clothes, and great buildings and aqueducts built in imitation of Rome.[38] He shows how this state of affairs leaves the early inhabitants open to Catiline's blandishments and how their participation leads to ruin. He concludes with an assessment of the effect of their defeat, again using moral terms. Their attitudes change; they become more sober, disciplined and moderate; this in turn makes them stronger in relation to their neighbors and more capable of supporting the large buildings and high standards of living which had previously ruined them.[39]

In relating this incident Bruni betrays a relatively simple moral sense, which equates certain virtues with certain inevitable practical rewards.[40] On the one hand, he does not see the virtues of modesty and sobriety as categorical imperatives; on the other, he does not elaborate the connection between virtue and the reward which justifies these virtues. Bruni's inquiring mind is not long satisfied, however, with assuming that relationship. In Book I he casts doubt on the extent to which the "virtus romana" saved Rome from the Etruscans, suggesting that the city's real savior was the width of the Tiber.[41] Throughout the first book, though, there are cases in which simple moral or immoral actions have simple effects and rewards or punishments,[42] and the book closes with a moralizing condemnation of Frederick II.[43]

As Bruni continues the narration, he deals with moral values more and more frequently in terms of their political meaning and importance. In Book II a rupture of treaty obligations calls forth

[37] Cicero, *In Catilinam*, II, 9.

[38] I, i, 60.

[39] I, i, 64.

[40] He has a similar approach to the problem when he recounts Camillus' return of the children to their parents after they had been betrayed by a greedy schoolmaster (I, i, 92).

[41] I, i, 84. Livy, *Ab urbe condita*, trans. B. Foster, F. Moore, et al. (14 vols.; London and Cambridge, Mass., 1925-1951), does not mention this consideration, stressing the *virtus* alone (I, ii, 10-13; hereafter Livy).

[42] For example, the faithfulness of Theodosius, which assures the friendship of the Goths (I, i, 110); Honorius' treachery, which excites them to a fury of destruction (I, i, 114); and the deviousness of Stilicho, which causes the sack of Rome (I, i, 116).

[43] I, i, 158.

not a simple condemnation, as it had in Book I, but a discussion of the practical consideration which made the break a foolish move.[44] When he considers the question of whether or not Florence should buy Lucca, his analysis concentrates on the advantages that would accrue to Florence from this action,[45] and when Mastino della Scala betrays Florence by keeping Lucca for himself, Bruni assesses the significance of the betrayal only in terms of the factors which permit Mastino to hold the city successfully.[46] A Florentine surprise attack on friendly Pistoia is condemned only when it is temporarily stymied. After Pistoia has been taken, Bruni comments, "By this means an affair badly begun has a favorable outcome."[47]

The subtlety of Bruni's understanding of the moral dimensions in history is perhaps most clearly manifest in his treatment of a diplomatic event toward the middle of the work. In 1351 the Archbishop of Milan, at war with Florence, sends legates to seek an alliance with the Pisans. The leaders of Pisa reply that they already have a treaty obligation to Florence and see no cause for breaking it, whereupon the Milanese legates appeal to popular passion. The magistrates permit the appeal but, in an oration of their own, convince the people that it would be dishonorable to join Milan against Florence. The two moral factors present here are skillfully intertwined. On the one hand there are the people, who decide against the war purely because it involves a breach of common honesty and trust.[48] On the other hand there are the magistrates, "led by a true assessment of the situation,"[49] who decide that the Archbishop's proposal would involve the surrender of Pisan liberty and refuse the alliance on these grounds, using honor only as a pretext. The situation is morally informed on both levels, but only the magistrates' reasoning reflects Bruni's concept of true morality; the people's reasoning is unsophisticated moralism, fit solely to move the lower orders.

In the last books of the *Historiae* Bruni explores with even greater frequency the relation between moral acts and their practical results.

---

[44] I, ii, 184. He calls the Pisan move an "impetus immaturus," since Manfred's power in Tuscany was still growing.

[45] II, vi, 168–192.

[46] II, vi, 220–229.

[47] "Per hunc modum res male coepta bonum tandem exitum habuit" (II, vii, 354).

[48] Bruni explicitly states the grounds on which the people are led to oppose the war, "pro honestate contra dedecus et infamiam" (II, vii, 378).

[49] "Verissimam rationem secuti" (II, vii, 370).

Bernarbo's ungrateful actions force Florence into alliance with his enemies and weaken his position.[50] The Florentines unjustly execute a group of citizens, infuriating the enemy's *condottiere* and rendering it impossible to buy off his army.[51] Florence's decision to abstain from taking Aretine castles which do not surrender of their own will has the effect of softening the king's enmity.[52]

Bruni, then, throughout the *Historiae* avoids unanalyzed moral categories which are not related to deeper historical considerations. The moral questions posed are political in substance and concern the viability of the state. They take this form from the very beginning of the work. The basic lesson derived from the early settlers and their intrigue with Catiline is that an excessively licentious and indulgent state is not a viable one. It will shortly collapse, undermined by internal problems exacerbated by external pressures.

Bruni's decision to write political history reflects a commitment on his part, just as does his decision to write Florentine history. To say that political history for Bruni is moral is not, however, to describe the substance of his historical understanding. It is rather to say that he regards political history as significant, that for him the description of political reality is an immediately valuable accomplishment, providing insights useful in the guidance of human conduct and leading toward the understanding of general truth. By understanding his commitment to political history one can grasp the importance Bruni affixed to his work, but one cannot penetrate thereby to his basic modes of perceiving historical reality. The substance which underlies these interrelated historical factors must now be sought.

Only in a very limited sense can the *Historiae* be seen as an exercise in institutional history. Bruni was deeply interested in institutional change and the workings of constitutional forms, for he devoted considerable sections of the text to their description. He seems to present institutional factors, however, not as elements of interest in themselves but as means for discovering and exposing the reality which lies behind them. He approaches the problem of exposing this reality, as he does that of the relationship between foreign and domestic affairs, slowly and deliberately.

In Book I, elaborating the means by which the Tuscan cities

[50] II, viii, 504–506.
[51] III, ix, 20–24.
[52] III, ix, 62.

acquired republican forms of government, Bruni suggests the effect
of this change in increasing Tuscan power.[53] That external power
should be a function of internal political organization follows from
the relationship between foreign and domestic history and should
cause no surprise. Here Bruni lets the matter rest, refraining from
an investigation of the nature of the interconnection and virtually
ignoring a similar change in Roman polity.[54] When he opens Book
II with a description of Florence's early political organization, he
posits the same correlation between the development of free institutions and augmented power in the foreign sphere.[55]

Bruni, however, is no more uncritical of received political categories than he is of received moral categories. If dishonesty has a
negative moral value, he must inquire into the reasons for this;
similarly, if free institutions have a positive moral value, he must
seek out with equal vigor the reality which explains this fact. After
stating that Florence's power grew after the creation of the *anziani*,
he shows that this increase was caused by the release of psychological energies untapped by the previous regime, which had given no
incentive to human effort. "Men who a short while ago served
either princes or their followers, as I have shown was the case,
once the sweetness of liberty was tasted, and the *populus* itself was
lord and bestower of honors, applied themselves with all their
strength in order to merit the respect of their own peers." [56]

The invocation of psychological elements to explain the inner
workings of historical phenomena and particularly of political institutions is of enormous importance for Bruni, and he soon takes
occasion to stress these elements in discussing the growth of faction, another political problem which can be dealt with by institutional means. In 1266, Novellus, administering Florence in Manfred's name and confronted with a popular uprising, grants certain
reforms including the creation of the Thirty-Six. By these measures
he hopes to both reduce the popular pressure and pacify the feud
between the Guelf and Ghibelline factions. Bruni shows how these

[53] "In tantas opes potentiamque accrevit, ut non solum urbibus passim oppor-
tunis locis per eam conditis, virisque et divitiis intra fines floreret, verum etiam
extra longe lateque dominaretur" (I, i, 68).

[54] I, i, 82.

[55] "Ea de causa robuste insurgens, domique et foris multa duxerat providendum"
(I, ii, 160).

[56] "Homines enim qui dudum aut principibus aut eorum fautoribus, ut vere
dixerim, inservierant, gustata libertatis dulcedine cum populus iam ipse dominus
auctorque honoris esset, totis se viribus attollebant quo dignitatem inter suos mereren-
tur" (I, ii, 162).

reforms not only lead to the restoration of popular government but also establish the government of the Twelve, which in turn is able to effect the recall of the exiles and a temporary pacification of the city.[57] He does not immediately explain how this psychological and institutional change proceeded from the first reform. Just as he did not elaborate the mechanism of the relationship between foreign and domestic affairs when he first narrated the increase in foreign power arising from the establishment of free institutions, so now he avoids probing the mechanism of the connection between psychological and institutional change. He is concerned only with recounting the interconnection as an historical phenomenon and with fixing it as an observed fact in the mind of the reader.

The next important institutional change [58] involves the establishment of the Ordinances of Justice. The actual crisis out of which the Ordinances are created is prefaced by an extended discourse on the state of anarchy and discord into which Florence has fallen. This preface concludes with an oration by Giano della Bella, who tries to persuade the people that the Ordinances are needed to correct the city's difficulties. Della Bella outlines the problem, and then he stresses the necessity for institutions to deal with it: "It seems to me that the liberty of the people is contained in two things: laws and judges." [59] After this general statement he goes on to propose detailed reforms.

Bruni uses the oration for several purposes. It summarizes and comments upon the condition of Florence previously described; it underlines the importance Bruni places on institutions; it introduces the account of the actual reforms. More important, Bruni uses Giano della Bella's words to suggest how institutions function. This is done obliquely by pointing out the circumstances under which they will not work adequately. "I seek to rouse your spirit to deal with the problem. Indeed, I see that certain things, more than men commonly think, depend not so much on the magistrates as on the vigor of the people. For if the people only wish to retain a fitting primacy in the republic, it will be easy to execute judgment even against the most powerful." [60] The value of institutions

---

[57] I, ii, 270–276.

[58] Technical changes in 1280 (I, iii, 354) and 1282 (I, iii, 364) are narrated in passing without suggesting a larger significance.

[59] "Mihi quidem videtur libertas populi duabus rebus contineri: legibus scilicet atque iudiciis" (I, iv, 432).

[60] "Ad exequendi vero difficultatem, quaeso, animos advertite. Quippe maius

lies, then, in the extent to which they draw on and promote fitting psychological attitudes — here in the case of domestic faction as formerly in the case of foreign policy.

Having established, in the two important categories of foreign and domestic affairs, the dependence of institutions on the attitudes and spiritual vigor of the human beings who use them, the historian analyzes and judges future institutional change in terms of that insight. When the Florentines initiate the practice of choosing magistrates by lot, they are making a mistake, according to Bruni, for this means of election has an unfortunate psychological effect: "It extinguishes the zeal for virtue, for if elections had to be contested and openly had to run all the dangers of publicity, men would be much more circumspect." [61] Here Bruni's sense of the place and importance of institutions emerges with even greater clarity. Though they cannot function by themselves to govern the state without reference to psychological factors, they can and should be used as a means of exploiting these human factors in the service of political order and for the achievement of common ends. Institutions are at best the instrument that combines human beings into an active unit; they are not the essence of the political union. The practice of choosing by lot is unfortunate — even though, as Bruni admits, it was a Roman political institution — precisely because it fails to fulfill the proper function of an institution.

Bruni has nothing but contempt for institutions which ignore or even attempt to suppress what he considers to be basic traits of human nature. In 1383 a pestilence breaks out in Florence, and many of the leading citizens seek to avoid contagion by fleeing the city, thereby exposing it to the unrestrained domination of the lower classes. Lest this should result in disturbances which will weaken the state, a law is passed forbidding a Florentine citizen to leave the city during the emergency. The law is totally ineffective in restraining the flight, and Bruni, rather than castigating the citizens for their lack of moral fortitude and civic feeling, simply notes the general impracticality of the measure. "But neither the law nor the

---

quiddam esse cerno quam homines opinentur, nec tam a magistratu quam a populi robore dependere. Si enim populus quemadmodum decet, praestantiam in republica retinere volet executio iudiciorum etiam contra potentissimos facillima erit." (I, iv, 438.)

61 "Extinguit praeterea virtutis studium, quia si suffragiis certandum foret, et aperte in periculum famae veniendum multo magis sese homines circumspicerent" (II, v, 82).

prohibition could restrain the flight; indeed to the fear of death, the fear of anything else will easily succumb." [62] Bruni, then, sees that just as institutions have psychological effects, so they themselves are affected by psychological realities.

After establishing this connection firmly in the first part of the *Historiae*, Bruni subsequently tends to narrate institutional change in terms of an accompanying change in the attitudes of the Florentines. His account of the opening of the Lucchese war in 1335 is a clear example: "And so, the treaty being broken, the Lucchese war began. The Florentines, though a great struggle was proposed to them and though a new war found them already exhausted, neither declined in spirit nor abandoned any of their original dignity but, carrying themselves fiercely and sharply and not in confusion or trepidation, provided for each contingency with mature council. They appointed ten men to the public power for securing money and six men to plan the conduct of the war." [63] Only after a thorough description of the Florentine spirit and a judgment on the quality of their decision in terms of that spirit does Bruni proceed to list the specific institutional measures adopted to face the crisis.

Clearly, behind the institutions, behind political history, behind the very moral concerns which inform the *Historiae* lies the vision of historical reality as fundamentally intangible, founded in human psychology — motivations, moods, character. This is the basic historical substance in terms of which all other elements need to be understood. The importance of that insight in understanding the substance of Bruni's work will emerge even more clearly in studying his presentation of two major historical events: the rise and fall of Walter of Brienne and the tumult of the Ciompi.

After a series of reverses and misfortunes in the Lucchese war the Florentines in 1342 call Walter of Brienne to take charge of the state. In the *Historiae* Walter's accession to power is explicitly set in the context of general popular discontent with the conduct of

---

[62] "Sed neque lex neque prohibitio tenere potuit fugas, quippe adversus timorem mortis propositae timor omnis alter tamquam levior succumbebat" (III, ix, 64).

[63] "Ita rupto foedere, bellum lucense ex integro nascitur, Florentini, etsi contentio magna proponebatur ac iam defessos novum excipiebat vehementiusque se attollentes, non trepide nec turbulente sed maturo singula providebant belli gerendi praefecerunt" (II, vi, 224–226). The close association of the spirit of the Florentines with the specific institutional measures adopted for the conduct of the war is striking. By comparison Villani, who devotes an entire chapter to the creation of the magistrates, says that it was "lo scampo" of the Florentines (XI, 45) but does not explain either the psychological context of the reform or the reason for its effect.

the war. The discontent, according to Bruni, manifests itself most directly in popular hatred of the responsible magistrates and generals.[64] Walter is no sooner ensconced in power than he begins to misuse it. Bruni, taking his facts from Villani, where they appear in the form of a disorganized catalogue,[65] describes Walter's abuse of power in terms of those acts which have political and constitutional significance. Walter expels the priors from the Palazzo della Signoria and robs them of all authority; he abolishes the *gonfaloniere*, deprives the citizens of arms, annuls all honors, takes money greedily, and imposes new taxes, using foreigners to collect them.[66]

The passage devoted to Walter's tenure of power is political in scope, wholly devoted to Walter's institutional changes. The reaction of the Florentines, in spite of Bruni's strongly implied disapproval of the Duke of Athens' conduct, is not given. The situation is represented statically, with no sense of growing outrage at each new transgression of Florentine custom nor of the increasingly serious nature of these transgressions. Having stated Walter's acts in a political context, however, Bruni narrates his actual overthrow psychologically. "Since all this seemed intolerable and the evils grew from day to day, hatred finally overcame fear, and at first there were various quarrels among the citizens; soon these were followed by conspiracies, indeed many at one time, each ignorant of the other." [67] Only then does he proceed to describe the course of the rebellion and the actual events leading to Walter's expulsion from the city.

This passage sheds considerable light on Bruni's perception of the real in history. The account of Walter's acts remains static and basically topographical, describing superficial alterations of a political nature and avoiding the suggestion that these are substantial. Only in dealing with the psychological dimension does Bruni attempt to narrate the change which gives reality both to the previously related background and to subsequent events. Once this change is stated ("superante iam odio metum"), the narrative assumes dimensions of substantial change — historical process, if

---

64 II, vi, 284. This interpretation is not unlike Villani's (XII, 1), but, typically, the relationship between the discontent and the accession to power is more clearly stated by Bruni, and all considerations not directly associated with it are omitted.

65 G. Villani, *Crònica*, XII, 8.

66 II, vi, 294.

67 "Cum intolerabilis videretur ac in dies magis crescerent mala, superante iam odio metum, variae primo querelae civium mox coniurationes sunt consecutae et quidem plures uno ignorantibus a aliis alias" (II, vi, 296).

you will — which it had not previously had. Whereas Walter's acts are not narrated in relation to one another but as an unconnected series, the conspiracies are described as growing in stages from small beginnings, a method that conveys a sense of real movement absent from the earlier section.

Bruni did not discover this mode of perceiving historical reality in his classical models. Livy, narrating a similar incident from Roman history, portrays the expulsion of the Tarquins in a significantly different fashion. Outlining Tarquin's actions in great detail, he includes for dramatic effect accounts of wars and portents which signify impending trouble.[68] Introducing with consummate skill the incident of Lucretia's rape, which provides the decisive act in Tarquin's overthrow,[69] he narrates it with sensual immediacy and dramatic import in order to underline the importance of this event in bringing down Tarquin. Bruni, of course, did not find in his sources an event of such notoriety and obvious importance as the rape, and consequently he does not suggest that any particular outrage was responsible for Walter's downfall.[70]

Livy, while concentrating on the specific event stressed in the legend, does not present any substantial psychological alteration as the cause of the revolt. Brutus is not transformed by the fate of his sister; he simply throws off his mask of indifference to reveal his true nature.[71] Livy has already prepared the reader for this revelation of Brutus' real character by describing his previous action: "Therefore, he abandoned industriousness and sought to feign foolishness so that under this guise the liberating spirit of Rome might bide its time." [72] Nor does the mood of the people undergo a real change. They are simply incensed by Brutus' oration [73] and are induced to do what they had always been inclined to do. The

[68] Livy, I, 49–56.

[69] He introduces the scene in the middle of a military event, the siege of Ardea, and gives no indication of its significance until the account of the events leading up to the rape is half finished (I, 57).

[70] In a less carefully constructed incident Bruni gives a precipitating cause. The narrative of the Sicilian Vespers contains all the elements found in his account of Walter's overthrow — the list of injuries, even the statement of a change in attitude ("superante patientiam magnitudine iniuria") — but he does narrate the insult to the woman at Palermo, which precipitates the revolt (I, iii, 366–368).

[71] "Ibi oratio habita nequaquam eius pectoris ingeniique quod simulatum ad eam diem fuerat" (Livy, I, 59).

[72] "Ergo ex industria factus ad imitationem stultitiae . . . ut sub eius obtentu cognominis liberator ille populi Romani animus latens opperiretur tempora sua" (Livy, I, 56).

[73] "Incensam multitudinem pepulit" (Livy, I, 49).

lack of popular affection for Tarquin has already been noted in Livy's remarks prefatory to the narration of the reign.[74] This popular dislike has not changed; it has simply been mobilized into action by an outrageous event.

The transformation of a monarchy into a republic is an historical change as real for Livy as the overthrow of the Duke of Athens is for Bruni. To Livy's mind, however, the reality exists in the concrete events, and the representation of this reality demands that these events be narrated in dramatic immediacy. For Bruni, on the other hand, the reality of the change is psychological, and the events themselves simply provide the context within which it is represented.

The psychological bases of political history are presented with even greater consistency in the section of the *Historiae* which introduces the Ciompi revolt. The crisis is institutional in origin, precipitated by an attempt to amend the law of Ammoniti in order to prevent its unjust use. In spite of its institutional character, Bruni develops the event exclusively in terms of the attitudes of the various groups into which he sees Florentine society divided. The causes of the revolt, moreover, are explicitly related to these attitudes. Though he introduces the section with a straightforward promise to explain its cause,[75] he apparently sees that the causality is too complex to be stated directly, for he proceeds with a narrative of the events.

The historian begins by noting that the eight magistrates who are directing the war against the Pope are considered by the upper classes to be too favorable to the plebs. The *optimates'* hatred increases as the magistrates' tenure in office is extended.[76] Although their unpopularity is further heightened by the papal interdict, the eight manage to retain the favor of the lower orders.[77] Next Bruni, having briefly delineated the psychological context of the event, describes the reactivation of the old anti-Ghibelline laws to be used by the *optimates* as a weapon against their enemies. Up to this point in the account he has followed his established practice of showing the significance of an institution in terms of the spirit in which it is administered.

When Sylvester dei Medici seeks to abrogate the law, the plebs

---

74 "In caritate civium nihil spei reponenti" (Livy, I, 49).
75 "Fluxit vero earum origo ex huiusmodi causa" (III, ix, 2).
76 "Attulerat ver carpendi improbandique materiam" (III, ix, 2).
77 "Eoque res gestas incredibile favore" (III, ix, 2).

and lower orders, "iam pridem infensa," come roaring to his support, and the *optimates*, "metu cedentes," flee the city. This is the first revolution of 1378, which has been narrated wholly in terms of the attitudes and motivations of the participating elements of the population. Bruni goes on to describe the new constitution which replaces the law of Ammoniti, interrupting his account to deal with the second revolution, that of the "urban multitude, now aroused by the discord among the greater citizens." [78] He narrates directly the actions of the revolutionaries and the formation, under pressure from them, of a new government under Michele di Lando.

One might expect that Bruni, after describing two revolutions, would pause to assess the concrete goals of the revolutionaries in order to show how political lines had changed. Instead of this he moves on immediately to the final revolution. "Meanwhile, new disturbances were arising every day. The lowest orders in the city were stirred up by new hope and some began to destroy the goods of the wealthy, others to take vengeance on their enemies, and still others quickly to appoint themselves to power." [79] An explanation for Bruni's haste is immediately forthcoming when he states the explicit lesson to be drawn from the affair. "It seems that the beginning of sedition among the first citizens ought rigorously to be avoided." [80] In telling us what the Ciompi revolt teaches, Bruni has also shown why he presented the crisis as he did. The events can be explained only by the spread of excitement and unrest and not by any specific issues.

A proper understanding of the psychological factors in the revolt teaches Bruni in turn to formulate general principles for dealing with bad laws. He freely admits that the law of Ammoniti was a poor law and should have been reformed. The leaders of the state, however, should never act in such a way that they show their disquietude openly, for open discontent spreads ineluctably through the classes of society. To underline the seriousness of the mistake made by the Florentine upper classes, Bruni says that it was only by chance that the revolt was suppressed, since Michele di Lando,

[78] "Multitudo urbana . . . iam pridem per discordias maiorum civium sublevat" (III, ix, 6).

[79] "Inter haec, motus quidam novi per singulos dies oriebantur, utpote in civitate populosa et multitudine concitata et ad novas spes erecta, aliis diripere bona locupletum, aliis inimicum ulcisci, aliis potentiam sibi comparare properantibus" (III, ix, 8).

[80] "Cavenda vero maxime videntur principia seditionum inter primarios cives" (III, ix, 8).

though from the plebs himself, was a man of virtue.[81] The reality of psychological change is stressed by this device, which suggests that no institutional form can deal with the consequences of spreading discontent. Popular unrest, once stirred up, is put down only by factors beyond human control.[82]

Bruni has thus presented two of Florence's most important domestic events in strongly psychological terms. In foreign affairs, as well, he sees the fundamental importance of psychological phenomena. In 1399 several of Florence's allies defect to Giangaleazzo.[83] All of the defections are explained by specific states of mind. The Pisans, fearing the instability of Gherardo d'Appiano, submit to Giangaleazzo, who in his turn has set his mind on taking them.[84] The Sienese go over to him because of hatred for the Florentines, the Perugians are fearful of Boniface IX, and the Lucchesi, "sive metu sive benevolentia," are more favorable to him after he seizes Pisa. None of these changes is directly related to a change in Giangaleazzo's actual power. The precipitating factor is his own animus, and the substantial change is grounded either in the hopes or fears of the defecting cities. Only in Lucca's case is there even a mention of actual political considerations, and Bruni is quick to suggest that the change is as much due to Lucca's own inclination as to the implied threat from Giangaleazzo's seizure of Pisa.

The discovery of a close association between the psychological and political dimensions of reality in Bruni strongly suggests that an exploration of his understanding of human nature, as it is displayed in the *Historiae*, would be fruitful. Two aspects of this understanding must be noted and elaborated. First, his treatment of human motivation reveals the depth and consistency with which he relates psychological to political matters. Second, his manner of dealing with specific historical characters casts new light on the strength of his political concerns.

The increasing sophistication of Bruni's critical approach to motivation is seen most clearly in his treatment of revenge. The importance of vengeance as a motivational category is established early in the work when Bruni, drawing directly from Livy,[85] describes the attack on Rome by the Veii, who are incensed that their

---

[81] III, ix, 10.
[82] "Divina sorte" (III, ix, 10).
[83] III, xi, 250–252.
[84] "Ad Pisas capiendas animum convertit."
[85] Livy, I, 15.

fellow Etruscans have been badly treated by the Romans. Romulus' counterattack is also motivated primarily by revenge.[86] Bruni regards this as an explanation invoking a perfectly normal mode of human behavior and needing no elaboration. He is similarly uncritical of the reasons behind the Florentine counterattack after Montaperti.[87] In narrating Henry VII's journey to Rome, however, Bruni places the desire for revenge in a more exact context. He expounds Henry's difficulties with the Romans, emphasizing the extent to which his dignity as emperor has suffered by his failure to be properly crowned.[88] In the context of this specific disgrace Henry, angry with his adversaries, turns against Florence because he is impotent to take revenge on King Robert, who has really caused his problems. Here Bruni, by accentuating the absence of sound policy, gives the motive of revenge a subtle but unmistakably negative moral significance.

This critical tendency grows stronger in the later books. In 1363 a Florentine army, trying to relieve Barga, is badly mauled by the Pisans. Piero Farnese, the Florentine general, "annoyed at himself and the enemy, . . . thinking of nothing other than how much it would be worth to avenge the slaughter," [89] immediately leads out the rest of the Florentine army against Pisa. Bruni's disapproval of such a rash and unconsidered act, undertaken for such an insufficient reason, is clear. Commenting on the success of the mission, he says, "And so fortune favored him in spite of his rash beginning." [90]

Bruni seems to grant man's natural greed an even more important place in the motivational hierarchy than the desire for revenge, and he is equally critical of its categorical use. Though he judges revenge by its practical effect, he tends to analyze the concept of greed in terms of its importance as a driving force relative to other motivations. At times, to be sure, he explains a man's actions by unqualified greed. It is the hope of gain that leads the Faliscian teacher to betray to the Romans the children in his charge.[91] Livy, in recount-

---

[86] The Veii attack "cum indigno consanguineorum casu permoti"; Romulus counterattacks "resistendi ulciscendique gratia" (I, i, 78).

[87] "Properantibus Florentinis arbiensem cladem ulcisci" (I, ii, 292). This is taken directly from G. Villani, *Crònica*, VII, 21.

[88] "Contra decus imperii" (II, v, 10).

[89] "Iratus quidem et sibi et hosti . . . nihil aliud meditatus quam quemadmodum acceptam cladem valeret ulcisci" (II, viii, 472).

[90] "Adfuitque fortuna illius coepto pene temerario" (II, viii, 472).

[91] "Mercedem sperans" (I, i, 92).

ing the incident, assigns no motive at all to the pedagogue, either in the narrative itself or in the man's brief oration before Camillus.[92] Bruni, however, feels the necessity of constructing a motive where the sources provide him with none, and he finds the most likely to be avarice.

As a strong human desire Bruni places greed for power alongside greed for riches. Stilicho could have defeated the Goths at any time and eliminated them as a threat to Europe, but, "imperio inhians," he allowed the opportunity to pass.[93] This time the motive of ambition can be found in Bruni's source, Orosius' *Adversus Paganos*, but Orosius buries the suggested motive under a mass of disorganized information on Stilicho — his origins, his character, and Orosius' own explicit condemnation.[94] Bruni makes Stilicho's personal ambition stand alone as the cause of Rome's future disasters.

In later books Bruni establishes both avarice and ambition as common human traits, applying to groups as well as to individuals. He sees ambition as a factor necessitating the institution of a limited tenure of office for the priorate.[95] He makes it the basic cause of an uprising in Florence in 1340.[96] He explains the fierce sack of Pecciole in 1362 by the fact that the soldiers were greedy for spoils.[97] In covering the very last years of the war with Giangaleazzo he says that the governor of San Miniato was bribed to surrender the town.[98]

From these examples it is clear that greed for power and wealth is an important motive for human action, both collective and individual. It occupies in Bruni's mind a more central place than the desire for revenge. Yet he is anxious to avoid using it uncritically as a category to explain any general class of actions; he prefers to analyze the importance of greed as a factor in terms of some

[92] Livy, V, 27.

[93] I, i, 116.

[94] "Interea comes Stilico, vandalorum inbellis avarae perfidae et dolosae gentis genere editus, parui pendens quod sub imperatore imparabat, Eucherium filium suum sicut a plerisque traditur iam inde christianorum persecutionem a puero privato meditantem in imperium quoquomodo substituere nitebatur" (P. Orosius, *Historiarum adversum Paganos libri VII*, in *Corpus scriptorum eccleseasticorum latinorum* [Vienna, 1882], book VII, chap. 38).

[95] "Cum ante quidem nulla lex vetaret se pudor tantum homines a petitione compesceret" (I, iv, 422).

[96] II, vi, 262.

[97] II, viii, 468.

[98] III, xi, 224.

specific situation. In 1291 the Pisans, at war with the Florentines, reduce the forces defending a castle, which the Florentines are then able to take because of its diminished strength. Giving the reasons for the Pisan action, Bruni says that they were driven to it "partim avaritia, partim ignavia." [99] The technique of suggesting two dissimilar but not wholly contradictory motives is one which he frequently adopts to bring into focus a situation for which a simple explanation is not available.[100]

Bruni's analytical use of greed to illumine a specific situation is even clearer in the section dealing with Louis IV, who stays in Italy long after his coronation, seeking to accumulate as much money as possible. Bruni does not rest with the simple statement that Louis is greedy but attempts to legitimize his desire by pointing out that in this instance he really needs money.[101] If Bruni's interests had lain solely in establishing categories and types of motivation, he would hardly have been interested in whether there were concrete circumstances to explain Louis' actions. Indeed, Bruni occasionally suppresses monetary factors which are explicit in his sources. Though Villani clearly presents the pecuniary reasons for the Sienese desire to do battle quickly in 1260,[102] Bruni is much more guarded, playing down the mercenary motives of the troops as much as he can without blatant inaccuracy. The Sienese, he says, must hasten to do battle lest "the King's forces, who had been directed to remain no more than three months in Tuscany, should depart." [103] The use of the verb *praescribo*, although it does not preclude the mercenary aspect, certainly does de-emphasize it, for Bruni does not mention money in telling how the Germans came to be sent to Siena.

[99] I, iv, 426.

[100] This technique is used often in describing fear. Though greed and revenge both evoke a reasonably well-defined set of psychological attitudes, fear must be placed in some sort of context in order to be given specific dimensions. One obvious method is to refer to the concrete circumstances which evoke the fear, as Bruni has done in describing the fears of defecting towns in 1399. At other times, however, he places fear in the context of other motivations (I, i, 80; II, v, 6–8; II, v, 16; III, xii, 268), thereby focusing the reader's attention on the motivations and stressing the complexities of motivation in specific instances. This technique is related to the dialogue form so common in humanist writings and finds further expression in Bruni's use of paired orations (see chap. iv).

[101] "Non tantum avidissimus tantum sed etiam indigentissimus erat" (II, v, 124).

[102] "I tedeschi non erano pagati per più di tre mesi" (G. Villani, *Cronica*, VI, 78). In the previous chapter he had made explicit their mercenary character and had noted the amount of money paid for them (VI, 77).

[103] "Auxilia regis, quibus tres dumtaxat menses nec ultra commorari in Etruria praescriptum erat se infecta discederent" (I, ii, 230).

Instead of employing greed to explain the action of the German troops, Bruni invokes the more positive motive of honor. Villani is not explicit in giving Manfred's reasons for sending aid to Siena, but Bruni brings out the honorary aspect of the act in Farinata's words preceding Manfred's decision.[104] When the decision itself is announced, however, Bruni notes the admixture of honor with more practical motives.[105] Honor, in fact, is presented in conjunction with other feelings throughout the *Historiae*. In Book VIII Bruni explains the Florentines' willingness to conclude peace with Pisa by their desperation over sedition in the army, their suspicion that Pisa is about to give itself to Milan, and, finally, their feeling that honor has been satisfied.[106]

Bruni, then, although he uses abstract categories of motivation — revenge, greed, fear, honor — to explain events, sees that these human motives exist in loose association with one another, and he seeks to root out the circumstances that determine the predominance of one over another in any specific instance. At times, indeed, he interprets events without resorting to types of motivation at all. Never ignoring the power of pure self-interest,[107] he often adopts the technique of discussing the political realities directly in order to explain an action, assuming that a man may act from no other motive than an intelligent and self-serving assessment of the specific circumstances. His analysis of Charles of Anjou's reasons for coming to Italy,[108] his statement explaining why the Tuscans remained with Charles even after an ostensibly disastrous defeat,[109] and his outline of the factors leading both Florence and Milan to treat for peace in 1353 [110] are examples of this approach.

Bruni's treatment of human motivation tends to bring out the psychological element of his historical vision; in his assessment of individual character, on the other hand, the political nature of his historical writing emerges most sharply. In delineating character,

104 Farinata promises to force Manfred to render aid "si modo ulla regiae dignitatis tuendae cura sit" (I, ii, 196).

105 Manfred sends the troops "quod non nihil dedecoris sibi inflictum existimabat et quod spes vindictae celerrima ostendebatur" (I, ii, 200).

106 II, viii, 492–494.

107 See the oration of the Guelfs to Charles of Anjou. The Guelfs, after dwelling at length on the evils of the Hohenstaufen race, conclude by admitting frankly their own self-interest in having the supporters of their factional rivals, the Ghibellines, driven from Italy (I, ii, 262).

108 I, ii, 286.

109 I, iii, 310.

110 II, vii, 416–418.

Bruni resorts most frequently to short appositive clauses which constitute epitaphs. This device, though present in classical authors, is more widely used by the chroniclers whom Bruni drew on as sources, and often he can be found copying from them the substance of specific characterizations, as well as the general form of the epitaph.

Though Tacitus and Sallust are both famous for their ability to characterize in a phrase, Livy, whose history the *Historiae* resemble most closely from a formal point of view, seldom resorts to this device.[111] Giovanni Villani, however, uses the technique regularly and without regard for the importance of the men involved. Clement IV, Martin IV, Farinata degli Uberti, Giano della Bella, and Corso Donati are all characterized with brief descriptive phrases.[112] Other Florentine chroniclers use the device with even greater regularity. Dino Compagni, for instance, seldom mentions any name without affixing to it a descriptive epitaph.[113]

One of the elements of Bruni's mode of describing individuals which immediately strikes the reader is the complete absence of physical characterization. Though Livy seldom includes a physical description, he does make exceptions in important cases, such as that of Hannibal. Villani notes the physical features of important men regularly.[114] Bruni never does. He is, in general, reluctant to endow the narrative with sensual dimensions. Since his basic historical reality is intangible, sensual data are utterly irrelevant, and Bruni's seriousness of purpose prevents him from including such details.[115]

---

[111] Livy almost never describes a really important man in this fashion. Fabius Maximus, for instance, is introduced without any indication of his character, which is suggested only by his actions (XXII, 7). Hannibal is first presented in a complex section involving narrated events, orations, and physical descriptions (XXI, 1–4). Typical of the occasions on which Livy uses the epigrammatic device is his description of an obscure young Argive named Damocles, who performs a rash act in the Macedonian war (Livy calls Damocles "adulescens maioris animi quam consilii" [XXXIV, 25]). An exception is found early in the work when he introduces Locumo, who will become king of Rome under the name of Tarquin I, as "vir impiger ac divitiis potens" (I, 34). At this point in the narrative, however, Livy is emphasizing precisely the obscure origins of the future ruler.

[112] G. Villani, *Crònica*, VI, 92, VII, 106, VI, 82, VIII, 1, VIII, 96. Bruni has clearly copied Villani in characterizing Corso Donati (see Bruni, I, iv, 474).

[113] D. Compagni, *Crònica*; see, for example, Corso and Cavalcante Cavalcanti in chap. XX, and Boniface VIII, Simone Gherardi, and Nero Cambi in chap. XXI.

[114] For instance, Charles of Anjou (VIII, 1) and Castruccio Castracani (X, 86).

[115] The avoidance of sensual imagery can also be seen in his description of objects. Buildings and walls tend to be described conceptually. Bruni mentions that the Palazzo della Signoria and the new walls are decorative but does not describe

His descriptions are not physical but political and moral. They evoke and reveal with greater clarity the content of Bruni's moral vision. In only two instances can an epitaph be found in which he attributes a simple, traditional, moral category to a man. He calls Gambacurta "a good man with a sincere soul," [116] though further on he places even this in a political context.[117] Turning to a less exemplary character, he calls Urban VI "a man free from simony but vehement and perverse by nature." [118] These two characterizations occur close together in the text and, significantly, concern non-Florentines.

Bruni finds the following questions most relevant in understanding a person's character: Where does this person serve within the political framework? How competent is he in this service? In answering the first question he is mainly concerned whether his subject is a warrior or a politician; seldom does he find one who is outstanding in both realms. Charles of Anjou is called "a man doubtless outstanding but more eminent in the arts of war than those of peace." [119] Gentile Orsini is called "a man outstanding in war and distinguished in factional zeal." [120] The *condottieri* Bonifacio Lupo, Pietro Farnese, and John Hawkwood are all praised for their military proficiency.[121] The citizens Ildebrandino, Giano della Bella, Giovanni Cambio, and Donato Acciaiuoli are lauded for their capacity to participate in governing the republic.[122] Particular political skills are also singled out. The Florentine legates

them (I, iv, 460), whereas Villani avoids passing judgment while describing the symmetry of the walls and the Palazzo and re-evoking the cornerstone-laying scene (VIII, 26 and 31). Other examples of Bruni's nonsensual descriptions are at I, i, 60; I, iii, 344; I, iii, 378; II, vi, 216; II, viii, 510. He would certainly have been surprised at the modern complaint that he is not "charming or engaging" in his details, for he would doubtless have considered the discipline with which he excluded such details to be a valuable asset to the work.

[116] III, ix, 100.

[117] "Is fuit modesti vir animi et florentino populo in primis amicus" (III, xi, 188).

[118] "Vir a simoniaca purus labe caeterum protervus natura atque perversus" (III, ix, 98).

[119] "Vir procul dubio egregius longe tamen belli artibus quam pacis insignior" (I, iii, 378).

[120] "Vir egregius bello a studio partium eximius." Other men similarly characterized are Piero Sacone — "vir bello quidem amodum praestans, ad urbanos vero conversiones non satis aptus" (II, vi, 218; see also II, viii, 436) — and Inghiramo, who is noted in both realms (III, ix, 64).

[121] Lupo (II, viii, 464), Farnese (II, viii, 470), and Hawkwood (II, viii, 500, and III, xi, 188).

[122] Ildebrandino (I, ii, 170), Giano della Bella (I, iv, 432), Giovanni Cambio (III, ix, 46), and Donato Acciaiuoli (III, xi, 210).

to the Pope, Antilla and Barbadoro, are called "men outstanding in the knowledge of law and capable both in doing and in speaking." [123] Finally, non-Florentines are frequently characterized by general canniness instead of specific political skills.[124]

Bruni devotes more than an epigram to both Walter of Brienne and Giangaleazzo Visconti. These men are highly dangerous enemies of Florentine liberty, and Bruni strongly disapproves of them. Describing the Duke of Athens, he begins, "Walter was a noble Frenchman." [125] It is unusual but by no means singular for Bruni to identify a man by his national origin — he notes the fact, for example, in Hawkwood's case [126] — but in referring to Walter of Brienne in these terms he has a definite purpose. After sketching Walter's life prior to his arrival in Florence, he goes on to show how his background is relevant. "For he was a Frenchman and accustomed to the ways of France, where the plebs has the place of servants. He therefore laughed at the name of the guilds and thought ridiculous that the city should be ruled by the will of the people." [127] No other aspect of Walter's personality, nor any of his features, is adduced to describe him. Bruni is solely interested in the political significance of his character, in the fact that he is intrinsically and personally hostile to Florentine republican attitudes and institutions. Bruni feels, however, that this hostility must be explained and clarified by reference to Walter's cultural background. Such a method of drawing out and deepening the picture of a man's character contrasts strongly with that of Giovanni Villani, who mentions Walter's ugly features and his qualities of greed and cruelty but ignores the historical background of the Duke. Even when Villani, on other occasions, elaborates on a man's origin, no connection is made between it and his actions.[128]

Here Bruni is much closer to Livy, who uses incidents from

---

[123] "Viri scientia curis clari et in agendo disendoque in primis efficaces" (II, viii, 516).

[124] Clement is called "vir procul dubio egregius ac multarum rerum experientiam callens" (I, ii, 252). Note the striking contrast with Villani's "uomo buono" (VI, 92). As another example, Guido Feretrano is called "vir callidate quidem astu profundissimus artifex sic ad aperta certamina parum audax" (I, iv, 428).

[125] "Gualterius erat gallus claro natus genere" (II, vi, 286).

[126] III, xi, 188.

[127] "Vir enim gallus et galliarum moribus assuetus ubi plebs pene servorum habetur loco, nomina artium artificumque ridebat; multitudinis arbitrio regi civitatem ridiculum existimabat" (II, vi, 286).

[128] See his discussion of the origins of Charles of Anjou, where Villani describes his genealogy and even his coat of arms (VII, 1).

Hannibal's environment to evoke without explicit statement the theme of his hatred for Rome. In the *Ab urbe condita* the role of historical events in the development of character is expressed by a complex series of narrative techniques, from digressions to orations, before Livy attempts a direct description of the formed character of Hannibal.

The subtlety with which Bruni develops historical character is even more apparent in his treatment of Giangaleazzo, the most fully drawn personality in the work, a contemporary of Bruni's, and a man whose character deeply impressed the Florentines. Giangaleazzo is introduced by an account of his seizure of the Lombard state from his uncle.[129] Then Bruni narrates briefly the history of Milan from the accession of the brothers Galeazzo and Bernarbo down to Giangaleazzo's coup. Without stating it explicitly, he brings out what he considers to be Giangaleazzo's predominant characteristic: deceitfulness. The historian reveals clearly his conception of this characteristic as not an ethical category but an historically developing and vitally personal trait. Giangaleazzo on the death of his father "was thought to be desirous of a tranquil life." [130] He manifests a hatred of controversy and war with a grave countenance, "seu vera seu ficta." He marries Bernarbo's daughter "pro stabiliori concordiae vinculo." But to no avail. "He could in no way alleviate suspicions. So faithless is the desire for power that Bernarbo, by nature harsh and hostile to him because of greed and because of the number of his own sons, must consider him a threat." [131] Fearing his uncle, Giangaleazzo flees to Pavia.

Bruni uses two devices in presenting Giangaleazzo's character, both of which contribute to its convincing reality. First, he avoids explicit description of Giangaleazzo's mental processes. The reader is not told that he is seeking to deceive Bernarbo, that his actions have hidden devious motives. Only the actions themselves are narrated; the intentions manifest themselves along with the results of Giangaleazzo's acts. In this manner Bruni draws the reader's attention by creating a tension between narrated appearance and historical reality. Secondly, Bruni creates a sharp contrast between Giangaleazzo's motives, which are hidden, complex, suggested, and

129 III, ix, 72.
130 "Tranquillioris vitae avidus putabatur" (III, ix, 72–74).
131 "Sed nec eo quidem modo sublatae suspiciones usque adeo infida est dominandi cupiditas, Bernarbos enim et naturae acer et cupiditate nimius et abundans filiis merito formidandus" (III, ix, 74).

Bernarbo's, which are explicitly and clearly stated in terms of abstract ethical traits, such as *acer* and *cupiditas*. The juxtaposition of Bernarbo's categorically stated motives and Giangaleazzo's concrete actions with implied motives serves further to reinforce as a significant personality trait the capacity to dissimulate.

Livy, too, is concerned with giving historical vitality and force to Hannibal's dominant characteristic, hatred of Rome. Having established this, however, he proceeds to a conventional description of physical and personal traits. Not so Bruni. He is not interested in representing Giangaleazzo in fullness as a human being, but in drawing out only those aspects which make him personally significant in a political context. Far more single-minded in his pursuit of political history than Livy, he forges on to narrate the political result of Giangaleazzo's seizure of power and to develop his deceitfulness in the context of the subsequent war with Florence.

After fleeing to Pavia, Giangaleazzo proceeds to gather support to overthrow Bernarbo, giving Bruni occasion to mention the personal charm and diplomacy which characterize this devious man.[132] When Giangaleazzo takes Verona and Padua, Bruni comments explicitly on the importance of the personality he has so carefully drawn. "Grown therefore first by taking power from Bernarbo, he soon was threatening the princes of Verona and Padua. Nor was he less formidable to free people, especially since in the cases both of Bernarbo and of Padua he had not shown in his face what he felt in his heart." [133] This explicit statement is elaborated in an oration delivered by Giovanni Ricci before the Florentine signoria. Here Giangaleazzo's rise to power is again recounted, but this time it is given the explicit meaning which has hitherto been only implied. Ethical categories are used, [134] and because of the previous narrative they now have concrete and vital content.

By a series of narrative devices, including the oration, Bruni has constructed Giangaleazzo's character along narrow yet vital and convincing lines, has placed him as a person in the context of Florentine political affairs, and has provided a framework within

[132] "Mansuetudine et clementia conciliare sibi animos hominum properabat" (III, ix, 74).

[133] "Auctus igitur primo Bernabovis potentia, mox insuper Veronensium principum accessuris etiam Patavinorum opibus formidabilis erat, nec immerito illius magnitudo a liberis populis formidabatur praesertim cum et in Bernabove et in Patavino deprehensus esset aliud fronte simulare aliud corde sentire" (III, ix, 84).

[134] "Inexplebilis eius cupiditas" (III, ix, 90).

which the subsequently narrated history of his relations with Florence can be understood. Nor does he allow the reader to forget this theme. He shows the distrust which Florence comes to have for the Milanese prince.[135] When Giangaleazzo forgives and even supports a Pisan uprising against his own troops, Bruni interprets it as a sign of his canny policy.[136] Finally, in an oration before the Venetian senate which concludes the work, the Florentines stress again and again the contrast between the appearance of Giangaleazzo's deeds and the reality of his dangerous intentions.[137]

This persistent and single-minded development of an historically founded character does not exist in the fourteenth-century chronicles, and, though the techniques are clearly present in Livy, he does not pay attention exclusively to those traits which are significant within the scope of political history. Not even Tacitus, in relating the effects of Tiberius' inscrutability and indecisiveness, is so immune to the attractions of a fully drawn and artfully elaborated personality.

The present chapter has sought to expose Bruni's vision of history. The investigation has proceeded by an analysis of the explicit scope of the *Historiae*, the development of this scope in the narrative itself, and finally the approach to human nature found in the work. A view of the moral, political, and psychological elements in Bruni's work reveals the existence of a picture of the intangible dimensions of history conceptualized in secular terms, with a rigor and coherence unprecedented in previous Florentine historiography.[138] This level of historical conceptualization is found only in the greatest classical historians, excluding even Livy.[139]

A final word must be added concerning Bruni's understanding of the place of fortuitous events in history. Given the nature of his historical vision, it is not surprising that he avoids a simple statement of the causes of important events. He frequently uses

---

[135] III, xi, 192.

[136] "Sed fuit Galeatius mirabile ingenio ad populos et amicos in benevolentia continendos" (III, xi, 242).

[137] III, xii, 300–306.

[138] R. Morghen, *La storiografia*, pp. 71–93, suggests that it was Villani's contribution to search out the deepest interconnections of events and explain them secularly. It seems to me, however, that Villani is more secular than his predecessors only in considering a larger dimension of history to be tangible. For him the intangible remains ineffable and is referred directly and simply to God.

[139] On Livy's inadequacies in this field, see R. Syme, *Tacitus* (Oxford, 1958), I, 139. Sir Ronald cannot completely evade the charge of bias in favor of his own hero, the author of the *Annales*.

the form with which he introduces the Ciompi revolt, saying that he will narrate its causes but then simply describing the course of events. This method, which allows him to express the causal structure with greater subtlety, can be observed in practice quite early in the work. Seeking to show the source of Charles of Anjou's discomfort before the battle of Benevento, Bruni first notes his two main problems: Conradin, and an uprising in Rome. Explaining how this uprising came about, he begins, "This was the cause of the revolution." [140] Then follows a long narrative, beginning, "There were two sons of the King of Spain." In the course of the narrative the political elements of the situation are gradually set forth in relation to one another, but without an attempt to explicate precise causal factors in spite of the earlier promise to describe the *causa*.

Reluctance to express directly the causal significance of specific events can also be seen in the section where Bruni deals with the death of the Florentine general Piero Farnese. He says clearly that Farnese's death occasioned a major turning point in Florentine affairs, but in the subsequent narrative, designed to explain the importance of Farnese's death, he avoids the problems posed in stating that a single event can deeply influence the course of history. Instead, he narrates the diplomatic and military situation in which the death has occurred, showing that it becomes important only in the context of the arrival of a group of English mercenaries shortly after Farnese's demise. [141]

In spite of his unwillingness to deal with causal problems, Bruni cannot, of course, ignore the fact that events are not always predictable from the general context in which they occur. Some events are unquestionably fortuitous. He will not, however, allow the possibility of accident to render the study of history nugatory. He suggests rather that those events which show most strongly the influence of fortune are precisely those which point up most cogently the importance of understanding general causes.

Fortune alone is not often invoked to explain events and is almost never used to explain domestic events. Bruni accepted the fifteenth-century humanist idea that chance is more active in war than in peace. [142] Yet even in explaining military events, Bruni is judicious

---

140 "Rerum novarum causa haec fuerat" (I, iii, 300).
141 II, viii, 474–476.
142 See M. P. Gilmore, *Humanists and Jurists* (Cambridge, Mass., 1963), p. 46.

in his use of fortune. Though he manifests that respect for the intervention of unpredictable forces which Gilmore has found in Guicciardini,[143] Bruni does not seem to prefigure his fellow Florentine's preoccupation with the inscrutability and capriciousness of fortune. Nor does fortune have the purposive quality found in Livy, who often speaks of the fortune of Rome in describing its steady rise to world domination. One cannot in the *Historiae* see a pattern or end in its action.[144] Not only is the work nonteleological, but fortune seldom assumes overwhelming significance. On occasion, to be sure, the seizure of a town or the acquisition of an ally will be narrated as a purely contingent happening.[145] For important events, however, Bruni tries to show the related fortuitous circumstances which interact and diminish one another's effectiveness, as he does in narrating the simultaneous death and victory of Henry VII.

Fortune is even used in the *Historiae* to reinforce and emphasize the importance of this causal perspective. The work begins with Catiline saving the Florentine colonists temporarily from the results of their disastrous conduct of affairs. Describing the situation, Bruni says, "By chance at this time Catiline was seeking to change things." [146] By emphasizing the element of chance Bruni underlines the implicit moral lesson that the Florentines' conduct was unwise, since it would have resulted in disaster except for an unusual circumstance. He uses this technique frequently in the history, stressing the folly of Florence's actions prior to Montaperti by saying that the city only escaped destruction by the intervention of Fari-

---

Narrating the sudden death of Henry VII, which renders vain the simultaneous victory of his fleet, Bruni observes, "Sed bellorum eventum nemo satis praedixerit quippe communis mars, ut aiunt magnique saepe terrores parvis momentis in irritum reciderunt" (II, v, 26). Dealing with an event in the Lucchese war he is even more explicit: "Magnam in bello vim habet fortuna, ut nihil tam exploratum videri possit, de quo non ante supremum sit eventum rei dubitandum" (II, vi, 194).

143 Gilmore, *Humanists*, p. 59.

144 There is one exception to this generalization. It occurs in Book I where Bruni talks of the fortune of the Romans, a usage clearly taken from Livy, for it forms one of the principal themes of the *Ab urbe*. An apparent exception occurs when Bruni suggests that the Duke of Athens was appointed "fato quodam impellente" (II, vi, 284), having previously referred to his arrival on the scene "quasi enim ira quaedam caelitus premeret" (II, vi, 282). In this case Bruni, as has already been shown, goes on to establish the significance of Walter's rule in the customary political and psychological terms.

145 For instance, the failure of the crusade in Tunis (I, iii, 326), Gambacurta's assumption of power in Pisa (II, viii, 498), the failure of the attack on Scarparia (II, vii, 404), and the betrayal and retaking of San Miniato (III, xi, 228).

146 "Forte per id tempus Romae L. Catilina res novare agressus" (I, i, 62).

nata.[147] The most effective example of this technique is his description of Michele di Lando's decisive role in settling the Ciompi revolt.[148]

In the foregoing analysis the conceptual nature of Bruni's historical vision has been established. The next two chapters will deal with the use of these concepts in understanding specific problems of concern to a fifteenth-century Florentine humanist, and with the new historical form through which Bruni expresses his understanding of history.

[147] I, ii, 234.

[148] III, ix, 10. Bruni strengthens his point still further by showing the weakness of these contingent forces. Though the chance interventions of Farinata and Di Lando manage to save Florence, Catiline's does not, nor can Pope Gregory save the city from its foolish factional strife (I, iii, 356).

Chapter Three

Bruni and the Problems of His Age

Moral commitment is not only the basis of Bruni's purpose in writing history but is an essential element in his analysis of historical events. His purpose is fulfilled not by invoking traditional moral standards but by interrelating all specific events through a coherent structuring of experience. The very thoroughness with which events are interrelated testifies to the strength of this moral commitment on Bruni's part. Irrevelant details, charming anecdotes, the simple chronicling of events, these are not goals Bruni considers worthy of his effort.

While the depth of the historian's moral concern has been suggested in Chapter Two, the precise nature of his commitment needs to be more carefully defined. According to Hans Baron, intellectuals in Florence in the early fifteenth century were acutely concerned with Florence's position as a free republic, with the nature of its institutions, and with the problems of preserving its hegemony in Tuscany and maintaining its independence from other Italian powers.[1]

Bruni's concern for these questions can be easily seen. His analysis becomes more rigorous when he is narrating specifically Florentine affairs. As he approaches broader topics, Bruni is less careful to interpret historical events in terms of the coherent concepts brought out in the last chapter. Accordingly, his most moralizing descriptions are those of churchmen. Urban VI, for instance, is described as a man free from simony but perverse and obstinate.[2] Bruni generally treats the church as just another Italian power and not as a corporate body possessing universal jurisdiction,[3] but when

[1] See chap. i at note 96.
[2] III, ix, 98.
[3] See, for instance, his treatment of the Pope's attempt in 1386 to retake his

he does deal with the spiritual powers of the papacy, he concentrates on personal considerations. He emphasizes, for example, that the pacification of factional strife in Florence was effected by the personal influence of Nicholas III and lasted only as long as he was alive.[4]

Bruni's fellow Italians, still a general if somewhat more precise group, are presented in almost equally uncritical terms in the *Historiae*. A sense of *Italianità*, the feeling that the northern races are more ferocious, cruel, rapacious, and greedy than the Italians, permeates the *Historiae*.[5] Bruni does not try to explain this in terms of political or even geographical factors. It is purely and simply assumed. So strong is his dislike of foreigners that he even expresses satisfaction when an Italian army defeats foreign troops in the pay of his own city. When Giangaleazzo in 1401 inflicts a series of reverses on the imperial troops coming to the aid of Florence, Bruni remarks, "After the Italian knights had attacked the Germans and light battles had begun, it was remarkable how the Italians seemed to be superior."[6]

One element of Bruni's Italian sympathy does lead to a deeper understanding of his thought and is closely associated with his Florentine patriotism. It is the feeling, which has already been seen in his treatment of the Duke of Athens, that foreigners have not had experience with free people and therefore tend to lack respect for the free institutions of Italy. This attitude finds expression in other sections of the *Historiae*. Bruni sees the Guelf-Ghibelline feud, for instance, in the context of foreign domination[7] and blames foreigners for the frequent revolts against papal governors.[8]

The sense of Italy as a place of liberty and free institutions is sharpened when the perspective is narrowed to Tuscany. Baron

---

former possessions in the Romagna (III, ix, 80), or his analysis of the causes of the disputes between Pope and Emperor (I, i, 152).

[4] "Hic rerum status fere biennium duravit; nec dubitabatur si is pontifex vixisset diutius, quin longe magis ea forma reipublicae fuerit durata" (I, iii, 358).

[5] There are numerous examples of this attitude. He describes the French as "viri gallici feroces natura atque superbi" (I, iii, 366), blames Henry VII's need for money on his barbarous soul (II, viii, 514), and reproaches foreigners for cruelty in the sack of Cesena (II, viii, 546). They are perfidious allies (see the Duke of Bavaria's threat to desert, at III, x, 128) and incompetent soldiers (see the impatience of the French troops, at III, x, 148).

[6] "Postquam contra Germanos equites Italici constiterunt ac levia praelia inniti coepta sunt, mirabile quantum Italici praestare videbantur" (III, xi, 284).

[7] "Germanos autem barbaros homines sub praetextu romani nominis dominari Italis, per indignum censebant" (I, i, 154).

[8] "Nec tolerabilis sane iam erat gallorum clericorum ambitio" (III, viii, 514).

has brought out clearly Bruni's attitude toward Tuscany and the relationship of this attitude to his republican sympathies.[9] Alongside Bruni's pride in Tuscan republicanism, however, stands his anxiety over the factional strife which constitutes another constant element in Tuscan history. He sees the problem, manifested in the early history of Tuscany, as an inability among the cities of the area to unite against a common foe. After describing the Roman conquest and subjugation of several such cities, he says, "And indeed there can be no doubt that, had all the Etruscans waged war with one plan, Tuscany could have defended itself magnificently and at length." [10] Approaching more recent events, he severely castigates Frederick II for his part in the promotion of internal strife among the Tuscan cities [11] and uses the zeal of faction as a keynote to affairs in Tuscany near the end of the thirteenth century.[12]

At first glance Bruni's loyalty to Florence seems to be as uncritical as his sense of *Italianità*.[13] On closer inspection, however, it is apparent that Bruni picks out the characteristics of fortitude and perseverance as Florence's particular traits. Of the city's success in investing Montecatino he says, "It was certainly a wonderful thing and must have been celebrated even among the Romans." [14] When in 1369 Florence has been badly beaten in the field and the enemy is before its walls, he observes, "The city in the situation was tenacious; it could be induced by no terror to surrender and persevered during the siege." [15]

In the war with Giangaleazzo the moral determination of Florence is highlighted. In the first place, Bruni stresses the fact that Florence wages the war almost singlehandedly. For instance, in describing the outbreak of hostilities in Arezzo and Bologna, he points to Florence's isolation in the face of these diverse problems.[16] Secondly, he seldom misses an opportunity to emphasize the

---

[9] See Baron, *Crisis*, 2nd ed., especially pp. 65 and 424–425.

[10] "Et profecto non ambigitur, quin si omnes Etruria populi uno consilio bellum gessissent, diuturnius ac magnificentius tota Etruria defendi potuisset" (I, i, 94).

[11] I, i, 156.

[12] "Ita cuncta vicissim Etruria studiis partium erecta conflictabatur" (I, iii, 398).

[13] On one occasion, discussed in chap. iv, he suggests divine favor for Florence because of a miraculous announcement to the priors of the victory at Campaldino (I, ii, 412).

[14] "Mirifica certe res ac vel apud romanum populum memoranda" (II, vi, 184).

[15] "Civitas in eo pertinax fuit; nulloque terrore potuit adduci, quin in obsidione perstaret" (II, viii, 502–504).

[16] "Itaque Florentini multis de rebus soliciti, uno eodemque tempore et de resistendo adversus propinquos hostes et de sociorum tutela curam suscipere cogebantur" (III, x, 114).

magnitude of the Florentine war effort. The Duke of Bavaria is induced to come to Florence's aid only "by being offered large sums of money and great rewards." [17] Shortly after hiring the duke, Florence sends ambassadors to purchase the aid of France; [18] when the French go down to defeat, the historian again draws attention to the great expense involved in prosecuting the war.[19]

It was suggested in the preceding chapter that the psychological characteristics manifested by a group of people are closely related to, even derived from, their form of political association. The fortitude of Florence derives from its free institutions, and Bruni's pride in Florence is a function of the city's republican tradition. His interest in establishing the firmness and constancy of this tradition is clearly illustrated by the care with which he explains each of Florence's temporary experiments with autocracy. In 1313 Florence, beset with internal and external problems, gives over control of the city to Robert of Naples. Bruni's narrative of this act differs in several important respects from the account to be found in Villani's chronicle.

First, Bruni puts the surrender in its true chronological order, before the death of Henry VII and while the imperial threat is still unresolved.[20] Villani includes it only after he has mentioned the death of Henry and shown the collapse of the Ghibelline hopes.[21] In the Villani chronicle the reader is given a picture of Florence voluntarily surrendering its liberty only after he has already been told that the political situation which compelled the surrender was ephemeral and not a real threat. Villani sets the reasons for Florence's actions in the vaguest and most general terms; [22] Bruni carefully and explicitly enumerates the city's problems: lack of money after a series of wars, desertion of the allies, incipient famine, and ever increasing danger from the enemy.

The two writers also choose different means to express the surrender. Villani bluntly says, "Si diedono." Bruni describes in detail

[17] "Magnis pecuniis magnisque praemiis ostensis" (III, x, 116).

[18] "Pecuniam abunde pollicentes ac insuper maxima praemia futura demonstrantes" (III, x, 142).

[19] "Decies centena et ducenta sexaginta sex millia florenorum auri expensa per eos menses relata ad aerarium comperio" (III, x, 150).

[20] II, v, 20.

[21] "Ne detto anno 1313 ancora vivendo lo'imperadore . . . [the Florentines] si diedono al re Ruberto per cinque anni" (G. Villani, *Crònica*, IX, 56).

[22] "Parendo a'Fiorentini essere in male stato" (Villani, IX, 56).

the constitutional processes invoked, together with the exact terms of the treaty, stressing the limitations placed on Robert's powers. Finally, Bruni and Villani differ in their judgment on the effect of Florence's actions; Villani remarks, "Certainly it was the salvation of the Florentines," [23] while Bruni only says, "And so the business of the city was transferred." [24] These differences of presentation tend to underline Bruni's feeling that it was striking and extraordinary for Florence to give up its liberty.

Bruni also takes care to stress the way in which the city's republican tradition affects its foreign policy. Speaking of its assumption of power in Arezzo, he says, "Indeed in setting up the republic, priors of the people and a *gonfaloniere* of justice were created so that by the name of these offices a tyrant would not be permitted to be in the city. This occasioned such joy that tears of rejoicing were seen. And so with glad spirits the Aretines first entered under the laws and power of the Florentine people." [25] By contrast, Villani does not stress this aspect of the Florentine take-over, including in the narration only a description of processions, a list of minor castles seized, and other details and anecdotes of dubious significance. [26]

The comparison with Villani into which this discussion of Bruni's loyalties has led represents another means of demonstrating the connection between Bruni's historical analysis and his moral commitment. There cannot be, nor should there be, an absolute standard against which the effectiveness of Bruni's approach to the problems and concerns of his age can be measured. It is clear, however, from this brief comparison and from the broader lines of difference suggested in the previous chapter, that Bruni departs from his fourteenth-century predecessors by offering insights that are based less on uncriticized moral judgments and more on a coherent analysis of the psychological and political dimensions of

---

[23] "Di certo fu lo scampo de'Fiorentini" (Villani, IX, 56).

[24] "Et civitatis quidem negotii si traducebantur" (II, v, 22). The verb *traduco* can have pejorative implications similar to those of the English "traduced" (see Livy, II, 38).

[25] "At vero in constituenda republica priores populi ac vexillifer iustitiae creati sunt quorum officiorum ne nomina quidem tyrannus esse in civitate passus fuerat, tanta repente laetitia est coorta vix ut lacrymae prae gaudio tenerentur. Ita laetis tunc animis Aretini primum in florentini populi jus potestatemque venire." (II, vi, 240.)

[26] Villani, *Crònica*, XI, 61.

history. Bruni's approach to the problems facing Florence in the fifteenth century is significant in comparison both to previous historians and to his own presentation of non-Florentine topics.

The particular problems with which he is most acutely concerned are related to the internal affairs of Florence and to her foreign policy. He seeks to deal in considerable depth with the problem of maintaining Florence's hegemony in Tuscany and with the larger issue of the city's relation to the other major Italian powers. Finally, he shows considerable interest in problems of military strategy and considers in some detail the advantages and disadvantages of the mercenary system.

Loyalty to Florence as the exemplar of the free republic is a constant factor in Bruni's thought, dating back at least as far as the *Dialogi ad Petrum Histrum* and the *Laudatio Florentiae urbis*. It also finds expression in his funeral oration for Nanni Strozzi and his Greek pamphlet on the Florentine constitution, composed in 1439. Baron places this aspect of Bruni's thought in the context of Florentine political development in the first half of the Quattrocento.[27] Furthermore, it is clear from the preceding chapter that Bruni's is not an uncritical prejudice but one which springs from his vision of the interrelation between political and psychological factors in history. The strength of republican institutions, it was pointed out, consists in their peculiar capacity to release the psychological energies of the citizens. Here this insight must be expanded. On closer inspection it is apparent that, although Bruni saw the competition for honors within a republic as a source of power both at home and abroad, he was by no means blind to the inherent weaknesses and drawbacks of a republican form of government.

His first and most direct statement of the association between a republic and virtue comes when he speaks of the beginnings of the Roman Empire. "I think that the decline of the Roman Empire must begin from that time in which, giving up its liberty, Rome began to serve the emperors." [28] Going on, he explains the reasons for this judgment: "For liberty ceased with the emperors, and with liberty, virtue departed. For previously the way to honors was through virtue; the journey to the consulate, to the dictatorship, and other great ranks of dignity was easy to those who by greatness

---

[27] See Baron, *Crisis*, 2nd ed., especially pp. 418–430.

[28] "Declinationem autem romani imperii ab eo fere tempore ponendam reor quo, amissa libertate, imperatoribus servire Roma incepit" (I, i, 98).

of spirit, by virtue, and by industry were superior to others. Soon, however, as the republic came into the power of one, virtue and greatness of soul began to be suspected by the rulers. Only those pleased the emperors who were endowed with the sort of temperament that concern for liberty could not move. And so the weak replaced the strong, and the courts of the emperors received adulators rather than energetic works, and the government of things passed to the worse elements, gradually working the ruin of the Empire." [29]

This interpretation is taken from a passage in Tacitus' *Historiae*, which Bruni had quoted in his *Laudatio*.[30] Baron has pointed out that Bruni took only one element of the Tacitean approach, ignoring the Roman historian's sense that the Republic had died from internal causes and that the Empire was an evil necessary in order to preserve some of Rome's former greatness. That Bruni took just one aspect of the Tacitean critique is true only in a limited sense. He does not, to be sure, consider in the passage quoted the cause for the demise of the Roman Republic, but neither does Tacitus in the corresponding section. The Roman historian's position is, in fact, less clear in the *Historiae* than in the later *Annales*, which he begins with a judgment on the decline quite similar to that found in his *Historiae*,[31] though he follows this negative criticism with a balanced account of the significance of Augustus. His treatment of the first emperor is so oblique and subtle, however, that it would be difficult to make any comment about Tacitus' opinions without following his search for the *arcana imperii* through the whole work.

It would be rash to claim for Bruni a Tacitean subtlety in this matter, but he does show a deep awareness of the problems intrinsic to a republic: mainly the tendency of a republic (already noted) to dissipate its strength in factional struggles for power,

---

29 "Cessit enim libertas imperatorio nomini, et post libertatem virtus abivit. Prius namque per virtutem ad honores via fuit iisque ad consulatus dictaturas et caeteros amplissimos dignitatis gradus facillime patebat iter, qui magnitudine animi, virtute et industria caeteros anteibant. Mox vero ut respublica in potestatem unius devenit, virtus et magnitudo animi suspecta dominantibus esse coepit. Hique solum imperatoribus placebant quibus non ea vis ingenii esset quam libertatis cura stimulare posset. Ita pro fortibus ignavos, pro industriis adulatores imperatoria suscepit aula et rerum gubernacula ad peiores delata ruinam imperii paulatim dedere." (I, i, 100.)

30 Tacitus, *Historiae*, I, 1. See Baron, *Crisis*, p. 461, n. 20.

31 "Sed veteris populi Romani prospera vel adversa claris scriptoribus memorata sunt; temporibusque Augusti dicendis non defuere decora ingenia, donec gliscente adulatione deterrerentur" (Tacitus, *Ab excessu Divi Augusti annales*, ed. J. Jackson [3 vols.; Cambridge, Mass., and London, 1931], I, i, 1; hereafter *Annales*).

but also the disadvantages encountered by a republic in the conduct of foreign policy. Bruni analyzes the causes and nature of these problems and suggests solutions for them in a way that evinces the thoroughness with which he applies the entire range of his historical insights to issues that touch him deeply and immediately.

The history of factional strife in Italy is for Bruni a tale of unmitigated disaster.[32] After outlining the issues in the Guelf-Ghibelline feud he remarks, "This factional zeal was the beginning of great calamity." [33] His readiness to blame the power of factional zeal for personal tragedies has already been noted in the case of Ugolino of Pisa,[34] and further examples of the calamitous nature of this problem can easily be found in the *Historiae.* Speaking of an outbreak of internal discord in famine-stricken Florence during a war with Pistoia, he considers the internal strife to be as hideous a scourge as either war or famine.[35] Faction is responsible for the loss of independence of many cities in Tuscany. The Pistoians surrender their liberty, "stirred up by discord among the citizens." [36] San Miniato requests a Florentine commander to settle its disputes.[37] Weakened from internal quarrels, Borga cannot defend itself,[38] and Volterra must also give up its independence.[39] Even the great city of Bologna falls to Giangaleazzo because of its own exiles, though neither faction in the city reaps any benefit from his rule.[40]

Bruni sees the worst effects of faction, however, in the history of his native city. Though he had come to Florence when he was hardly twenty, his affection for the Arezzo he had left continued

[32] He devotes so much attention to this problem that students of Bruni have occasionally considered faction to be the basic subject of the *Historiae.* See, for instance, P. Joachimsen, *Geschichtsauffassung und Geschichtschreibung in Deutschland unter dem Einfluss des Humanismus* (Berlin, 1910), p. 20. In spite of his misreading of Bruni in this particular case, Joachimsen's section on him is quite sound. He understands the importance of Bruni's classical form, for example, better than did either Santini or Fueter, who were contemporaries of Joachimsen (see p. 19).

[33] "Hinc studia partium coorta magnarum calamitatum initia fuere" (I, i, 154).

[34] See chap. ii at note 35.

[35] "Cum et bello et fame civitas premeretur, intestina insuper oritur seditio, haud minor sane pestis quam duo superiora incommoda" (I, iv, 488); and further on, referring to the same incident, "Urbs eodem tempore ardebat et vicatim oppugnabatur, non secus ac si hostis entrasset" (I, iv, 502).

[36] "Commoti ob discordias civium" (II, vi, 200).

[37] "Dedentibus oppidanis ob intestinas seditiones et nobilitatis iniurias fatigatis" (II, vii, 332). Colle and San Gimignano follow suit shortly thereafter, "domesticis seditionibus laborantes" (II, vii, 338).

[38] II, vii, 396.

[39] II, viii, 460.

[40] III, xii, 310.

throughout his life. It is seen both in his frequent references to Arezzo's loyalty to its allies and in his emphasis on the city's unswerving Guelfism. After Charles of Anjou's early defeats, Arezzo remains loyal, even though the victorious enemy is in Aretine territory.[41] The imputation of loyalty to the city in this case is significant, for Villani does not mention the Aretines' constancy,[42] and Bruni could easily have found another motive, such as fear of Charles's army, which, though beaten, was still capable of inflicting damage. The Guelf sympathies of Arezzo form the subject of an oration of Domitiano asking Florence for aid on behalf of the Aretine Guelf exiles.[43] Here again, this theme is not to be found in Bruni's source.[44]

Having, early in the work, established Arezzo as a loyal Guelf ally of Florence, Bruni continues the account of his native city with a series of disasters, evoking a sympathy for its fate which is felt for no other town in the whole of the *Historiae*. First, in 1336 Arezzo, pressed by its own exiles in league with the Perugians, gives up its independence to Florence. Such a voluntary surrender was, of course, common in the fourteenth century and does not serve to set Arezzo apart from other Tuscan towns. In 1343, after the expulsion of the Duke of Athens, Arezzo, along with the rest of Florence's dependent cities, declares its freedom.

Arezzo has not profited from its experience of the pernicious effects of internal discord, and the succeeding years see the problem intensified. The first indication that the city is again in difficulties comes during Charles of Hungary's campaign in Italy in 1380, when, Bruni abruptly announces, the Aretines, fearful of their enemies, ask the Angevin to assume command of the town. Pausing to explain the circumstances leading up to this second cession of independence, Bruni describes the Aretines' inability since 1343 to establish a government which could satisfy all factions. But calling in Charles does not solve the problem, and in the following year the storm breaks, prompting one of Bruni's few overt expressions of sympathy for the subjects of his narrative.[45]

---

[41] I, iii, 310.

[42] G. Villani, *Crònica*, VII, 24.

[43] I, iii, 384–386.

[44] Bruni's source for the oration is not Villani but Dino Compagni, who fails to refer to Arezzo's tradition of loyal Guelfism (Compagni, *Crònica*, I, 6).

[45] "Cum esset prosperitas summa regi secundusque rerum cursus Aretinorum supervenit calamitas, miserandi quidem ac deflenda" (III, ix, 40).

After a series of frantic attempts on all sides to pacify the city, one of the factions calls in a force of mercenary troops, who sack Arezzo, occupy it for six months, and leave it in ruins. Bruni stresses the outrages of the situation: the soldiers give no excuse for refusing to leave and make no attempt to justify their presence; the faction that has invited them in suffers as much as the others.[46] And this is not the end of Arezzo's trials. During a Florentine attempt to retake the city for the Guelfs, it is attacked and seized by French troops, who finally sell it to Florence. Despite Bruni's respect for a city's independence, despite his concern for the final, irrevocable subjugation of his native city, his only comment when the Florentines assume control seems to be an expression of thanks and relief that Arezzo is at last free from its curse of internal strife.[47]

Bruni's sensitivity of the evil effects of faction is deepened by his awareness that it constitutes an essential companion to liberty. If the strength of a republic rests on general competition for honors, then the psychological attitude informing republican institutions must perpetuate the struggle and inevitably lead to the creation of factions. Bruni explicates the line of reasoning which connects liberty with faction when he deals with the re-establishment of the republic after the expulsion of Walter of Brienne. "Yet envy and contention, long an accustomed disease of the state, returned to the city together with liberty." [48]

Causal relationships and moral judgments are seldom simple for Bruni. Though factional zeal is used as a basic type of motivation,[49] it only becomes harmful to the state when it is accompanied by certain specific attitudes. The first of these attitudes is stated in Giano della Bella's oration. "I think that when a good citizen advises his *patria*, he should never turn to consider his own utility nor govern his public counsel by his private interests." [50] The explicit opposition of private to public interests is a theme strongly

[46] III, ix, 44.

[47] "Ita Aretium cum omnibus oppidis suis in Florentinorum potestatem, tamquam in portum aliquem deveniens a longis iactationibus et acerbissimis tempestatibus requievit" (III, ix, 72).

[48] "Caeterum, invidia atque contentia, consueti dudum civitatis morbi, una cum libertate in urbem redierant" (II, vii, 310).

[49] See, for example, II, vi, 186, where factional zeal is used in company with greed: "Peditum vero multitudinem ex pisano lunensique agro, vel praemiorum pollicitatione vel studio partium maximam cogunt."

[50] "Verum boni civis esse nequaquam arbitror, dum patria consilium poscit, in propriam utilitatem intuitum retorquere ac ex suo privato commodo publicis consiliis moderari" (I, iv, 434).

implied throughout the *Historiae*. Giano della Bella himself, when he goes into exile in spite of the fact that he could easily have defended himself, provides an example of action motivated by valuing the public good more than his own interests. He explains his conduct by saying, "No citizen by my example should seize arms against public authority." [51]

Both Arezzo and Bologna provide concrete instances of how much a city can suffer from external disaster due to the willingness of a faction to overlook the best interest of the city as a whole by inviting in a foreign power. The Ghibelline threat to dismantle Florence after the battle of Montaperti is used by Bruni as a further example of this principle. He employs his technique of emphasizing the element of chance in Florence's survival in order to point out the foolishness of the city's previous conduct.[52] Bruni understands that this readiness to put private above public interests is grounded in basic psychological realities which make factional strife an unavoidable historical fact. Explaining the failure of an attempt to settle Florentine internal discord in 1266 by a marriage between the rival factions, he says, "For the disease was too great to be cured by this medicine," [53] and he goes on to describe the rancor and suspicion which remained even after the marriage and eventually broke the peace.

An incident during Florence's war with Castruccio in the early fourteenth century further reveals the profoundly historical nature of faction as Bruni understands it. After a surprise retreat by Castruccio a dispute arises among the Florentines concerning the best way to exploit the situation. Bruni describes the argument in the following manner: "For the plebs and the urban multitude thought that the enemy ought to be followed immediately. The nobles, however, whether because of indignation against the plebs or because, expert and skilled in war, they did not trust the hastily collected militia, thought that the forces ought now to be led home and, if it seemed opportune after the alllies had been collected and the forces solemnly drawn up, only then to invade the enemy's territory.

---

[51] "Nec meo quisquam exemplo civis adversus publicam auctoritatem capiet arma" (I, iv, 454). This opposition of public to private interests is also in Toso's oration recommending the purchase of Lucca (II, vi, 176).

[52] "Vicisset tandem ea sententia ne unus Farinata contra omnium impetum restitisset" (I, ii, 234).

[53] "Enim vero maior erat morbus quam ut ex huiusmodi medicamento sanitas illi posset afferi" (I, ii, 284).

Since the variety of opinions induced discord — the plebs distrusting the good faith of the nobles, and the nobles the temerity and madness of the plebs — serious hatred arose." [54] The dispute is referred to the priors and the immediate attack which they decide upon fails, mainly because of the undercurrent of mutual distrust. Bruni presents the incident as one in which the valid arguments of both sides are buried under the weight of the existing partisan passion. Villani, who is less aware both of the causal complexities of history and of the importance of the psychological states described here, affixes the blame squarely and simply on the "vizio de' nobili." [55]

The passions which lie at the base of factional strife are, then, historical realities whose existence precedes and underlies any given situation. Although for this reason faction cannot be eliminated, it can, according to Bruni, be controlled. While he offers no simple solution to the problem, the *Historiae* contain implied judgments on good and bad remedies. He clearly disapproves of two institutional practices often used as checks on factional strife. The first involves summoning a foreign lord to pacify the city, and this is obviously no solution at all. Indeed, one of the evil effects of passion is this very loss of independence, with the suffering and injustice which usually accompany it. Florence has had two singularly unfortunate experiences with such a remedy, first with Charles of Valois [56] and later with the Duke of Athens. But even in the most advantageous of circumstances, where the city has been fortunate enough to find a just and beneficial arbiter, it is not a wise method of resolving factional strife, for it does not attack the root of the problem. The psychological realities involved can be temporarily repressed; they cannot be eradicated. Both Gregory X and Nicholas III, with the very best intentions,[57] fail utterly in their attempts to settle Florence's domestic struggles.

[54] "Plebs enim ac urbana omnis multitudo sequendum e vestigio hostem censebat; nobilitas autem, sive indignatione adversus plebem, sive quod experta et bellorum gnara in subitaneo collectitioque milite non multum spei collocandum putabat, reducendas tunc domum copias et alio si videatur tempore sociis convocatis apparatuque solemniter facto, vadendum in agros hostium suadebat. Cum varietas sententiarum discordias induxisset, ac plebs fidem nobilitatis nobilitas vero temeritatem ac vaesaniam plebis incusaret, odia graviter exarsere." (II, v, 64.)

[55] G. Villani, *Crònica*, IX, 214.

[56] See I, iv, 478.

[57] Of Gregory, Bruni says, "Cum amoenitate urbis delectatus in illa resedisset amor coepit si qua fieri posset studia partium ac discordias civium sedare eiectosque dudum reducere" (I, iii, 328).

A second means of dealing with faction consists in the exclusion from power and, if necessary or convenient, the expulsion from the city of all but the leading faction. This is equally inefficacious and can have consequences as disastrous as calling in a foreign lord. The first disadvantage is that the practice not only weakens the city but strengthens its enemies. There are numerous instances of this adverse effect in the *Historiae,* beginning with the first time the Florentines see their exiles augment the strength of Siena and Pisa.[58] In the last section of the work, one of Florence's weapons in the war against Giangaleazzo is Bernarbo's son and the faction supporting him,[59] and the Bolognese exiles are a crucial factor in the fall of that city.[60]

Bruni's objection to the tactic is, however, deeper than this. Not only does the oppression of a particular faction weaken the city, but it does so in vain. Domestic discord cannot be effectively eliminated by such a means. On the contrary, exclusion from power exasperates and augments those very passions which form the bases of factional strife. Bruni makes this point very early in the work when he explains the nobles' discontent with Florentine popular government. "They grieve both on account of factional zeal and because, while their enemies had returned, they themselves were excluded from the republic." [61]

Throughout the *Historiae* Bruni consistently expresses approval of those measures designed to provide for a government on the broadest possible political basis, and he attacks with equal regularity those which seek to exclude a particular element. Noting the reception of the nobles into the government upon the expulsion of Walter of Brienne, he says, "Two reasons for this plan were given. One was the respect for civil peace, for thus at long last the spirits of the citizens were quieted and pacified. It was believed that the republic would be tranquil if no faction were excluded from honors in such a way that it would be compelled to hate the present state of the city because of its own injuries." [62] Bruni severely criti-

---

[58] I, ii, 64.

[59] III, x, 116.

[60] III, xii, 310.

[61] "Cum ob partium studia tum quod reductis adversariis se ab republica exclusam dolebat" (I, ii, 186).

[62] "Causa vero huius consilii duae potissimum ferebantur. Una concordiae civilis respectus. Ita demum enim quietis pacatisque civium animis tranquillam fore rem publicam credidere si nulla in ea pars honore exclusa, praesentem civitatis statum odisse per suam iniuriam cogeretur." (II, vii, 306.)

cizes the immoderate use of legislation against the Ghibellines in 1357;[63] in the same manner he associates the creation of stability after the Ciompi revolt with the reassimilation of the exiles.[64]

There is a limit, however, to the extent to which factions can be included within the body politic. Bruni was loyal to the Florentine Guelf tradition and realized that, at least in a city which was as historically Guelf as Florence, the Ghibelline nobles could not easily be admitted. Several of his comments stress the deep split between the nobles and the rest of the population. He notes, for instance, that the papal legate sees this split as the most fundamental of the various divisions in Florence.[65] In the case of Arezzo, where Bruni has stressed the bankruptcy of trying to drive out rival factions, the recall of the Ghibelline exiles in 1381 is considered the result of "malignitas regis" and it has unfortunate consequences.[66] He further emphasizes the unreasonable opposition of the Aretine Ghibellines during the Giangaleazzo war.[67] Bruni sees this fissiparous tendency as an essential element of the noble class,[68] who are wont, more than others, to place their private interest above the public good.[69]

The practical explanation for Bruni's approval of governments comprehending all factions lies in his feeling that human jealousy renders internal discord inseparable from republican institutions. Factions cannot therefore be permanently excluded from the city, for new ones will continually spring up to replace the old ones which have been driven out. Bruni's most explicit acknowledgment of this process occurs in Book IV, where he says that one of the great occasions of civil strife finds outstanding men insisting upon just rewards from the state. The people, considering these men arrogant, refuse to grant the desired rewards, and the outstanding citizens in their turn think the people ungrateful.[70] Here is another

---

[63] II, viii, 438.

[64] III, ix, 52. See also his complaint about unfairness to the white faction (I, iv, 508), and his satisfaction with the broadly based government after the expulsion of Novello (I, ii, 276).

[65] I, iv, 492.

[66] III, ix, 40.

[67] They create trouble "studio magis partium quam ulla probabili ratione inducti" (III, x, 384).

[68] "Nam peculiarem nobilitatis malum, superbia et ambitio conflictare dominantes coepti" (I, iii, 384).

[69] For instance, they oppose the creation of a *gonfaloniere* simply because they want to retain the power to avenge their private wrongs (I, iv, 420).

[70] I, iv, 524.

case in which neither faction is really wrong but in which enmity is inevitable.

Deeper, however, than this practical reason for Bruni's insistence on a broadly based government is his concern for the integrity of the body politic itself. After describing the punishment of a conspiracy in 1340, he says, "For citizens ought to be hated in such a way that we still remember them to be citizens." [71] This attitude of Bruni's cannot be explained by reference to any obvious practical consideration. Instead, his statement points toward a more subtle dimension of his historical understanding. Despite the limitations and disadvantages of the republican city state, it is an institution which deals with what Bruni considers to be the basic political and psychological factors of human government and hence demands moral commitment. His concept of faction, as well as any other major idea in his *Historiae*, cannot be fully understood until the level of moral sensitivity and concern has been reached, however deeply the historian has hidden it.

Bruni, then, consistently grasps internal affairs in terms of a well-defined and coherent set of factors. Since faction is derived from basic traits of human nature, the specific historical institutions determined by faction or seeking to restrain it take on significance only in relation to constant psychological elements. To combat the problem of internal divisions the state should not depend on transforming competition for honors into another personality trait. In foreign affairs, however, in spite of the fact that the psychological underpinning of relationships with other cities is clearly articulated, Bruni is far more concerned with the specific, empirically derived elements of a diplomatic situation.

Two themes of diplomatic policy predominate in the work, and both of these are understood more in their historical context than in relationship to fundamental psychological or political categories of understanding. The first to be developed is the theme of Florence's domination over Tuscany. Bruni considers critically both the process by which it came about and the historic means by which Florence has exercised it. His conceptualization here is clear; the predominance of Florence in Tuscany was, after all, a long-established fact by the mid-fifteenth century. The second theme concerns the part Florence is to play in Italy at large, and on this issue

---

[71] "Cives enim sic odendi sunt, ut tamen cives illos esse meminerimus" (II, vi, 264).

Bruni is less definite. Italian politics assumed a greater and greater proportion of Florentine energies in the fifteenth century, a process which would climax, a decade after Bruni's death, in the city's participation in the general league of the five great Italian powers. This process interested and puzzled Bruni. There is a tension in his work between an acute awareness of the dangers implicit in Florence's wider involvement in Italian affairs and the realization that the city cannot avoid and should, in fact, exploit its general Italian responsibilities.

Diplomatic relations do have psychological and political underpinnings. Such is the psychic force of competition that the mere fact of contiguous boundaries is a cause for friction leading to war. Very early in the first book Bruni establishes a sense of geographical causation, beginning his first war narrative: "The first war between the Romans and the Etruscans started from this cause. The Tuscan colony of Fidena was across the Tiber between the fields of the Crustumerians and the Romans." [72] Shortly thereafter he finds the same cause for a war between the neighboring Veii and Romans.[73] Although in later books he avoids stating so baldly the function of geographical proximity as a cause for war, such a consideration continues to weigh heavily in diplomatic decisions. Though the Florentines are not directly involved in the Bolognese war, they are concerned because of the proximity of Bologna and are ready to take measures to protect their interests.[74] The Venetians seek an alliance with Florence partly because they desire peace and see Giangaleazzo as the chief obstacle to its conclusion, but also because they find "his proximity and hostile power threatening." [75]

As an added complication in foreign relations and a cause for war between those who are not neighbors, the political factor of factional strife must be taken into account. Though faction in a domestic context is predominantly a psychological fact, in foreign

[72] "Fuit autem inter Etruscos Romanosque prima belli origo ex huiusmodi causa. Fidenae Tuscorum colonia trans Tyberium fuit inter crustumerinum romanumque agrum." (I, i, 76.) Livy (I, 14) explicates the suspicions of the Fidenates, whereas Bruni considers proximity alone a sufficient explanation for the war.

[73] "Firma hinc pax quiesque romano populo et Etruriae fuit quem ad extremum veientes turbarunt. Haec enim civitas agrum Romanis finitimum habens, ex communione ut saepe fit discordiis haustis . . . cum Romanis contendit." (I, i, 86.) Livy (II, 42) does not give a cause for the outbreak of hostilities.

[74] "Erat tamen sic animata civitas, ut ecclesiam mallet quam Bernabovem in propinquo habere" (II, viii, 460).

[75] "Propinquitatem vero illius et potentiam nimiam formidantes" (III, xi, 242).

affairs it takes on more narrowly political dimensions. Establishing the issues in the Guelf-Ghibelline struggle, Bruni calls the Guelfs protectors of liberty and the Ghibellines followers of imperial domination.[76] This characterization governs his treatment of the feud in later books.[77]

The importance of faction as a cause for war is stressed in Count Ugolino's oration to Florence, in which he pleads for a peace treaty that will spare the Pisans total defeat. Ugolino points out a number of practical considerations which should, ideally, form the basis of a peaceful relationship between the two cities. Among the most important of these is the fact that Pisa abuts on the Florentines' own territory. Ugolino then reviews the issues and shows that Pisa has nothing Florence wants; the war can be explained only by "foolish factional zeal."[78] Villani mentions Ugolino's peace mission but makes no attempt to relate it to the issues, saying only that the Pisan emissary sought his ends through bribery.[79] In part, Bruni is seeking here to underline the foolishness of faction, a constant theme in the *Historiae* in both the domestic and foreign spheres. He is also stressing the innate character of the zeal derived from factional feuds, for he goes on to narrate the oration's complete lack of effect, saying that the Florentines only decide to treat with the Pisans after the Ghibellines have been expelled from Pisa.

Florentine diplomacy is consistently narrated in terms of these two factors of geography and faction.[80] The very first Florentine

---

[76] Of the Guelfs he says, "sed ea quam imperatoribus adversam supra ostendimus, ex iis fere hominibus conflata erat, qui libertatem populorum magis complectebantur," and of the Ghibellines, "alia vero factio ex iis erat qui imperatorio nomini addicti, libertatis et gloriae maiorum immemores obsequi externis quam suos dominari malebant" (I, i, 154).

[77] Partisan zeal has already been seen by Bruni as the cause of disturbances in several post-Carolingian cities. After stating that Siena and Pisa were separated from each other by the territory of Volterra, he explains the friction which nevertheless existed between them: "Sed haec vel studia partium, vel factionum respectus saepenumero variebant. Etenim quod cuiusque rationibus aptissimum est, id promptissime populi amplectuntur." (I, i, 152.) Later on in the work he calls the Ghibelline faction at Arezzo "libertatis hostes" (I, iii, 386).

[78] "Inane partium studium" (I, iii, 374-376).

[79] G. Villani, *Crònica*, VII, 98.

[80] As would be expected from the discussion in chap. ii, the conduct of diplomacy in terms of self-interest is assumed. The stress on self-interest in the alliance between Charles of Anjou and the Tuscan Guelfs has already been mentioned (at I, ii, 264). In another case the Sienese and others join Florence against Castruccio simply because she seems the stronger: "Cum fama florentinis prospera in dies vulgaret, conciti, eo decucurrerunt" (II, v, 94). Dealing with the reasons behind Florence's attack on Lucca, Bruni gives only the considerations relevant to its suc-

foreign adventure recounted shows their influence. Shortly after establishing its independence, Florence launches an expedition against the Pistoians, "not indeed from ambition or the desire to dominate, but to take care for preserving its liberty." [81] Bruni goes on to explain that Pistoia had followed the opposite faction and that "upon hearing of the advent of Charles IV in Italy, Florence was forced to attack in order to preserve its own independence and to restore a Guelf government to neighboring Pistoia." [82] Florentine aggression in support of both its own independence and the Guelf faction is a continuing theme in the second book.[83]

Florence's wars, induced by factional zeal, geographical considerations, and the instinct for self-preservation, result in the establishment of Florence's predominance among the cities of Tuscany. Its hegemony, in turn, determines the broad lines of subsequent Florentine foreign policy. At first found in the narrative only by implication, this ascendancy is explicated in the orations, particularly the one which Farinata degli Uberti delivers before Manfred on behalf of the Tuscan Ghibellines.[84] Finally, the position of Florence is stated in explicit form in the narrative itself when Bruni, giving the reasons for the Ghibellines' desire to destroy Florence after its defeat at Montaperti, says, "That city was the center of Guelfism in Tuscany, and its ruin would involve the ruin of that whole faction." [85]

In the *Historiae* Bruni is more attentive to the concrete problems facing the city in attaining its leading position among Tuscan powers than to the underlying cause of the phenomenon.[86] The cities with

cess: the departure of Lewis of Bavaria, the collapse of the anti-Pope, and the treaty with Pisa (II, vi, 192).

[81] "Nec ea quidem ambitione vel dominandi cupiditate sed provida cura libertatis retinendae" (I, ii, 162).

[82] "Ad huius igitur rei famam exercitus florentinus populus, civitatem tam propinquam durare in partibus sibi periculosum arbitratus reducere Pistoriensium exules perfactionem dudum pulsos, populum ac libertatem in ea quoque urbe assere constituit" (I, ii, 162).

[83] Arezzo (I, ii, 164), Volterra (I, ii, 168), Pisa (I, ii, 174), and Orvieto (I, ii, 176). In 1312 the Florentines even send aid to the Roman Guelfs "ne communis partium studio deessent" (II, v, 8).

[84] "Florentia autem quasi domina quaedam regiones est, et quacumque inclinant magnam eius partem quo velut pondere secum rapit. Nec regionem unquam tecum habere videberis nec ulla ipsa quae adhuc in partibus durant consistent, nisi Florentiam habeas." (I, ii, 196.)

[85] "Eam urbem caput diversae factioni in Etruria esse . . . eius enim casu et ruina penitus obrui diversam in Etruria factionem stante vero" (I, ii, 232).

[86] He intimates the cause at the beginning of Book II, suggesting that it lies in the liberty of the Florentine *populus*, a characteristic which gives the commune great

which Florence has to deal fall into three categories. In the first are those which, because of either size or location, can be easily and directly subjugated to Florentine control. The second includes cities that are too strong to be brought readily under Florentine rule but which because of factional zeal are fundamentally hostile to Florentine interests. The third covers a group of cities that are too large to be smoothly assimilated into Florence's sphere of influence but which are not necessarily hostile to Florentine interests.

Among the cities that Florence can easily overcome are Pistoia and Prato; Florentine policy here is simple and direct, depending on the use of whatever means is necessary to achieve domination. The policy is clearest in the Florentine recovery of the two cities after the expulsion of the Duke of Athens. Prato is simply bullied into surrender by a show of force; [87] Pistoia, being stronger and more distant, is attacked first by an ill-conceived and poorly executed trick. When this fails, Florence is forced to undertake a long and eventually successful siege. Bruni does not imply that Florence is mistaken in its general strategy. When the attempt to trick Pistoia fails, there is an oration in which its perpetrators are castigated, but more on tactical than strategic grounds. The oration suggests that, although perhaps Pistoia ought not to have been attacked in the first place, now that the Pistoians' suspicions have been aroused the city definitely ought to be taken. Bruni's final assessment of the affair reflects his basic approval of Florentine conduct in this particular instance.[88]

Florence can treat her weaker neighbors in a blunt and high-handed way because she can act largely free from the intervention of outside forces. The second type of city, represented by Pisa, demands equally blunt treatment but for quite another reason. Pisa is, on both strategic and psychological grounds, hostile to Florence and must be directly and forcefully opposed. Bruni, beginning the *Historiae* a decade after the capture of Pisa, knew the

advantages over its neighbors: "Ab his initiis profectum mirabili dictu est quantum adoleverit populi robur" (I, ii, 162). In the *Laudatio*, composed some years before this book, Bruni had already explained at some length the sources of Florence's strength, including both its institutions and its strategic geographical position. See Baron's analysis of this explanation together with his exposition of the continuity between the *Laudatio* and the *Historiae* (*Crisis*, 2nd ed., pp. 61–62 and 199–211).

[87] II, vii, 344.

[88] "Per hunc modum res male coepta bonum tandem exitum habuit" (II, vii, 354).

outcome of this long and bitter antagonism and profited from his hindsight, commending Florence's policy of consistent opposition and likening the struggle between the two powers to that between Rome and Carthage.[89]

The theme of Pisan antagonism to Florence, founded on the rock of partisan zeal, runs constantly through Bruni's work. Pisa is among the cities receiving the Pistoian Ghibellines after Florence has driven them into exile.[90] In 1270 only the insistence of the royal legates induces the two rivals to make peace.[91] The Pisans take advantage of any opportunity to launch an attack on Florence; for example, the mere presence of Manfred causes them to disavow a Florentine alliance and attack Lucca.[92] Faction alone does not suffice to explain this antagonism. Pisa and Florence are commercial rivals, a fact which is seldom noted directly but which tends to emerge in peace treaties, such as the treaty of 1292, which provides exporting and importing rights for the Florentines,[93] or the treaty of 1366, which provides for a restitution of the immunities.[94]

The relatively inflexible policy forced on Florence in the case of Pisa leads to more difficulties than had a similar policy when applied to such lesser powers as Pistoia and Prato. Pisa alone cannot seriously damage Florence, but its reaction to Florentine threats is often to call in other powers, particularly Milan. In describing Giovanni Visconti's attempt to secure Pisa's alliance in 1351 Bruni most clearly acknowledges the dangers arising from this reaction. "About this time the Bishop sent legates to the Pisans to persuade them to undertake a war against the Florentines. Although there was a peace between Pisa and Florence, he was convinced that it would be easy to persuade them to go to war, because he knew of the long hatred between them which arose from factional antagonism. He was especially sure of himself since he was offering such

---

[89] I, Proèmio, 50.

[90] I, ii, 164.

[91] "Praesentibus ac iubentibus legatis regis" (I, iii, 324).

[92] "Spreto foedere cum Florentinis sociis que nuper icto" (I, ii, 182).

[93] III, xi, 250. For an explicit reference to Pisa's hostility, see Toso's oration (II, viii, 494).

[94] II, viii, 494. In narrating the causes for this particular war, Bruni deals more explicitly than usual with commercial factors: "Florentinis enim ad Talamonem emporium celebrantibus, angebantur Pisanorum animi, cernentes urbem suam quae portus Florentinorum esse consueverat, per illorum demigrationem in solitudine destitutam. Simul enim cum Florentinis negotiatoribus caeteri quoque illiusmodi homines secuti negotiorum commoditatem, relictis Pisis, Talamonem petierant." (II, viii, 460.)

a good opportunity." [95] The fear that Pisa would give itself to Bernarbo Visconti was one of the basic considerations inducing the Florentines to make peace in 1361.[96]

Florentine policy toward the first two types of cities is properly rigid, in the first case from politic self-interest, in the second from necessity. A third class of city, represented by Arezzo, Lucca, and Siena, demands a more judicious approach. These cities are not irrevocably hostile to Florence and may presumably be developed into faithful and valuable allies. It is with Arezzo that Florence has been most successful in implementing this policy. Arezzo, torn by internal strife, had surrendered completely to Florence in the fourteenth century, but after the expulsion of Walter of Brienne the city had declared its independence along wtih most of Florence's other subject cities. The reaction of Florence, in marked contrast to its policy toward Pistoia and Prato, was to recognize voluntarily the Aretines' freedom and even to congratulate them on it. Bruni remarks that this generous action had the effect of making the Aretines firmer allies, more useful to the Florentines than they had ever been as subjects.[97] The Aretines finally surrender their independence after a disastrous occupation, but their friendship with Florence stems from the time when they were treated and respected as confederates.

Florentine policy is least successful in dealing with Siena, which, after a period of occasional alliances,[98] is driven into open and nearly unremitting hostility to Florence, with much the same dangers as those produced by Pisan antagonism. It is Siena's invitation to Giangaleazzo, prompted by Sienese annoyance with Florence for receiving Cortona and Montepulciano under its protection, that provides the pretext for the Milanese intervention in Tuscany.[99]

By the time of the Giangaleazzo war, and even more clearly by the 1420's and 1430's, Florence's relations with other Tuscan cities have been stabilized. The one major exception is Lucca, strategically

---

[95] "Per hoc ipsum tempus, praesul, oratoribus ad Pisanos missis ut bellum adversus Florentinos susciperent flagitabat. Etsi enim pax erat civitatibus, tamen, quia audierat pervetustas utrique populo inimicitias fuisse studiaque, partium omnino diversa persuaserat ipse sibi perfacile eos tali praesertim opportunitata oblata ad capessendum bellum impellere posse." (II, vii, 368.)

[96] II, viii, 492–494.

[97] "Aretini vero, haec audientes, laetati sunt et omissa suspitione, fidem florentini populi maiorem in modum complexi in amicitia perseverarunt" (II, vii, 320).

[98] Siena is, in fact, included in the Aretine alliance just mentioned.

[99] III, ix, 186.

important because of its position guarding the passes from Lombardy into Tuscany. It has yet either to be subjected to the Florentine yoke, or turned into a reliable ally, or irrevocably antagonized. During much of Bruni's chancellorship, however, it seems that Florence's attempts to conquer Lucca are fast driving the city into permanent hostility. War begins in 1429. Florence, exhausted by the recently concluded war with Milan, seeks to rob its neighbor of independence in order to bolster Florentine prestige in Tuscany and to prevent Milan from gaining an entrance into the region by means of an alliance with the Lucchese leader Guinigi.[100] Distracted by other interests and plagued by internal revolt, Florence cannot subjugate Lucca even after the fall of Guinigi, and an inconclusive peace is signed in 1441.

The sixth book of the *Historiae* was written shortly before the outbreak of the war, and here the question of Florentine policy toward Lucca is treated at great length. In the fifth book, written in the same years (1421–1426), Bruni deals with the Castruccio war of the fourteenth century as a more or less personal problem, hardly considering the extent to which Lucca poses a special strategic difficulty. However, in the sixth book, when he comes to deal with Mastino della Scala's seizure of Lucca and the city's eventual surrender to Pisa, he dwells at some length on Lucca's historical significance to Florence. "Indeed the Florentines were led into the Lombard war because of Lucca; for the same reason they undertook the war against Mastino; similarly because of Lucca the Pisan war broke out." [101] Shortly afterwards he further underlines Lucca's importance by listing the reasons for Mastino's confidence in being able to hold it against Florence. These include the strategic position of Lucca, allowing him to bring his own troops down from Lombardy, together with the aid Pisa will inevitably be able to bring.[102]

It is also in this section that Bruni, in the course of an oration advocating the purchase of Lucca, makes his clearest general statement of the true aims and objectives of foreign policy. "I confess that I am moved by what men think good: to extend one's borders, to increase one's power, to extol the splendor and glory of the city,

[100] For a narrative of the war, see C. Bayley, *War and Society in Renaissance Florence* (Toronto, 1961), pp. 98–177.

[101] "Lucae siquidem causa in Gallicum bellum se coniecerant Florentini; eiusdem Lucae causa aliud rursus bellum adversus Mastinum susceperunt. Lucae etiam causa pisanum postea bellum exarsit." (II, vi, 220.)

[102] II, vi, 229.

to look after its utility and security." [103] This conception of foreign affairs implies, above all, efficacious action, which Florence is unwilling to take. Refusing to buy Lucca, Florence sees it go to the Pisans and is forced to undertake a huge and unsuccessful military effort to seize it. Bruni's comment on all this expresses clearly his disappointment with Florentine policy.[104] His sense of the foolishness of war with Lucca continues, and he lauds every attempt to negotiate with the city during the fourteenth century.[105]

In describing Florence's relations with the larger powers in Tuscany, Bruni is primarily concerned with penetrating to the realities of the political situation and bringing out the necessary interrelationships among the historical elements involved. The particular element which stands out most clearly is the intervention of other powers, both Italian and foreign. No decision can be wisely made without taking this into consideration. Florence's high-handed treatment of Siena is unwise in view of the threat of Milan. So is the decision to assault Lucca directly, when it probably could have been bought without alienating the Lucchese. Florentine aggression against Pisa is necessary but should be prosecuted in the light of Florence's total Italian policy. The successful incorporation of Arezzo into a friendly dependency lessens Florence's danger from foreign intervention, for Arezzo defends itself obstinately against Giangaleazzo's troops and its own exiles.[106]

Florence's responsibilities in the politics of Italy are unavoidable. Bruni dwells on them, not to suggest that Florence should withdraw into Tuscany but to clarify the implications of Florentine actions. His awareness of the ramifications of the city's status among the leading powers of Italy emerges most clearly in the passage describing how the Pope and the Emperor seek Florence's help against Milan. Florence refuses because of an existing treaty with Milan. Bruni makes the point that Florence is too large to remain neutral and that by refusing to join the Pope it has effectively stymied the combination against Bernarbo.[107] And yet Florence incurs the en-

---

[103] "Me moveri fateor quae bona apud homines putantur; extendere fines, imperium augere, civitatis gloriam splendoremque extollere, securitatem utilitatemque asciscere" (II, vi, 172).

[104] "Per hunc modum primis florentini populi ad Lucam, plenus dudum bona spe in irritum recidit ac maiora subsecuta certamina dispendiis et periculis mali poenas consilii a populo exegerunt" (II, vi, 196).

[105] "Ita ut minus gloriosa si magis certa visa est pactionis via" (I, vi, 266).

[106] II, x, 118.

[107] "Quasi libente fundamento nihil superaedificari solidum potuit" (II, vii, 496).

mity of the Pope by refusing to join him. Both the impossibility of remaining inactive in Italian affairs and the advisability of regulating conduct by well-considered self-interest are strongly implied.

If inaction can breed difficulties, ill-considered action can invite disaster. Florentine aid to the Guelfs in Lombardy is an example of such rash action, for it causes the Lombard Ghibellines to incite Castruccio into breaking the peace, thus pushing Florence into a long and dangerous conflict.[108] The last books of the *Historiae* see the development, finally, of a coherent and sophisticated policy for intervention in Lombardy. (This will be taken up a little later when military history is discussed.)

Florentine foreign policy, especially in the case of Lucca but also on a wider scale, evinces a failure to appreciate the realities which necessarily inform the relations between states. Bruni sees an explanation for the failure in the very republican constitution which provides Florence's strength, both internally and externally. This is strongly suggested in the previously noted oration advocating the purchase of Lucca. Pinio Toso suggests that one possible reason for the reluctance of the people to buy the city is their lack of foresight and their failure to understand the necessity of preventive action.[109] It is clear that Bruni considers such policy to be extremely unfortunate, and, indeed, he has Toso go on to condemn it, pointing out that in their private affairs the citizens would never be so shortsighted.[110]

This is not the only reference in Bruni's work to the disadvantages of a republic in the conduct of foreign affairs. Noting Florence's reaction to a military defeat, he says, "As happens among the people, some blamed the leaders themselves and others the soldiers. They preferred to think themselves tricked rather than beaten." [111] A Florentine attempt to secure Arezzo through negotiation with King Charles fails, "for those cities who are ruled by the people cannot hide what is done. Indeed, in single decisions the deliberations are conducted with the knowledge of many." [112]

[108] II, v, 50. The theme of rash Florentine intervention in Lombardy is also stressed in Azzo Visconti's oration to his troops (II, v, 106).

[109] "Sunt qui satis vos habere monentes, id quod est tuendum censeant et nec impensis nec coeptis sese novis onerandum" (II, vi, 174).

[110] "Quasi vero ista susceptio non pro tutela fiat eorum quae possidemus, aut superiora bella nobis illata non in periculum haec ipsa amittendi coniecerint" (II, vi, 174–176).

[111] "Ut fit in populis, alii duces ipsos alii milites accusabant proditos denique se credere malebant quam victos" (II, viii, 478).

[112] "Civitates enim quae populanter reguntur neque celare sciunt quod factum

The problem is dealt with most fully, however, in two important orations. The first is the Florentines' reply to a Bolognese delegation claiming that Bologna is exhausted by the war with Giangaleazzo and must soon seek a truce. Florence answers that war is hard on all classes, but particularly on the lower orders,[113] who do not understand the issues. It is the duty of the governors of a city to force the lower orders to support the war effort.[114] The inclusion of both the *populus* and the *multitudo* in the same category is significant, for Toso's oration had referred principally to the commercial classes, who would understand an analogy drawn from business practices. Here Bruni uses a medical metaphor, which would be more easily understood by the lower classes.[115]

The posture of a popular government in foreign affairs is dealt with most fully in the eleventh book, by a Florentine, Gianfigliazzo, who criticizes the conduct of the war with Milan. He evokes in explicit, clear terms all the themes relevant to this issue which Bruni has developed through the work. Florence's problems, he says, stem more surely from its own customs than from its enemies. In the first place, the city is always tardy in preparing for eventualities because the people [116] do not look into the future and do not see the danger until it is upon them. Secondly, there is the practice of branding as a warmonger anyone who proposes specific actions in preparation for war. Gianfigliazzo illustrates his point by noting the recent situations in which Florence has found itself frustrated by unpreparedness.[117]

Having established the problem, Gianfigliazzo proceeds to sug-

---

sit neque possunt quippe multorum deliberatione et coscientia in singulis decretis opus est" (III, ix, 62).

[113] "Populus et multitudo."

[114] III, x, 134–138.

[115] "Verum tamen ut medici quos curant aegrotos urere interdum ac secare compellunt et partem corporis cum dolore abiicere quo caetera conserventur, ita gubernatores reipublicae futurum periculum instar medicorum praevidentes etiam cum dolore cogere debent populos partem facultatem suarum pro conservatione caeterarum partium erogare" (III, x, 134–136).

[116] Again, "populus ac multitudo."

[117] III, xi, 254–258. This sense of the lower orders as a peaceful force, opposed to warlike endeavors, is a continuing theme in the *Historiae*. One of the effects of the change from monarchy to popular government is peace: "Qualis concordiae fructus esse solet" (I, i, 68). After the Ordinances of Justice are passed, Florence makes peace with Pisa, "sed ne nobilitas, quae belle clarescere solebat, per occasionem militiae aliquid moliretur et plebs nusquam a reipublicae custodia abscederet, pacem potius visum est quam bellum expedire, teneris adhuc legibus et reipublicae statu nondum solide stabilito" (I, iv, 444).

This point of view in the *Historiae* contrasts with the position Bruni takes in his *Difesa contro i riprensori del popolo fiorentino nella impresa di Lucca*, ed. P.

gest a solution. The first thing to be done, since Florence's antago-
nist is not hindered by the ignorance and unwillingness of the
people, is to narrow the basis of power. Councils are too unwieldy
and should be reduced in size and number. Decisions must be made
silently and swiftly, without publicity. Only when these reforms
are undertaken at home can Florence proceed to attack its foreign
problems by gathering troops, placating Siena and Perugia, and
seeking an alliance with Venice.[118]

A study of Bruni's treatment of foreign affairs has led to the
conclusion that the problems involved are too complex to be solved
without limiting the basis of power to those capable of understanding the issues. A balance must be sought whereby the energies re-
leased by republican institutions will not dissipate themselves in
policies that ignore the interrelated causal complex of political and
psychological factors constituting the substance of the historical
process.

Properly limited and controlled, a republic is much wiser in policy than a single ruler. The very oration which points up the weaknesses of popular involvement in foreign affairs begins with a
passage extolling the virtues of decisions made only after general
counsel has been taken.[119] One of Bruni's chief criticisms of the
Florentine surprise attack on Pistoia is that it was made by the
priors without consulting anyone on the councils.[120] By the same
token, he is quick to point out a single ruler's rash decisions, which
are usually influenced by the circumstance that the ruler is sur-
rounded by courtiers and sycophants rather than genuine counselors.
One of Mastino della Scala's considerations in thinking he could
hold Lucca was the advice of his adulators, "of which the courts of
rulers are full." [121] The Archbishop of Milan becomes willing to
make peace with Florence when he sees that he has been deceived

---

Guerra (Lucca, 1864), quoted by Bayley, *War*, p. 99. Here he maintains that the
Lucchese war is caused not by the intrigues of the leading Florentines but by the
bellicose temper of the plebs.

Yet, it is only fair to say that on occasion Bruni does portray the people as
warlike in the *Historiae*. For instance, they are furious at the peace treaty signed
with Pisa in 1366, even though the terms are singularly advantageous to Florence
(II, viii, 494).

[118] III, xi, 258–264.

[119] III, xi, 254.

[120] "Quippe caeteri quidem omnes ante rem consultare solent; vos autem (quod
bona venia dictum sit) post rem actam consilium postulates" (II, vii, 348).

[121] "Quibus dominatorum atria sunt referta" (II, vii, 416).

by his courtiers.[122] Finally, Bruni proudly notes occasions when a republican city has used its intelligence to solve a problem. When the legate cut off its grain supply, Florence, according to Bruni, would surely have fallen had it not adopted a wise policy.[123]

Though Bruni focuses on specific problems in narrating the history of Florentine foreign relations, his analysis in terms of general themes makes him somewhat insensitive to concrete political factors. Little or no attention is paid to the specific attributes of Florentine power and none at all to its vicissitudes. No real change is seen, for instance, as resulting from the black death, nor is the massive change in Florence's position after the expulsion of the Duke of Athens recognized.

Bruni emphasizes rather the psychological elements in foreign affairs, holding the major objective of diplomacy to be the establishment of an attitude of trust and friendship among allies. By the same token, traditional opponents are assessed in terms of mutual antagonism and hatred. In keeping with this practice a strong emphasis is placed on such factors as *dignitas* and *auctoritas*. The Pistoians, in choosing an ambassador to ask peace of the Florentines, select a man "of great authority in the republic at that time." [124] Dignity constitutes an important strategic objective in military campaigns. The Florentine *dux* leads a force out into the Mugello, relieves a castle, and leads it back again, "since he thought that enough had been done for the dignity of the republic." [125] Florence rejects the possibility of buying off a band of German marauders because such a policy would not be worthy of the city, and, speaking of the effect of its stand, Bruni shows his awareness of the value of *dignitas*.[126] One consideration in making peace with Pisa in 1366 is that a recent victory has made Florence "satisfactum dignitati." [127]

---

122 "Cum enim cerneret se ab adulatoribus deceptum" (II, vii, 416).

123 "Nisi civitas prudenti consilio obviam iisset . . . Hoc periculum tunc civitati imminens non armis sed consilio depulsum est." (II, viii, 512.) His approval of Florentine negotiations with Lucca has already been mentioned.

124 "Per ea tempora magnae in republica auctoritatis" (I, ii, 170).

125 "Cum satis pro dignitate reipublicae factum dux existimaret" (II, vii, 408).

126 "In dignitate enim atque constantia non cedendi magnam sibi gloriam fore propositam haud falso existimabat . . . Nomen certe ac fama florentini populi ex hac una re mirum in modum apud cunctos accrevit plurimamque exinde civitas est auctoritatem et gloriam consecuti." (II, viii, 450.)

127 II, viii, 494. That such considerations do not constitute uncritical moral imperatives in Bruni can be seen in several instances where he allows other considerations to outweigh them. For instance, though he specifically says that the

Florence's wealth, the one definite source of its power which is consistently noted, tends to be seen in the light of the energy and vigor which have produced it. This perspective emerges most clearly in the oration in which the Bolognese claim that they are exhausted by the war effort. The orators begin by saying that if their city were as rich as Florence there would be no problem, but it is not. "For our men do not have the temperament to exert energy in acquiring things, nor do they carry on business in France and England. They are simple men content with what they have and delighting with joyful spirit in what they possess at home." [128] From this passage it is clear that Bruni sees the Florentines' wealth in the context of their character. Not only does the commercial strength of Florence rest on psychological factors, but it can be adversely affected by them. He explains the fall of Florentine banking houses in the 1340's not by unwise investments or external pressures but by the fear that arises among their creditors when Florence seems to be turning away from the Pope and King Robert to the Emperor.[129]

A third contemporary problem in which Bruni is interested is the military one. Though closely related to foreign policy, the actual conduct of war is sufficiently important to merit independent discussion. Two aspects of Bruni's position on this matter are worthy of note: first, his emphasis on strategic and tactical considerations, to the exclusion of personal valor and glory, in narrating military campaigns; second, his deep sense of the advantages as well as the disadvantages implicit in the mercenary system.

If Bruni's purpose in relating military events is to provide models of virtuous action, he chooses an odd means of doing so. In the case of a joust between two Bretons and two Florentines he describes the actual combat very rapidly and sketchily, saying simply that the *virtus* of one of the Florentines was responsible for the victory.[130] He makes no attempt to suggest that the incident had any larger significance for the outcome of the war. The historian tends in gen-

---

Florentines cannot desert Montepulciano "cum honestate," they do not hesitate to do so in the light of the more pressing need to conciliate Siena after the fall of Giangaleazzo has made it imperative to obtain the good will of the major cities in Tuscany (III, ix, 96).

128 "Non enim eo ingenio sunt homines nostri ut industria multa in aquirendo utantur, nec ulli eorum per Galliam et Britanniam negotiaturi discursant; simplices magis homines ac suis rebus contenti, eo quod habent domi laetis animis perfruuntur" (III, x, 132).

129 II, vi, 278.

130 II, viii, 542.

eral to de-emphasize the role of personal valor or cowardice. For instance, in narrating a battle between the Pisans and Florentines in 1341, he blames the Florentine defeat on a tactical mistake, the failure of the second line of battle to join the first when it was hard pressed.[131] His source for the battle is Villani, who stresses the military importance of personal acts by specifically condemning the standard bearer.[132] In comparison with Villani, Bruni's emphasis on the simple tactical consideration that a second line should always support the front line is striking.

Personal valor alone seldom causes a victory or personal cowardice a defeat. The successful defense of Ferrara in 1333 is explained by both the bravery and energy of the Florentine leaders and the fortuitous collapse of a bridge, and the historian maintains that without the latter accident the former vigor would have been in vain.[133] He does credit the "virtus et ardor" of the *dux* for a victory over the Pisans in 1363, but again he is careful to point out the great importance of *fortuna*.[134] Bruni is interested in valor and other moral qualities only on a general scale, where they take on tactical significance. Describing the respective strengths of Florence and Pisa, he notes that one is "recenti victoria superbus," while the other is "odio doloreque incensus." [135] Even here, however, he does not show that these psychological states influenced the battle in any direct and meaningful way.

It would be fruitless to extrapolate a detailed military strategy from Bruni's history, which was obviously not intended to present anything of the kind. Only a few examples need be given to show how Bruni uses strategic factors to organize the military sections of the narrative. The basic military strategy developed through the *Historiae* involves repelling an attack through a counterattack into enemy territory. This is, in many ways, typical of Bruni's general type of insight. Sensitive to the advantages of defense in fifteenth-century warfare,[136] he seeks to penetrate beyond the obvious strategy

131 "Victoria haud dubie parta erat, si alterum agmen prosecutum fuisset; sed stetit immobile nec post suos incessit" (II, vi, 272).

132 "Ma dissesi che fu per difetto di messer Gianni delle Bellina di Borgogna ch'avea l'insegna reale chi non volle andare contra l'insegna di messer Luchino peri il saramenti ch'avea fatto essendo suo prigioni in Lombardi" (G. Villani, *Crònica*, XI, 134).

133 II, vi, 208–210.

134 II, viii, 472.

135 I, ii, 166. See also his judgment of the place of *virtus* in the battle of Benevento (I, ii, 268).

136 When, for instance, Florence besieges Pistoia: "Cum moenia dumtaxat

of static defense to a sounder and more dynamic plan. In earlier books, when Florence is involved almost exclusively in Tuscany, warfare is narrated in terms of simple sorties into enemy territory, both for revenge and to create pressures leading to the withdrawal of enemy troops from one's own lands. This technique is particularly emphasized in the war with Castruccio,[137] but it also figures in smaller operations.[138]

The strategy of sorties into enemy territory emerges most clearly in Bruni's narration of the war with Giangaleazzo. Florence, reacting to Giangaleazzo's thrusts into Tuscany and his attack on Bologna, seeks to defend itself by widening the war into Lombardy, and it purchases the services of the Duke of Bavaria for this purpose.[139] The nature of the pressure placed on Giangaleazzo by the maneuver has psychological as well as purely military dimensions.[140] Hence, even though the endeavor results in military disaster when the Duke of Bavaria refuses to join Hawkwood, who is compelled to retreat,[141] it is strategically successful in forcing Giangaleazzo to remove his troops from Tuscany.[142] The strategy is employed again in the following year (1391) with equal success [143] and remains a consistent theme in the war. A Florentine victory at Mantua in 1397, for instance, forces the removal of Milanese troops from Tuscany and leads to a major Florentine victory there.[144]

In the predominance of conceptual over personal dimensions, in the attempt to penetrate beneath surface appearances to more broadly conceived realities, in the relation of strategic considerations to psychological realities, Bruni's vision of military history reflects his general historical perspective. The necessity for grasping the larger strategic aspects of military affairs leads Bruni to see in turn the value of professional military leaders. Bayley has found in both the *Historiae* and the *De Militia* that Bruni is a strong advo-

---

tutaretur hostis nec fortunam praeli tentare vellet nihil aliud profectum est quam ut agri hostiliter vastarentur" (I, iv, 486).

[137] II, v, 521–554.

[138] See the defense of Barga by attack on the Lucchese town of Ceruglio (II, vi, 200), or the use of the technique by Pisa against Volterra (II, viii, 466).

[139] III, x, 116.

[140] III, x, 120.

[141] III, x, 128.

[142] "Quippe mediolanensis domi percussus non eadem qua prius alacritate subsidia in Etruriam submittebat" (III, x, 130).

[143] "Galeatius autem, cum ex magno periculo domi respirasset, quo parem Florentinis cladem inferret ac Senenses oppressione hostium liberaret, victrices copias suas Etruriam mittere constituit" (III, x, 160).

[144] III, xi, 238.

cate of the citizen army and an unqualified opponent of professional condottieri.[145] The passages he quotes from the *Historiae*, however, admit of a broader interpretation and are all taken from the first half of the work.

In later sections Bruni, however much he has extolled the virtues and accomplishments of the thirteenth century civic militia, consistently supports the professional soldier against his civilian critic. In 1362 Bonifacio Lupo becomes embroiled in an argument with the commune over military policy. Bruni supports Lupo on the ground that his technical acumen makes him a surer judge of military affairs than those skilled in the arts of peace.[146] Considering the historian's feelings against princes who take no counsel, his remarks here constitute a striking affirmation of the value of a professional soldier in dealing with necessarily complex and sophisticated military problems. Again, speaking of 1369, Bruni recounts an incident in which the *dux*, Giovanni da Reggio, is right and the citizens are wrong.[147]

Bruni is hardly blind to the faults of mercenary troops: they are often motivated only by greed for booty and pay;[148] the consequences of allowing them into even a friendly city can be disastrous;[149] the leaders are occasionally quite untrustworthy;[150] and the difficulties of disbanding mercenary troops at the end of a war render the maintenance of peace more difficult.[151] None of these drawbacks, however, affects the capacity to provide skilled leaders which is the basic virtue of the mercenary system.

Bruni clearly believes that the skill of the leader is a credit to the commune which hires him and that of this kind of glory is as sound and meritorious as the more obvious type manifested in the valor of a citizen body.[152] Bruni's pride in the amount of money

---

[145] See Bayley, *War*, especially chap. 4.

[146] "Scientia enim rei militaris vix illis qui tota vita nihil aliud meditati sunt contingit, ne dum homines plebeii et otio mercaturisque assueti illam possideant" (II, viii, 466).

[147] II, viii, 500.

[148] II, viii, 468–470.

[149] See the experience of Pisa (II, viii, 500), Hawkwood's sack of Faenza and Cesena (II, viii, 516, and II, viii, 544–546), and the sack of Arezzo (III, ix, 42–44).

[150] See his consideration of the value of the Emperor Robert to Florence (III, xii, 280–288).

[151] See the causes given for the revival of hostilities after the truce of 1392 (III, xi, 174), or the problems of enforcing the truce of 1398 (III, xi, 246).

[152] The idea that effectiveness is as glorious as valor is suggested also by Bruni's method of treating sneak attacks and subversion as genuine military tactics. After describing the skill of the Florentine *dux* Peter Farnese, he narrates his first act,

Florence is willing to spend in its war effort has already been noted. His sense of the glory of hiring a brilliant condottiere is seen most clearly in his treatment of Hawkwood. When Bruni first introduces the English mercenaries, he shows them to be motivated by other factors than base greed, saying that they would have preferred fighting for the Florentines to fighting for the Pisans because they had friends among Florentine businessmen in England. He goes on to call the earlier Florentine decision not to hire them "malo consilio." [153] In describing their service under Pisa, Bruni emphasizes their skill and effectiveness, so that when Florence finally does hire them the wisdom of the decision is clearly seen.[154] Once Hawkwood begins to fight for Florence, Bruni concentrates more fully on his personal brilliance. Particularly impressive is his strategic retreat after a major defeat.[155]

The importance of particular leaders is stressed by Bruni in other cases as well. The major battle of Altopascio is lost when the *dux*, whether by incompetence or betrayal, turns and flees.[156] Villani assigns the same cause for the defeat,[157] but, because of Bruni's tendency to change personal causation into general causation, it is significant that he accepts Villani in this instance. Again, in emphasizing the importance of the captain, Bruni has the surprise attack on Pistoia fail because the *dux* who is leading out reinforcements from Florence loses his way.[158]

This chapter has not tried to present a systematic view of Bruni's thinking on any of the major fifteenth-century problems. It has sought instead to show more precisely the nature of Bruni's commitments and the manner in which he brings his historical analysis to bear on them. His commitment to Florence, to republican institutions, and to liberty is an inextricable part of his moral purpose in writing history. His achievement cannot be understood without reference to these loyalties.

"Is ergo . . . principio veris Lucam per proditionem occupare tentavit" (II, viii, 470). On other occasions as well, he relates such tactics as treachery and betrayal in a military context (see III, x, 118).

[153] II, viii, 474.

[154] See Hawkwood's temporary defeat of a larger number of Florentine troops by means of a skillful sneak attack (II, viii, 488–490).

[155] Bruni's comment on this is, "Illud autem censuerunt omnes, non alium quemquam ducum, praeter unum augutum, ex tantis difficultatibus servare exercitum potuisse" (III, x, 156).

[156] II, v, 102. Previously Bruni had noted the significant role played by the *dux* in a minor night-time maneuver.

[157] G. Villani, *Crònica*, IX, 306.

[158] II, vii, 346.

Chapter Four

The Development of the New Style

Bruni's historical insight, embodying an approach different from that of previous Florentine historiography, necessitated a new mode of expression. The new content implied a new form. It is unfair to speak of the rhetorical form of humanist histories as if it were an independent factor imposed arbitrarily on the received body of pre-humanist historiography, and recent scholarship has tended to emphasize the inaccuracy of such treatment.[1] Once the import and nature of Bruni's historical conceptualization have been grasped, it becomes clear both that his research beyond the basic chronicles was undertaken to answer new questions arising from this conceptualization and that the modifications of form — however much they may be uncritical imitations of classical historical techniques — reflect his desire to present these new concepts with cogency and lucidity.

Though the importance of accuracy to humanist historians in general and to Bruni in particular has been shown in Chapter One, it remains to be dealt with here in more specific terms. Santini devotes much of his study of the *Historiae* to this problem, establishing both that Bruni was faithful to his sources [2] and that he sought beyond his basic source, the Villani chronicles, taking facts from other narratives and even from archival evidence. While Santini's observations are hardly in dispute, their significance remains prob-

---

[1] Baron has done this by implication in pointing out the civic humanism peculiar to at least the early Quattrocento Florentine thinkers. Gray has done it more directly in her doctoral thesis.

[2] See Santini, *Leonardo*, pp. 82–88, where he shows that in narrating military events Bruni does not resort to "uno schema fisso fornitogli dagli storici Latini," but is sensitive to the peculiarities of each battle as it is found in the Villani chronicles. G. Salvemini, *Magnati e popolani in Firenze dal 1280–1295* (Florence, 1899), p. 243, also stresses the accuracy and specificity of Bruni's accounts of wars and institutions.

lematic. Felix Gilbert expresses the problem succinctly when he suggests that, although Santini's work is a valuable contribution to the understanding of Bruni's stature as an historian, Santini has created more problems than he has solved.[3]

Santini's critical edition of the *Historiae* thoroughly documents Bruni's regular use of the Villani chronicles for the period they cover. But the editor neglects to consider why Bruni felt it necessary to go beyond the chronicles. What answers did Bruni seek in vain from Villani? What types of historical facts are most consistently drawn from other sources?

Once the problem is posed in this manner, the answer becomes clear. Bruni's research beyond the Villani chronicles directly reflects his political interests.[4] He was anxious to determine the precise details and dates of constitutional innovations.[5] On several occasions he sought to establish a proper chronological order for institutional changes. For example, speaking of the election of Guelfs to the *buonuomini* in 1267, he says that some authorities date the influence of the Guelfs from this event, but he must disagree on the grounds of his researches.[6] He establishes the date of the first priors from the ancient annals.[7] On at least one occasion he corrects Villani's dating without explicitly noting that he has done so.[8] Bruni also investigates the context of factional strife — even when it occurs outside Florence.[9] Still in relation to domestic affairs, he wants more information on Florence's rewards to its citizens after a victorious military campaign.[10] In the same vein, he brings out the extent of Florence's war effort by discovering the exact sum paid for the emperor's help against Giangaleazzo.[11]

---

[3] Gilbert, *Machiavelli*, pp. 334–335.

[4] Santini (*Leonardo*, p. 59) has observed that Bruni's researches fall into political, military, or diplomatic categories but has not drawn conclusions from this.

[5] For instance, Villani does not elaborate on the reforms of 1311, and Bruni was compelled to use another source (see *Historiae*, I, iv, 544). Whether he went directly to the archives for his information is of course difficult to say, but in any case the account in the *Historiae* corresponds exactly to archival sources (*Archivio di Stato di Firenze, Consulte e Pratiche*, C. 8v, quoted by Santini, *Leonardo*, p. 60).

[6] "Ego vero et diu ante hoc tempus fuisse duces partium in civitate comperio. Idque publicis annalibus multis extat locis." (I, ii, 292.)

[7] I, iii, 362. He is content, however, with a simple confession of ignorance on the question whether the second or third walls of the city were built in 1284 (I, iii, 378).

[8] I, iv, 422.

[9] He has, for instance, gone to the *Storie Pistoresi* to find information about a disturbance in 1301 (I, iv, 174; see Santini, *Leonardo*, p. 61).

[10] II, vii, 390; Santini, *Leonardo*, p. 73.

[11] III, xii, 280; Santini, *Leonardo*, p. 92.

Villani is particularly lax in reporting the names of ambassadors and the details of peace treaties, and here, even more frequently than in matters of domestic policy, Bruni was driven to supplement him. Several instances of these additions are noted by Santini.[12] Still other cases appear in which Bruni, drawing on other sources, has either expanded the details of diplomatic negotiations or listed the names of diplomats; these have not been pointed out by Santini, probably because he could not locate the specific source Bruni used.[13]

Not only did Bruni's researches take place in response to clearly articulated questions dictated by the disciplined scope of the *Historiae*, but these researches reflected his concern to elaborate the causal relationships he saw among historical events. This particular aspect of his investigations emerges most clearly in the few military details he took from other sources. They serve to support the claim that interest in tactical considerations predominates in his narrative of military matters. Among the events for the year 1317 is included a change in armor dictated by previous experience in battle and intended to increase the tactical value of the cavalry.[14] Speaking of 1325, Bruni even names the men appointed to inspect Florentine fortifications.[15] His desire to include the most specific facts which are relevant to his own concerns is clearly manifested.[16]

[12] According to Santini (*Leonardo*, p. 61) Bruni has gone beyond Villani, Dino Compagni, and Stefani to find the names of the ambassadors to Robert of Calabria; he has listed, presumably from archival sources, the alliances in Tuscany (*Leonardo*, p. 75); and he has named the ambassadors to King Robert in 1401 (*Leonardo*, p. 92). Other instances, not mentioned in the monograph, appear in the course of Santini's edition of the *Historiae* for the new series of *RR.II.SS.* For example, Bruni has taken the details of Walter of Brienne's treaty with Lucca from the *Storie Pistoresi* (II, vi, 299; Santini ed., p. 163, n. 3); the particulars of the peace of 1353 with Milan, though partly from Villani, have been taken also from other sources, possibly archival ones (II, vii, 418; Santini ed., p. 190, n. 1). Other examples are the details of a negotiated peace with Pistoia in 1253 (I, ii, 170; Santini ed., p. 85, n. 1); details of the city's agreements with King Robert (II, v, 22; Santini ed., p. 110, n. 1). Santini has also found cases where Bruni includes from other sources both the names of ambassadors and the particulars of treaties (see I, iv, 462, Santini ed., p. 87, n. 1; I, iv, 510, Santini ed., p. 98, n. 3; II, v, 18, Santini ed., p. 110, n. 1; I, v, 116, Santini ed., p. 129, n. 2).

[13] These include the terms of an Aretine treaty in 1313 (II, v, 32; the relevant sections in Villani are IX, 61 and 64, and do not include the particulars found in Bruni), and the conditions of the league with the legate against John of Bohemia (II, vi, 202, not found in the relevant sections of Villani, X, 212).

[14] II, v, 46. The relevant sections of Villani are IX, 80-90.

[15] II, v, 110; Santini ed., p. 127, n. 4.

[16] This tendency to elaborate details relevant to Bruni's own historical conceptualization appears also in his geographical narrative. He does not usually go beyond the descriptions found in Villani, but when he does the description has strategic —

Santini is convinced that, in addition to chronicles besides Villani's,[17] Bruni used the archives for his research. The mere fact that one can find data in the *Historiae* which are not to be discovered in any of the chronicles does not prove conclusively that Bruni used the archives, but it suggests very strongly that he did have recourse to archival material. In any case, he explicitly refers to authority on several occasions when he establishes facts. In the very first book, when assessing the length of the war with Servius Tullius, Bruni implies that he has consulted more than one authority.[18] He also mentions specific sources in the work, employing a letter of Dante's to support his account of the battle of Campaldino [19] and narrating Giangaleazzo's dismissal of troops in terms of a report from the Florentine ambassadors at Milan.[20] On one occasion, he quotes an entire document, a letter written by Giangaleazzo in defense of his conduct.[21]

Bruni not only collected data from a wide variety of sources to answer his questions; in isolated instances he also analyzed his sources critically. Charlemagne's reconstruction of Florence, described at length in Chapter One, is the most obvious example of this practice. Bruni shows a readiness and a capacity to reason from a coherent reconstruction of past events to demonstrate that a given source either should or should not be granted credence in a specific instance. Another example of the critical method occurs in Book II. After noting the claim of earlier historians that Charles of Anjou came into Tuscany because he was invited by the Florentines,[22] Bruni proposes what he considers to be the actual causes, not by drawing on other sources but by analyzing what Charles's real interests were in the light of the political situation.

The extent to which Bruni represents an advance in critical method over the previous chroniclers can be indicated by a passage in the *Historiae* which, at a superficial glance, seems to make him less critical and more credulous than Villani. This passage re-

---

usually military — significance. See, for example, his description of Montecatini (II, vi, 184), which Villani omits (X, 136).

[17] Santini, *Leonardo*, p. 61.

[18] "Viginti annos continuatum a Servio id bellum quidam auctores sunt" (I, i, 82).

[19] I, iv, 220.

[20] III, xi, 220.

[21] III, ix, 104–106.

[22] "Postulatum hoc a florentinis civibus regis amicis quidam auctores sunt, eorumque precibus adductum regem copias suas in haec loca misisse" (I, ii, 286).

lates the story that news of the battle of Campaldino was miraculously announced to the priors by a mysterious voice at the very hour of victory. Villani substantiates the event by first showing that the Florentines took all possible measures to discover a natural source for the voice, and then vouching for the truth of the report by his own witness to it.[23] Bruni does not elaborate the priors' attempt to discover whence the voice came, nor does he say that there are reports from reliable eyewitnesses which testify to its authenticity. Instead he frankly acknowledges the abstract possibility of miracles in general and buttresses his willingness to accept them by referring to similar happenings reported by historians of Rome and Macedon.[24]

On the surface, this means of explanation seems to come near the credulity of those chroniclers who preceded the Villani. Provided with the evidence of a reasonably dependable eyewitness who has, after all, furnished most of the data for his own narrative,[25] Bruni ignores this evidence in favor of a broad predisposition to accept the validity of extranatural phenomena. On deeper analysis, however, a critical judgment can be found. Bruni, not an eyewitness himself, will not accept a statement merely on the evidence of an eyewitness. Rather, he raises the question of the meaning and context of the event and finds that the miraculous announcement of a Florentine victory is significant in terms of his own understanding of history. "For it is not strange to believe that the same divine grace by whose favor victory was won, should by the same favor give swift news to those whom he has helped." [26] One of the basic, concrete themes growing out of the complex of historical factors in Bruni's work is the moral pre-eminence of Florence, and the miracle is comprehensible in terms of this theme. Bruni in criticizing his sources regularly asks whether a reported occurrence blends coherently with the conceptual structure of his narrative. The complete destruction of Florence by Totila, which does not make sense in the light of a coherent understanding of history, is

---

23 "E questo fu il vero, ch'io l'udii e vidi" (G. Villani, *Crònica*, VI, 131).

24 I, iv, 410–442.

25 There is nothing in the textual tradition of the Villani chronicles to suggest that Bruni's copy of the work did not include the anecdote. Only the last two books of the chronicle seem to be excluded from manuscripts with any regularity. (See I. Moutier's preface to the *Crònica*.) Bruni throughout this section is relying on Villani.

26 "Nec sane alienum credere divinum numen qua benignitate victoriam praestat eadem per famam ocissimam favore propitio illis ipsis quibus favent nunciare" (I, iv, 412).

rejected. The announcement of Florence's victory at Campaldino does make sense and is accepted.

On another occasion in the work, Bruni shows more clearly his use of divine favor within his general causal perspective. Coming to the sudden death of Castruccio Castracani, Bruni narrates it briefly without assessing its significance and proceeds directly to mention the simultaneous death of Galeazzo Visconti. After this, the historian deals with Castruccio's two sons and the failure of their efforts to retain their father's dominions, suggesting the reasons for their incapacity. He sums up this whole series of narrated events by saying, "And so the danger threatening the city was removed not so much by human effort as by divine favor." [27] By presenting the incident in this way Bruni explains the significance of Castruccio's fortuitous death both in conjunction with other events and in terms of larger themes inherent in the *Historiae*, showing that the outcome is not to be understood wholly in terms of accidental factors. Villani, on the other hand, fills his account of Castruccio's death with details of his own experience of the event, without suggesting that the dramatic change in Florence's position was significant in terms of any systematic understanding of the historical process. [28]

The problems connected with Bruni's research techniques and critical method diminish in importance when assayed from a less positivistic point of view. He sought new facts when his new concept of history posed questions that could not be answered from the material in the chronicles. He criticized his sources in terms of his own presuppositions about the nature and structure of history. At no time is the technique abstracted into a general principle; at no time is research pursued for its own sake, independent of an immediate sense of significance. Bruni's critical method, the aspect of his researching practice most suggestive of modern techniques, is used without rigor. The collection of data, though pursued with energy and great effort, is not the chief element of the new form the humanist historian sought to create as a vehicle for his new historical insight.

If Bruni's contribution to historical method depended only on those few occasions when he researched in archival material, or on

[27] "Ita imminens civitati periculum non tam humana ope quam divino est benificio sublatam" (II, v, 158).
[28] G. Villani, *Cronica*, X, 86.

the isolated cases which suggest a critical approach to his sources, it would be minor indeed, and the criticisms of nineteenth-century historians would be more nearly justified. To discerning contemporaries such as Machiavelli, however, as well as to some modern students of the subject, the true significance of the humanist contribution lies elsewhere.[29] It is found in the order and clarity with which the historical events are structured. Humanist historians sought to develop, both through patient imitation of classical historians and through the application of their own creative imaginations, narrative techniques that would capture the interest of the reader and focus his attention on those themes and ideas which the historian considered most important.

The humanist historian did not see himself as a collector of facts but as an artist who organized the facts into a coherent and attractive form. He might have discovered the facts for himself, to be sure, but they could just as easily have been gathered by someone else. Gilbert has brought out this peculiar attitude toward the assembling of factual material by studying the relation between the Venetian humanists Sanudo and Bembo. Although Sanudo spent a great deal of his life in compiling the annals of Venice, he recognized that his work was not "true history" but "the raw material on which later he would build a 'true history' of Venice." [30] He was bitterly disappointed when Bembo was appointed official historian of Venice, believing that his own life work had been done in vain. Mrs. Gray has persuasively described the humanist attitude: "Events attain historical significance not simply because they happened or because they were reported in documents or in tradition. It is the historian who gives them historical existence . . . endows them with life." [31]

This conception of the historian's task, explicit in theoretical works of the late Quattrocento, is also found in Bruni. His most obvious statement of the position occurs in his *Praefatio in vita M. Antonii ex Plutarcho traducta.*[32] Dedicated to Coluccio Salutati

---

[29] C. Vasoli, *Storia e politica nel primo umanesimo fiorentino* (Genoa, 1955), p. 9, has seen that Bruni's great contribution to historical method lies in his structural innovations, though Vasoli does not discuss these with precision. K. Brandi, *Geschichte der Geschichtswissenschaft* (Bonn, 1952), p. 69, also suggests that Bruni's chief advantage over his predecessors lies in organization, though he also does not specify what he means.

[30] See Gilbert, *Machiavelli*, pp. 225–226.

[31] Gray, "History and Rhetoric," p. 43.

[32] In Baron, *Leonardo*, pp. 102–104.

and written before 1405,[33] the translation of Plutarch's life of Mark Anthony is preceded by a discussion of the duties and function of a translator. Bruni begins by emphasizing the difficulties of translation in comparison with the small satisfaction it brings, dealing with these difficulties in much the same way that he stresses the difficulties of writing history in the Proèmio to the *Historiae*.[34] If a writer succeeds in making a good translation, everyone credits the original source; if he fails, he must take the blame himself. Bruni suggests that for these reasons translation is an even more difficult and thankless task than the writing of history, though of equal value. "Indeed, in history, in which nothing is invented, I do not see what it matters whether you write of deeds or what has been said by others. In each case the labor is the same, and even greater in the latter." [35]

Though Bruni assumes here a pose of complete passivity before the historical facts, the import of his statement is quite the opposite, as a glance at his own translations will show. Beatrice Reynolds has compared Bruni's translation of the first books of Polybius with that done by the mid-century humanist Perotti.[36] In the preface to his work Bruni frankly admits that he has taken great liberties with the original text and has even supplemented it with material from other sources. In fact, he is hardly more dependent on Polybius here than he is on Villani in the early books of the *Historiae*. Reynolds has studied some of the ways in which Bruni modifies Polybius' account: he adds a description of Sicily; he tends to emphasize the bravery, resourcefulness, and importance of Rome at the expense of Carthaginian glory.

Of even greater significance than the fact that Bruni changed Polybius is the fact that all these alterations, according to Reynolds, tend to make the narrative read more like Livy.[37] Polybius' generalizations are omitted, and the translator concentrates on developing the lines of the narrative and on clarifying the chronology. Descriptions of battles, where tactics and strategy are stressed by Polybius,

---

[33] Baron, *Crisis*, pp. 161–162.

[34] "Nec tamen a principio ignorabam me eam rem suscipere in qua summam esset labor gratia nulla corruptissimum vero omnium ferme iudicium" (Bruni, *Praefatio*, in Baron, *Leonardo*, p. 102).

[35] "In historia vero, in qua nulla est inventio, non video equidem quid intersit, an ut facta, an ut ab alio dicta scribas in utroque enim par labor est aut etiam maior in secundo" (Bruni, *Praefatio*, in Baron, *Leonardo*, p. 104).

[36] B. Reynolds, "Bruni and Perotti Present a Greek Historian," in *Bibliothèque d'humanisme et Renaissance*, 16 (1954), 108–118.

[37] Santini, *Leonardo*, p. 23, also makes this observation.

are used in the translation to emphasize the carnage and horror of war. Since Bruni's concept of the historical process is much closer to Polybius than to Livy, it is striking that Bruni, in translating the very historian who had so deeply influenced him, should have reworked him by using Livy as a model.

One of the means Bruni chose to bring his translation into the form of a Livian history has not been noted by Reynolds. He achieves chronological order by emphasizing the consular elections, so that the narrative proceeds from year to year in a distinctly annalistic form. The year 263 B.C., at the beginning of the work, is introduced, "And so M. Valerius and C. Octacilius, consuls of the following year . . ." [38] and is concluded, "The year having passed, he left the province." [39] Polybius mentions the election of the consuls not as an ordering event of interest in itself but in connection with more important military events.[40] Similarly, he does not conclude the year, though from his narration Bruni could easily have told that a year had passed.[41] Bruni continues throughout the first book to follow the events from year to year, clearly delineating the beginning and occasionally the termination of each period.[42]

Returning to the *Historiae*, one finds that here also Bruni has carefully organized his work by moving from year to year, plainly marking the boundaries between the years. Apart from the first book, which is introductory in character — and its organization seems to have troubled Bruni [43] — the *Historiae* cover a period of 152 years. Of these years, over two thirds (108) are dealt with individually, introduced with a phrase like "in the next year," and usually concluded by a remark such as "these things were done in

---

[38] "M. Valerium et C. Octacilium, sequentis anni consules" (*Polybii Historici de primo bello punico* [Paris, 1515], p. 4).

[39] "Circumacto anno e provincia decessere" (*Polybii*, p. 5).

[40] Polybius, *Histories*, I, 16, 1.

[41] Polybius, *Histories*, I, 17, 6.

[42] The year 262 B.C. begins with choosing the consuls (p. 5); 261 B.C. starts by specifying the passing of a year (p. 6ᵛ); 260 B.C. begins with the election of consuls (p. 7); 259 B.C. is noted for being insignificant (p. 8); 258 and 257 B.C. are introduced by the change in the consulship (p. 8). Polybius, though he occasionally narrates the election of consuls as an independently significant event, tends to mention it only in passing in a sentence devoted to a more strategically or politically important fact (I, 20, 4, or I, 21, 4).

[43] "Pervagatiorem nobis historiam superioris libri necessitas fecit. Nam neque tantum opus aggressos originem urbis indictam illibatamque praeterire fas putavimus neque post illam enarratam statim sine aliquo nexu rerum ad propria tempora siccis, ut dixerim, pedibus, transeundum. Itaque brevi discursu longa pervagata tempora quaecumque an notitiam dicendorum necessaria fuerunt quasi argumentum pretexentes uno in libro collegimus . . . Iam vero non cursu, sed incessu erit utendum." (I, ii, 160.)

this year." The remaining 44 years are divided into 23 periods, eight of which cover only two years. Even in the longer periods, where Bruni compresses an average of three years into one chronological division, he more often than not keeps the semblance of annalistic form by introducing and concluding the section as if it included only one year.[44]

Bruni has often been criticized, even by those who seek to defend his reputation as an historian, for his consistent reliance on the annalistic form. Both Ullman and Fueter, however much they may disagree in their general interpretations of Bruni, are in accord on this point. Fueter, correctly locating the source of the annalistic treatment in the classical historians whom Bruni imitated and not in the chronicles which served him as sources, says, "Bruni took over from the classical form a second damaging principle: the rigidly annalistic structure."[45]

To criticize Bruni for his annalistic mode of composition is, however, to ignore the reasons inducing him to choose this form. If one is interested in clarity of organization and a mastery of the order of events, permitting the development of themes through the narrative, the annalistic form offers distinct attractions in contrast with the narrative style found in prehumanistic chronicles. The Villani chronicles, for example, are not formless, but they are certainly lacking in discipline. Though the narrative proceeds in rough chronological order, the amount of skipping back and forth makes it often difficult to say which of two events happened first. This defect, along with the tendency of all the Villani to jump widely from one geographical point to another in relating what interested them, may contribute to the charm of the narrative, but it is hardly conducive to a lucid understanding of the events. Livy, on the other hand, understood and exploited the organizational advantages of the annalistic form.[46] Polybius, for all his superiority

[44] For example, the long period between 1256 and 1261, which has no chronological indications within it, is introduced, "sequentis anni initio" (I, ii, 182), and ended, "haec eo anno fere gesta sunt" (I, ii, 232). The period between 1340 and 1343 is similarly narrated (II, vi, 262; II, vii, 320). Bruni's longest lapses from the annalistic form can be explained by lapses in his sources. He misses a period of nine years in transferring from Villani to Stefani between 1364 and 1372 (II, vii, 482–508).

[45] Fueter, *Geschichte*, p. 19. Ullman, "Leonardo Bruni and Humanistic Historiography," *Medievalia et Humanistica*, 4 (1946), pp. 45–61, implies that Bruni got this from his sources.

[46] See P. G. Walsh, *Livy: His Historical Aims and Methods* (Cambridge, Eng., 1961), pp. 174–175.

to Livy in the realm of historical conceptualization, tended to be clumsy and profuse as a narrator. His lack of discipline forced him into lengthy digressions to explain in abstract terms what he might have expressed through the structure of the narrated events. Livy, in seizing upon the annalistic form as one means of organizing and mastering his data, was responding to a general feeling among the first-century Romans, exemplified in the very theoretical works on historical writing which influenced the humanists,[47] that historians should develop techniques of literary presentation which would compensate for the deficiencies of previous historians.

Bruni's obvious preference for Livy over Polybius as an historical writer can be understood in terms of the presuppositions about the importance of an attractive narrative style which underlay the historical approach of both the age of Livy and the fifteenth century. Felix Gilbert has pointed out that, at least by the end of that century, the division by years was one of the ideal forms through which humanists imitated the ancients, and that this practice of division was clearly influenced by the example of the *Ab urbe condita*.[48]

The annalistic form is valuable, first, in that it relates events to one another in terms of a firm and well-articulated chronological structure. In the few instances where it is necessary to break chronological order to narrate the background of an event, clarity is easily preserved by a simple statement that the author is digressing.[49] But true annalistic structure involves more than the simple division of the narrative into separate years. It also implies an account of each year ordered in terms of the principal historical elements which comprise the body of history. In Livy's case, according to the latest student of his narrative technique, these include "the inauguration of magistrates, the allotment of provinces, the disposition of troops, the enumeration of prodigies, the petitions of embassies . . . [followed by] the year's military campaigning and the depiction of other noteworthy events, and finally . . . details of political elections and sacerdotal matters."[50]

These elements are related to one another by their relevance to

---

[47] See Cicero, *De oratore*, I, 37, and II, 54. See Walsh, *Livy*, pp. 33 and 173, for the influence of these ideas on Livy.

[48] Gilbert, *Machiavelli*, pp. 208–209, where he is drawing on Pontano's *Actius*.

[49] There are several instances of this in the *Historiae*, mostly in the later books, where Bruni was working independently of the Villani chronicles. See, for instance, II, vi, 198; II, viii, 424; III, ix, 30; III,, ix, 72; III, xi, 188.

[50] Walsh, *Livy*, p. 175.

Livy's two basic themes: on the one hand, external warfare, diplomacy, and expansion; on the other, internal discord and constitutional development. Livy seeks to inject interest into his narrative by alternating these elements with one another, observing a classical technique known as *variatio*.[51] This stylistic canon dictates that, although a year inevitably begins with the consular elections and generally proceeds to distant and then to closer military campaigns and finally to political events, this schema need not be followed religiously. Political events may break into military ones as long as there is justification. Religious portents may interrupt political narrative. Livy had at his grasp, and used with great resourcefulness, a wide range of possibilities for providing a varied, attractive, and yet coherently structured narrative.

Bruni follows Livy in principle; that is, he divides his work according to the two basic themes of internal and external affairs. He also seeks to structure the year in terms of the relations between the various elements comprising these themes. When he tries to use the annalistic form to structure his own concepts, however, he runs into difficulties arising basically from the schematic and superficial manner in which he imitates Livy. Livy's selection of the annalistic form was not entirely arbitrary. The political life of the Roman Republic was made annually periodic by the consular elections, which, due to the consuls' functions, were events of both political and military significance. Livy uses the division of years to reflect concrete historical considerations. First, he does not begin to organize annalistically until the beginning of the republic (Book II).[52] Secondly, whenever the consular election is delayed, he starts the new year not from the Ides of March, the normal date for the event, but from the date of the actual election.[53] Moreover, the consular election offers him a useful fixed point from which to begin to organize the year, leading off into the activities of the new consuls.

Bruni easily adapted the Roman annalistic form to the Florentine calendar, which dated the new year from the Annunciation, less than two weeks after the Ides of March. There was, however, no

[51] See Walsh, *Livy*, p. 174.

[52] It would have been extremely difficult, of course, to do so without the consular lists, but, had Livy conceived of the annalistic form as abstractly valid, he could easily have organized from the beginning of the military season, as Bruni does.

[53] For instance, the elections for 401 B.C. are delayed until October. Livy makes no mention of the passage of the Ides but begins the year in October with the election and military actions of the new consuls (V, 10).

significant annual event in Florentine political life. Several elections
to the priorate occurred in one year, and in any case the position
of the priors of Florence was not nearly so significant as that of the
consuls of Rome. Bruni could give substance to the annalistic division only by relating it to the opening of a new military season,
which, of course, came every spring. Indeed, the end of winter,
accompanied by renewed military activity, constituted the only
tangible event associated with the new year.[54]

Bruni did not, however, seem to see that Livy had used the
annalistic form strictly in conjunction with the historical reality
it reflected. Bruni himself uses the coming of spring to break up
the narrative of a campaign, even if there has been no cessation
of military activity.[55] The annalistic division refers to nothing which
is essential to Bruni's political and psychological concerns. It can
help him to structure events in good order, but it cannot help him
to master them in such a way that they illustrate and give concrete
reality to his historical conceptualizations.

Not only was this form, as Bruni understood it,[56] inimical to
his historical concepts, but the fact that it did not spring from any
important Florentine historical phenomenon seriously diminished
its value as an organizing principle. For Livy, the year by definition
starts with a concrete event: the consular elections. Nevertheless,
Livy's literary abilities were too great for him to rely on this, and
more often than not the election of the consul is not the main subject with which the year is opened.[57] Whenever there is no event
of obvious significance, however, he can fall back on the consular
elections and structure the year in terms of the activities of the
consuls.

This means was not open to Bruni, who could not begin the

[54] For instance, under the year 1312 Bruni follows the military movements of
Henry VII through the middle of the winter. Only with the spring and the beginning of a new Florentine military campaign does he announce the passage of the year:
"Proximi anni principio Florentinorum copiae Lucam transmissae" (II, v, 24). See
also I, iv, 400, and I, iv, 512.

[55] See, for instance, his narration of the war with Castruccio for the years 1323–
1324 (II, v, 84). In the period from 1350 to 1353 the narration of both a specific
legation and a siege is explicitly broken up in deference to annalistic structure (II,
vii, 402, and II, vii, 408).

[56] The obvious point must be stated that the annalistic form is not intrinsically
unfit for Bruni's use. Tacitus, for instance, uses it to convey a highly conceptualized
and sophisticated understanding of history. It is not the form but Bruni's limited
understanding of it which is at fault.

[57] See, for instance, Book VII, where, of thirteen years presented, only six are
introduced by sentences in which the principal clause concerns the elections. In
the other seven the elections are only mentioned in passing.

year with a fixed event, simply because there was none except the opening of the military season.[58] Considering that the spring military campaign constituted the only annual event available to Bruni, however, it is somewhat surprising that he does not use it more frequently to introduce the year. Even during periods of peace he could have begun by stating that there was no military action that year. On one occasion he does precisely that,[59] but most of the time he introduces the year without mentioning military events. More than once he even uses the simple statement that nothing at all happened that was worth writing about.[60]

The cause of Bruni's unwillingness to use exclusively military events as principles of organization is readily seen. Military events do not constitute a major concern; they do not convey his causal principles so well as either internal discord or diplomatic relations. It is not, then, surprising to discover that the vast majority of years not introduced by military events begin with facts of either internal or diplomatic significance.[61] Considering the nature of Bruni's historical understanding, his attempt to emancipate himself from a military calendar is not strange. He is not observing the principle of *variatio* but is straining to attract the reader's attention to his central themes within a recalcitrant mode of organization.

If Bruni felt uncomfortable within this form during the early books, he sought to overcome its disadvantages in the section of the work composed in the 1430's and 1440's. Military events are narrated first in well over 50 per cent of the individual years in the first six books. In the last six books this percentage declines, until by the end of the work the practice has been completely abandoned.[62]

---

[58] Bruni does use a military event frequently in the first half of the *Historiae*. Always leaving aside Book I — which presents totally different structural problems — of the six years in Book II, the years so introduced are 1252, 1256, and 1262; of the twelve in Book III, 1269, 1275, 1276, 1285, 1288, and 1289 are so introduced; of the thirteen in Book IV, 1290, 1291, 1302, 1303, 1305, 1306, 1308, and 1310; of the fifteen in Book V, 1313, 1315, 1316, 1320, 1321, 1323, 1324, and 1326; of the ten in Book VI, 1329, 1334, 1335, 1336, 1337, and 1338. In all 56 years in Books II through V, 28 are introduced by military events.

[59] "Proximo dehinc anno quies fuit ab externis bellis" (I, iv, 524).

[60] For the years 1293, 1318, 1339, 1360, 1373, 1393.

[61] In Book II there are three nonmilitary introductions, of which two are political and one diplomatic; in Book III, of six nonmilitary, two are diplomatic and three are concerned with internal strife; in Book IV, of five, three are of internal strife; in Book V, of seven, six are diplomatic; in Book VI, of four, two are diplomatic.

[62] The seventh book is not a good indicator, since the four consecutive years of pestilence and famine from 1346 to 1349 are narrated separately, and each one is begun with a reference to the famine. Even if this period is taken as one year, however, the nonmilitary outnumber the military introductions three to two. In

This abandonment of military introductions is striking in the light of the fact that the explicit subject of the last three books is the Milanese war, which should presumably have rendered a military organization even more expedient.[63]

In these last books Bruni, concentrating on his more basic concerns, not only ceases to structure the year around a military introduction but changes perceptibly the nature of the nonmilitary events used as focal points. There is a distinct tendency to introduce a year, not with a concrete event, but with an abstract statement embodying an historical judgment based on several concrete facts. In the first six books, putting aside the years in which nothing worth mentioning happened, there are four examples of abstract statements out of twenty-five nonmilitary introductions.[64]

Among these the treatment of the year 1340 is especially significant. Bruni uses a number of devices to emphasize the importance of that year. In the first place, he dates it. Until Book VI he seldom dates anything but events of note, and, though he occasionally dates by lustrum in the last half of the work, 1340 is the first round-numbered year to be so marked. After the date there comes the statement that the year was *insignis* because of many things. A comet appeared, followed by a plague. It is apparent, however, that neither of these events constitutes the importance of the year, for Bruni goes on immediately to narrate an internal disturbance followed by the outbreak of a serious war over Lucca, both of which contribute to the accession to power of Walter of Brienne, the event that Bruni explicitly considers to be most important.[65] The period from 1340 down to the expulsion of Walter of Brienne is narrated without any chronological indication and constitutes the longest period so treated between 1280 and the period 1364–1372, when a break in the sources forces a departure from rigid annalistic form. This deliberate decision to narrate the period as a whole gives unity to the story of Walter's rise and fall as well as added meaning to Bruni's original statement of the importance of the year 1340.

Book VIII there are four military to eight nonmilitary; in Book IX, three military to six nonmilitary; in Books X, XI, and XII only one year (1398) is introduced by a tangible military event.

[63] He begins Book X, "Bellum mediolanense quod nunc scribere aggredimur" (III, x, 110).

[64] The year 1267 is introduced by "Turbulentos habuit motus"; 1284, by "Insignis multis rebus"; 1283, by "Domi quies fuit"; and 1340, by "Hic annus insignis fuit multarum rerum novitatibus."

[65] "Res enim digna est quae literis annotetur" (II, vi, 290).

In a sense Bruni abandons the annalistic form in narrating this period. Yet he seeks to operate within it, treating the four years as if they were one.[66] The introduction of the year by means of a comet serves as a literary device to draw the reader's attention to the importance of what follows. Bruni, however, is not confident of the efficacy of this device alone and feels the necessity to add a specific, abstract statement that the year is important. To make such a statement is to make an historical judgment based on several factors, which may or may not be capable of annalistic presentation. In this particular case Bruni avoids the problem by grouping several years into one period. But the annalistic form does not lend itself easily to the expression of historical concepts, and Bruni experiences increasing difficulties in the latter half of the *Historiae*.

In Books VII and VIII generalizations are used to introduce the years just as infrequently as in the first half of the work. In Book IX, however, of the six nonmilitary introductions, five involve generalizations. In two of these cases Bruni is attempting to generalize in terms of the psychological concepts which lie at the base of his historical approach. The year 1379, which begins, "In the next year all was quiet abroad except for fear of the exiles," [67] shows how exile activity around Figline creates a difficult situation for Florence. The year 1382 is introduced in a similar fashion by noting the suspicions of the citizens of Florence.[68]

Such psychological terms as *metus* and *suspicio* not only represent a process of historical judgment and reconstruction but cannot be easily tied down to a concrete historical event. The difficulty is particularly acute for an historian of Bruni's subtlety, who sees such psychological states in a broad context of political, diplomatic, and military causative factors. For this reason their incorporation into an annalistic structure presents certain problems. Bruni does not think it adequate to say that in 1379 a certain band of Florentine exiles from Siena seized Figline, causing fear among the Florentines. The "exulum metus," fear of exiles, is not explained by this seizure alone, or by any of the other events narrated in this year,

---

[66] As in previously noted instances where more than one year is treated, he begins, "Sequitur annus" (II, vii, 262), and ends, "Haec eo anno qui tyrannus pulsus est domi forisque gesta" (II, vi, 320).

[67] "Alter dehinc anno foris quieta omnia praeterquam ab exulum metu" (III, ix, 16).

[68] "Principio insequentis anni multa simul premebant civitatem. Nam et domi res admodum solicitae et foris suspicio ingens." (III, ix, 52–54.)

or even by all of them taken together. It is rather a product of the diplomatic situation in which Florence finds itself externally and of the internal weakness of the republic following the upheavals of the previous year. Ultimately, this fear is founded on the accumulated historical experience of the damage which can be done by exile activity abroad, an experience which takes the reader back at least as far as Montaperti and which informs so much of the narrative of the *Historiae*, beginning with the very first act of the free city when it seeks to restore its own faction to power in Pistoia in 1250.

To express an event of this subtlety and complexity without blurring chronological lines is difficult indeed. Not only is "exulum metus" a generalization, but, unlike the statement "hic annus insignis fuit" which introduces 1340, it transports the reader beyond the year to which it refers. Bruni, in seeking an adequate means to express his historical insights, is carried further and further from a rigidly annalistic form into an historical narrative which, however much it holds fast to chronological indicators,[69] increasingly deals with realities that do not admit of precise chronological orientation.[70]

In the last three books Bruni repeatedly follows the practice of introducing a year with generalizations that represent creative historical judgments which transcend chronological limits. For these books, covering the period between 1390 and 1402, the historian had to work without the support of a major chronicle. He did not use Gregorio Dati's history as consistently as he had used the Villani chronicles. In spite of the great similarity between Dati's his-

---

[69] Bruni's dating becomes far more frequent in this section. There are only three dates in the first six books (1260, 1306, 1312). There are two in Book VII (1340 and 1350), three in Book VIII (1355, 1375, 1378), three in Book IX (1381, 1385, 1390), and nearly half of the years in the last three books are dated (1391, 1395, 1396, 1398, 1400, 1402). He is generally not dating significant occurrences but round-numbered years, to clarify the progression of events in the narrative.

[70] The technique of introducing a year with a general statement of its significance followed by another generalization pointing beyond the year is even more clearly present in his treatment of 1387. In this case he explicitly maintains the basic thematic division between domestic and foreign affairs by describing each sphere in terms of a distinct psychological reality which characterized that year. He then is driven to refer to events which took place in the preceding year and which determined these realities. Still unsatisfied with his statement, Bruni follows with two periods, introduced by *cum* clauses, showing why the events occurring in 1387 induced these suspicions, explaining the predicaments into which Florence had been thrown, together with the limited expedients open to the city for eluding the difficulties. Only then, with a further indication of a psychological change, does he begin a narration of the concrete diplomatic events of that year (III, ix, 54).

torical ideas and those which are found in the *Historiae*, neither Santini nor Baron has been able to discover clear proof that Bruni borrowed any of the details of the period from Dati. Perhaps this independence from a major source allowed Bruni to impose a more personal order on the material. In any case, of the twelve introductions in this section, only one involves the type of self-contained concrete event which dominated the introductions in the earlier sections of the work.[71]

Some of these introductory statements are simple generalizations summarizing the events about to be narrated. For instance, the year 1391, the only example in Book X, is introduced, "In the next year there were great disturbances and battles as never before." [72] Even here, however, Bruni goes on to describe the Florentine attitude and to relate it to an event which had occurred in the previous year. In one case, which would otherwise be a normal military introduction, Bruni deliberately blurs chronological lines so that the action of one year is carried over into the next.[73] Most of the years between 1390 and 1402, however, are introduced by generalizations which cannot be grasped solely in reference to any one year.[74]

Book XII affords an illustration of Bruni's technique in its full maturity. The book deals with the collapse of Bologna, and two of the three years it covers are introduced by references to this particular theme. The year 1401 begins, "In the next year, as soon as it was spring, more serious disturbances broke out among the Bolognese." [75] The comparative degree is used because, in narrating

[71] "Altero dehinc anno . . . comites pupii et balnei, itemque ubertini cum omnibus eorum castellis ad mediolanensem defecerunt" (III, xi, 244). This is the sole military event used as an introduction in the last books.

[72] "Altero dehinc anno . . . maximi insuper motus et quanta nunquam prius certamina exstiterunt" (III, x, 140).

[73] "Facta sunt autem haec in extremo anni nonagesima sexti, ut etiam principium insequentis anni circa Florentia has copias reperiret" (III, xi, 230).

[74] *Suspicio* is used twice in this fashion (1392 and 1399). In other cases a series of events is compared to previous ones. For instance, 1395 is begun, "Eo qui secutus est anno . . . eadem contentiones civitate fuere" (III, xi, 200); 1396 commences, "In eo rursus anno, quanta nunquam prius certamina parabantur" (III, xi, 214). Introducing 1400, Bruni frankly admits his intention to make an historical judgment. After a section in which he has dealt with the state of mind of the Florentines, has described the diplomatic situation in which most of Tuscany is hostile to Florence, and has noted that all the signs were unfavorable to the city, he says, "Haec erat conditio rerum, cum annus millesimus quadrigentesimus supervenit" (III, xi, 268).

[75] "Altero dehinc anno, statim ver primo turbationes in Bononiensibus graviores exortae sunt" (III, xii, 278).

1400, Bruni had told of the seizure of power in Bologna by Benti-
voglio. By connecting the two years in this fashion he is able to
stress the city's internal weakness, which contributes greatly to its
fall. In passing to 1402, Bruni widens the geographical scope of
the problem by including the threats to the city emanating from
the surrounding region.[76] This introduction leads to an account of
several past events which bear upon Bologna's plight. Only after
mentioning these incidents does Bruni describe the particular strife
of 1402. By thus connecting Bologna's internal and external history, he can present the period of its attack and fall coherently,
drawing out fully the various historical themes which are illustrated
in its collapse. In this way he seeks to teach historical lessons through
the narrative itself.

The specific problems Bruni encountered in appropriating Livy's
annalistic form to organize his own historical vision are most
clearly apparent in the means by which he effects the passage from
year to year. The stylistic demands of this particular type of transition force into relief the tension between the temporal, tangible
dimensions of the annalistic form and the conceptual nature of
Bruni's historical understanding. A consideration of his general
organizational technique reveals an attempt at a more thematic
presentation, especially in that section of the *Historiae* which describes Florence's struggle with Giangaleazzo of Milan.

The last four books concern this war with Giangaleazzo. In narrating the conflict Bruni divides his attention between the periods
of actual, declared war and the periods of uneasy peace, diplomatic
maneuver, and minor skirmishes. He divides the narrative in such
a way, however, that large sections, and even whole books, are devoted to only one of these two themes. While dealing with those
years in which the war is actually being waged, he tends to pass
over or to greatly de-emphasize diplomatic events, while in the
other years military actions are either ignored or related as minor
skirmishes.

This is not simply a topical division; it reflects a concern with
different historical realities. The periods of uneasy peace and preparation for war are narrated in psychological terms, while during
the periods of war strategic and tactical factors are stressed. Diplomacy (especially in these last books) is presented in a manner

[76] "Eo qui secutus est anno . . . circa Bononiam magnis contentionibus belli-
geratum est" (III, xii, 306).

similar to the way in which the Ciompi crisis was depicted. There the determining factor in the rebellion was the gradual spread of unrest and discontent through the classes of the city, and the concrete events of the revolt were implicitly seen as manifestations of this psychological element. Similarly, here in the last books, the historical reality underlying diplomatic activity is found in the mutual fears and suspicions of the various cities, and the concrete diplomatic events are directly related to these attitudes.

It is nearly always more difficult to present intangible historical realities than to describe temporal and spatial phenomena. One of the many modes Bruni has chosen for dealing with this problem sheds considerable light on his narrative technique in the last books of the *Historiae*. Throughout the work he makes frequent use of the noun *suspicio* to characterize the psychological attitude informing the diplomatic maneuvers which precede a state of active war. The value of words of this nature in permitting Bruni to conceptualize emerges clearly when his method for introducing particular years is analyzed. The word *suspicio*, while it is by no means the only device Bruni employs to deal with conceptual or psychological factors, is used with sufficient frequency so that valid generalizations can be built upon it.[77]

A close relation between the word *suspicio* and the type of diplomacy which forms a prelude to war characterizes the entire work. Bruni first uses the term to show the Sienese reasons for sending a legate to Manfred, and shortly afterward he uses it to suggest the background to an Aretine attack on Cortona.[78] The word is employed to explain the Ghibelline alliance against Charles of Anjou,[79] as well as Charles's reaction.[80] *Suspicio* frequently lies behind Florentine military and diplomatic initiatives,[81] as well as behind the motivations of her enemies.[82] At times, even in the earlier books, it is used not to explain a specific course of action but simply to sum up a general state of affairs.[83] Only occasionally is it used to describe a battle.[84] Suspicion explains or characterizes events of external significance far more frequently than internal events. The

[77] The word occurs an average of six times in each book.
[78] See I, ii, 182, and I, ii, 184.
[79] I, ii, 284, and I, iii, 302.
[80] I, iii, 322.
[81] I, iii, 360; I, iii, 396; I, iv, 538; II, vi, 202; II, vii, 344; II, vii, 354; II, viii, 460.
[82] I, iv, 484; II, v, 36; II, vi, 340.
[83] II, v, 86; II, v, 158; II, vi, 260; II, vii, 494; II, viii, 508; II, viii, 510.
[84] II, v, 36; II, viii, 490.

word is used approximately fifty times in the first eight books; it applies to domestic events less than ten times, and these occur almost exclusively in the first four books.

Not only does Bruni's usage of *suspicio* remain constant, but the word occurs with impressive regularity. Of the first eight books none has less than five occurrences; on a reasonably careful count, none has more than seven.[85] With Book IX, however, one notices a significant change, for the word appears eleven times, or nearly double the average. Even more surprising, it does not appear at all in Book X, is used sixteen times in Book XI, and only once in Book XII. This obvious pattern of alternation can be explained away neither by new uses of the word nor by new subjects being narrated. Such explanations would only be satisfactory if there were an absolute increase in the number of times the word is used, while in fact it occurs with only slightly greater frequency in the last four books than in the first eight. Nor does a study of the way in which the word is employed in Books IX and XI reveal any new usages. *Suspicio* either explains a diplomatic event, is caused by a diplomatic maneuver, or provides the general background of foreign-policy decisions.

Bruni's usage of *suspicio* in the last books is significant not because it reflects new subject matter but because it illuminates an increased tendency on the historian's part to narrate thematically across chronological lines. The term conveys one of Bruni's deepest historical concerns, the psychological reality which informs historical change, and hence it appears most frequently in those sections of the work devoted to elaborating this reality.

In the last part of Book IX and all of Book XI Bruni is dealing with periods of uneasy peace leading to open war.[86] These books cover the periods 1378–1389 and 1393–1399 respectively: the ninth book ends with a declaration of war; the eleventh, with an oration outlining a plan for open war. The fundamental subject of each book is the growing uneasiness of the Florentines at the Milanese threat, and the events of the period covered are viewed in the light of this developing attitude. Military events are infrequently narrated, and, when they are recounted, strategic considerations are ignored.[87] These years are treated, then, from the perspective of a

---

[85] Always excepting the introductory first book, where it does not occur.

[86] The first part of Book IX concerns the Ciompi.

[87] For instance, Florence's attack on Urbino in 1386 is not narrated in the context of the geographical consideration which will dominate the books covering the

distinct and specific theme: the development of Florentine disquietude.[88] *Suspicio*, used by Bruni throughout the *Historiae* to express this theme, appears much more frequently.

By contrast, Books X and XII deal with the war periods 1390–1392 and 1399–1402. The change in subject matter is apparent from the opening sentences of Book X. Though Bruni alludes to the Florentine animus in describing the magnitude of the war, he emphasizes the power and size of the two combatants. To do this, he outlines the forces Florence is able to field, and he begins the war with the mustering of troops around Siena. The narrative brings out the Florentine strategy of creating pressure in Lombardy to draw Giangaleazzo away from Tuscany. The military talents of Hawkwood are elucidated through a tactical narration of his campaign in the plain of the Po. The nature of the war is further elaborated by a Bolognese oration, complaining not that the people of Bologna lack the animus to fight but that only a great commercial power like Florence can long wage a struggle of these dimensions. The book concludes with the making of peace.

During this period of three years almost no attention is paid to the psychological element so predominant in Books IX and XI. There is no sense that the attitudes of the people involved in the struggle may be changing. The diplomatic moves by which Florence tries to bring first German and then French troops into the conflict are introduced without reference to possible motivations. The peace itself is presented abruptly in a purely tactical context, with no allusion to the possibility that both sides may be weary of war.[89] Under these circumstances it is not strange that during the entire narrative of Book X the word *suspicio* does not appear, though

war period, but in terms of the *indignatio* of the Florentine people at the illegal seizure of two of their ambassadors (III, ix, 78–80); similarly, Bruni's narration of the military actions of 1396 lacks the precise and sophisticated strategic grasp that either the previous or the following book possesses (III, xi, 214–232).

[88] It is significant that Bruni understood the outbreak of war in each case to be due to this factor, not to specific provocations by Giangaleazzo, and certainly not to any overt act of war on his part. Concluding Book IX with a review of the various provocative gestures narrated in it, the historian says, "Atque ita bellum magno elatoque animo est a florentinis receptum" (III, ix, 108). In like manner he concludes Book XI with an oration showing that the initiative in resuming the hostilities lies on the side of the Florentines (III, xi, 254–264).

[89] "Stante igitur per lucensem pisanumque agrum exercitu hostium, nostris vero per ea loca adversos eos oppositis, Ranio autem in Aretinis obsesso, pacis mentio exorta est. Erat iam autumni extremum frigoraque et pruinae deducendum in hiberna militem suadebant. Belli autem clades hinc inde inflictae, pacem aequabilem recipere posse videbantur." (III, x, 168.)

at the beginning of Book XI, which covers the period between the wars, the reader is again confronted with this term, expressing a reality profoundly psychological.[90]

Book XII reveals the same inattention to psychological factors that characterizes Book X. Bruni makes the transition between Books XI and XII by describing a religious movement which has brought temporary peace. His avoidance of psychological references in the narration of this movement is striking. He depicts in sensual terms the dress of the pilgrims, their origins, and their path through Italy, but he only states explicitly that they have had a profound spiritual effect when narrating the resumption of war after their departure.[91] The book then stresses the same historical elements which have been found in Book X, avoiding the narration of psychological elements. For instance, when Bruni comes to deal with the growing power of Giangaleazzo in Tuscany in 1401, he refers to it simply as a fact, whereas in other books he tends to concentrate on the suspicion or fear created by this mounting power.[92] Significantly, in Book XII the word *suspicio* occurs only once.

Bruni's later method of organization — broadening the perspective of the narrative to cross chronological lines — stands in marked contrast to earlier sections of his work. The conflict between Florence and Castruccio Castracani between 1320 and 1328, which is described in the last two thirds of Book V, provides an excellent comparison. Except for the last year of the war, which is included in the previous year, annalistic form is rigidly maintained. Every year begins with a concrete event, and military, diplomatic, and domestic events are narrated with equal stress under the years in which they occur. Bruni does not hesitate to break up a military operation in order to describe a minor domestic change.[93] Diplomatic moves are given both a psychological [94] and a strategic [95]

[90] "Principio insequentis anni etsi pax erat, suspiciones tamen nequaquam parvae exortae sunt ex huiusmodi causa" (III, xi, 174).

[91] "Dum religio tenuit animos, de periculis belli nihil cogitabatur, sed postquam finis fuit dealbatorem fervori ad primas rursus curas animi redierunt" (III, xii, 268). The word *animus* has not previously been used in this book.

[92] "Per Etruriam vero manifestum non erat bellum, sed ita dies crescebat mediolanensis potentia ut tandem apprehensura omnia videretur" (III, xi, 280). Note how he uses *videretur* to avoid narrating the dread as a direct historical fact.

[93] See II, v, 80, and II, v, 88, where important military and domestic activities are interrupted two years in succession in order to discuss minor constitutional changes.

[94] "Per idem tempus gravis suspicio civitatem habuit ne Pistorienses ad Castrucium deficerent" (II, v, 86).

[95] See the battle of Altopascio (II, v, 102).

background, and military actions are occasionally narrated psychologically.[96] The principle of presenting each event within the year in which it occurs is observed religiously, at the expense of the thematic development which enriches the last books.

Nor is Bruni's technique in his last books to be compared with that of the first book, where annalistic form is completely sacrificed in favor of a broad, thematic sweep. Any unity which this first book may have is not temporal but spatial, for it begins and ends with Tuscan events. Though there is a general chronological progression in the book, the historian continually moves back and forth to take up the origin of a new factor. There are seven separate historical narratives in Book I, related in this order: (1) the foundation of the city and the social wars, 80–65 B.C.;[97] (2) the foundation of Tuscany and its history down to the Roman conquest, 1370–283 B.C.;[98] (3) the emperors to Constantine, 31 B.C. to 315 A.D.;[99] (4) barbarian invasions, 300–774 A.D.;[100] (5) Holy Roman Emperors, with a brief look at the entire tradition beginning with Augustus, 1–1000 A.D.;[101] (6) events in Tuscany since the Roman conquest, 300 B.C. to 1200 A.D.;[102] (7) introduction of Frederick II. Though some of the themes which are to emerge during the course of the work are present in this early part, any attempt to encompass such great periods of time within broad, clearly defined historical categories is subordinated to the treatment in depth of empirically derived topics.

Bruni, then, in order to convey his historical concepts cogently and clearly, modifies the annalistic form in two major respects.[103] In the first place, he develops a technique for suggesting the significance of a year, presenting an introductory generalization which draws the reader's attention to events and historical realities transcending the particular year. Secondly, he tends in the last books, while maintaining a rigid annalistic division, to narrate thematically in a manner which crosses annual boundaries and binds several years together through the development of an important theme.

[96] "Hoc detrimento accepto, rursus Castrucii spes debilitari est coepta" (II, v, 86). The Florentines march into battle "spe sublatus" (II, v, 100).

[97] I, i, 56–68.

[98] I, i, 68–98.

[99] I, i, 100–104.

[100] I, i, 104–136.

[101] I, i, 136–148.

[102] I, i, 148–154.

[103] Rossi, *Il Quattrocento*, p. 171, notes the critical element of Bruni's classical imitation in the *Historiae*.

Bruni took more from classical sources than the annalistic form. His second major borrowing is the practice of including orations in the narrative. Since this practice is far more suited to his needs than the annalistic structure, there is little attempt on his part to modify the classical technique. His inclusion of orations, however, has scandalized those modern historians who operate under the positivistic notion that the historian should play a passive role by reporting only the concrete facts to be found in his sources. Typical of these modern historians is the late-nineteenth-century scholar Venturi, who, studying the orations in Cavalcanti's works, makes no attempt to find value in them but addresses himself solely to the measure of their factual reliability.[104] Santini, defending Bruni's use of orations, concentrates less on their positive value than on the fact that, after all, even the chroniclers of the thirteenth and fourteenth centuries used them,[105] and that in any case Bruni's are more firmly based on factual evidence than are Poggio's.[106]

Bruni's speeches, in spite of Santini's suggestion that he might have taken his inspiration from the chronicles, conform to classical models. Whether he patterned them directly on Livy or composed them from the rhetorical canons of Cicero and Quintilian is difficult to say. Nor is it of crucial importance, for Livy certainly relied on Cicero's precepts for writing the speeches in the *Ab urbe*, while Quintilian doubtless used Livy's orations as a guide in constructing his own rules.[107] Classical orations are of three types: judicial, ceremonial, and deliberative. Bruni's fall exclusively into the third category. This type of speech is divided into three major parts: the introduction (*exordium*), the statement and discussion of theme (*tractatio*), and the conclusion (*conclusio*). Furthermore, the *tractatio* generally discusses the proposition from the aspects of expediency and honor.

Most of Bruni's formal speeches conform to this model; one example, the first in the work, will suffice. This is an oration delivered by Farinata degli Uberti to Manfred, asking help for the Tuscan Ghibellines.[108] Farinata begins by saying that even if those

104 A. Venturi, *Le orazioni nelle istorie fiorentine di Giovanni Cavalcanti* (Pisa, 1896).

105 Santini, *Leonardo*, p. 77.

106 Santini, *Leonardo*, p. 81.

107 See Walsh, *Livy*, pp. 219–244, for Livy's relation to the classical canons of oratory and for the following summary of classical practice. See also J. F. D'alton, *Roman Literary Theory and Criticism* (New York, 1962), for a discussion of classical oratorical styles.

108 I, ii, 190–194.

standing before Manfred were completely unknown to him, he should still give them aid. In this way Bruni constructs the *exordium* to lead directly into the *tractatio*. He then moves into the development of the theme, having Farinata bring up reasons why Manfred should help — moral reasons (gratitude) and practical reasons (utility and possibility). The *conclusio* is expressed in a simple sentence reiterating the request for aid.

The particular relation between considerations of practicality and morality which inheres in the form of a classical oration is extremely well adapted to the expression of Bruni's ideas, and hence the oration provides an excellent vehicle for his historical conceptualization. Exploiting fully the possibilities inherent in this form, Bruni frequently expands the *tractatio* to include an explicit interpretation of past events from the perspective of his basic themes. In the example given, for instance, Uberti explicates the strategically important position of Florence in Tuscany, as well as the polarization of the Tuscan cities by the Guelf-Ghibelline struggle. Though these points can be extrapolated from the preceding narrative, the oration serves to clarify and stress them.

Throughout his work Bruni uses the oration to express directly the deeper substance of the narrative. Ugolino's speech to the Florentines develops the impracticality of factional strife as a principle of diplomacy.[109] Strategic considerations, including the advantages of a strong defensive position, are brought out by Aldobrandini's oration, seeking to convince the Florentines not to launch the campaign which does in fact lead to the disastrous defeat at Montaperti.[110] The psychological dimensions of governmental institutions emerge most directly in Giano della Bella's oration.[111] The principles of diplomacy are also a frequent subject of the orations, particularly that of Pinio Toso advocating the purchase of Lucca.[112]

In the course of the work Bruni's style of oration changes only in becoming more complex. The basic tripartite form is maintained, but the *tractatio* is enlarged in scope, frequently embracing several themes which grow out of one another. For instance, in one of the last orations in the *Historiae* Gianfigliazzo deals with the problems presented to the city by Giangaleazzo's growing power.[113] After an

[109] I, iii, 374–376.
[110] I, ii, 204–214.
[111] I, iv, 432–442.
[112] II, vi, 170–176.
[113] III, xi, 254–264.

exordium in which he thanks the priors for asking counsel and praises his own sincerity in giving it, Gianfigliazzo begins the *tractatio* on the theme of Florence's difficulties, which are explained by the city's own customs and traditions. This interpretation, in turn, is developed in moral and practical terms. Then the orator goes on to a consideration of specific situations in which Florence has acted unwisely. At this point he introduces the theme of the city's strength and develops it in terms of what Florence must do to bring its power to bear on the present situation. Many of Bruni's presuppositions about both constitutional government and diplomacy are woven into the oration.

Another technique Bruni uses is that of the dialogue oration. There are seven examples of paired speeches in the work. They tend to be true dialogues, each part being complementary to the other rather than mutually contradictory. For instance, one of the earlier pairs is formed by the orations of Castruccio and the Bishop of Arezzo before the Emperor.[114] Castruccio's is almost completely practical in development, pointing out that the bishop has proved unreliable on several occasions and that the emperor ought not to trust him. The bishop makes no attempt to meet these charges but counters with a moral line of argument, saying that he has protected Castruccio on occasions when he was otherwise defenseless, and that he could not support Castruccio in his war with the Florentines because of a previous treaty. The bishop even alludes to the emperor's own greed and trickery.

This attempt to divide the material in the oration thematically foreshadows Bruni's success in organizing the entire narrative in the last four books. The dialogue in Book VIII between the Florentine ambassadors and the Pope is an excellent example of the way in which later paired orations are structured.[115] The Florentines emphasize the ideal of good government and then rehearse the previous loyalty of Florence to the Pope, stressing the injustice of the Pope's aggression toward them, The papal reply ignores all the Florentine arguments, stating that Florence has taken arms for aggressive ends and virtually admitting tyrannical government but claiming it as a necessity. The paired orations of the Bolognese and Florentines (discussed in Chapter Three) betray a similar division.[116] The final orations of the book, also in dialogue form, find

114 II, v, 134–136.
115 II, viii, 518–538.
116 III, x, 130–138.

Milanese and Florentines defending their conduct before the Venetians.[117] The Milanese stress the moral outrage of Florence's conduct, specifically the calling in of barbarian troops. The Florentines, in turn, seek to bring out the practical effect of Giangaleazzo's actions, showing that their responses were both essential and justified.

Bruni makes little attempt to use the orations for emotional effect.[118] He occasionally notes that a speech had a strong impact, but in the one instance where he describes the effect on the auditors explicitly, the decision goes against the orator.[119] Furthermore, there is in the work only one military exhortation on the field of battle, that of Jordanus to the Sienese, and Bruni conspicuously avoids depicting its impact.[120]

Besides annalistic structure and orations, Bruni profitably imitated one other classical technique: battle narratives. Felix Gilbert, drawing on Pontano's *Actius*, has described most clearly the classical form: "Pontano suggested that the historian begin the story of a battle with an account of the omens presaging the outcome of the struggle. The next requirement was a precise topological explanation of the area where the battle took place; that should be followed by brief character sketches of the chief military leaders, a detailed recital of the way in which the troops on the opposing sides were arranged, and a description of the war machines of the two armies." [121] This ideal permits the historian to gain and convey to his reader a well-articulated, studied grasp of the important facets of the battle.

Bruni's dependence on classical models is revealed by a comparison of his battle narratives with Villani's. The first major battle in the *Historiae* is the Florentine defeat at Montaperti. Bruni introduces the battle with the skillful device of a Florentine oration opposing it, a stratagem which has the effect of convincingly portraying the advantages of the enemy. Then he recounts the hortatory oration of the Sienese commander within Siena. Immediately following this, he begins the battle with the opening of the gates.[122]

---

117 III, xii, 294–306.

118 Ullman has seen that their function cannot be understood as related to the tragical in history ("Leonardo," p. 53).

119 The previously mentioned oration of the Florentines before the Pope (II, viii, 532).

120 I, ii, 218–220.

121 Gilbert, *Machiavelli*, p. 210.

122 "His dictis, aperiri portam iubet" (I, ii, 220).

He does not, however, narrate the rushing out of the Sienese forces but instead describes in a leisurely fashion the formation of the Sienese battle lines, explaining briefly why each unit was placed in its specific position. Next he relates the effect of the Sienese troops' appearance on the Florentines. Only after this does he narrate the actual physical clash of the troops, concentrating on the tactical difficulties created for the Florentines by the surprise attack of the enemy. He then describes the struggle for the Florentine standard, the loss of which precipitates the flight which leads to defeat. He concludes by stating the number of men killed and captured.

By comparison, Villani [123] begins the section on the battle with a period seeking vainly to encompass all the Florentine preparations together with his own judgment on the wisdom of the attack. He describes the departure from the city with the Caroccio; he interrupts the narrative with the report of a ruse attempted by the Sienese. Moving directly into the battle he narrates it breathlessly, not stopping to describe it in such a way as to gain perspective, not outlining the battle lines but mentioning the troops as they pour forth from the city. Each sentence begins with an *e* to connect it closely to the previous sentence, for such is Villani's fear of losing the momentum of the narrative that he willingly sacrifices clarity — the clarity Bruni gains by a more studied, less immediate recounting.

Bruni's narratives of battles increase in complexity through the work, though here again, the classical model being well suited to exposing the strategic and tactical elements which interest him, he does not substantially modify the basic form. His version of the first major battle in the Giangaleazzo war is an excellent example of the sophisticated technique which characterizes the last books of the *Historiae*.[124] He first states the strategic objective of the battle — unification of the French troops with those of Hawkwood; then he mentions various minor skirmishes which bear upon this strategic objective. Following this he traces first the paths of the French and then those of Hawkwood, in their respective attempts to unite. Finally, he describes from the standpoint of military topography the place where the battle is fought. Only after all this does he begin the narrative proper by describing how the battle lines are drawn up. He goes on to point out the tactical advantages of each

[123] G. Villani, *Crònica*, VI, 79.
[124] III, x, 142–156.

side, taking the weather into account, showing how the French fail to exploit their position, and concluding with a summary statement of the size of the victory. To include these factors in the narrative of a battle would have been exceedingly difficult for Bruni if he had not had the classical models to work from, for the hurried style of Villani, however engaging it might be, did not permit this sort of consideration.

To summarize, the form Bruni created to convey his new historical concepts consisted of three major elements, all abundantly present in his principal model, the *Ab urbe condita*. First, and probably most importantly, he organized the material annalistically in the interests of clarity. Since the annalistic form found in Livy did not easily convey the conceptual element of Bruni's historical vision, he was forced to modify it in certain important respects. These modifications were to assume increasing importance in the later Quattrocento, as historians sought further to perfect their narrative techniques. Second, Bruni adopted the practice of including orations to expand and clarify his fundamental historical themes. Third, he adopted from Livy a means of narrating the military sections of the history in such a way as to emphasize strategic and tactical elements and to describe battles in a more lucid, well-structured manner than had been possible with the Trecento mode of presentation.[125]

Finally, it is clear that Bruni's narrative technique underwent an unmistakable development in the course of the *Historiae*. He gradually impressed his personal conceptions upon the classical techniques and forged thereby an instrument which conveyed his historical

[125] This survey does not, of course, exhaust Bruni's narrative techniques. The chapter has not sought to engage in general literary criticism but only to study the extent to which Bruni's major borrowings from the classics aided him in expressing his own thoughts. The elements in Bruni's style which were meant to, and probably did, entertain his contemporaries are not relevant to this central question, and hence his use of such literary techniques as *variatio* has not been considered.

A very sensitive interpretation of narrative style from a more literary but nonetheless historical point of view is found in E. Garin, *Medioevo e Rinascimento* (Bari, 1961), chap. 1. Garin shows the close relationship between the rhetorical style and the humane concerns of the Quattrocento. He also finds that the style improves as the author is more and more drawn into concrete problems and away from the imitation of traditional form. In this chapter Garin draws heavily on R. Spongano, *Un capitolo di storia della nostra prosa d'arte* (Florence, 1941), who should be consulted for a technical criticism of Renaissance prose. See also Paul van Tieghen, "La litterature latine de la Renaissance," in *Bibliothèque d'humanisme et Renaissance*, 4 (1944), 177–419, and G. Vallese, "Retorica medievale e retorica umanistica," in *Delta*, n.s., 2 (1952), 39–58, who also stresses the existence of more than purely technical concerns in the Renaissance approach to style.

vision with greater accuracy and cogency than had been possible at the beginning of the work. This increasing sophistication should not be confused with a change in basic concepts. The fundamental outlines of Bruni's historical approach are strongly intimated in the very first books and probably dated from the early years of the century. However impressive this approach may be in terms of the mature grasp of intangible dimensions in history and of the rigor with which this grasp is applied, it is matched in significance by Bruni's contribution to historical writing in the development of narrative techniques from his classical models. The importance of this contribution emerged as the subsequent humanist historians of Florence sought to improve on these techniques and assembled a vehicle in which both the form and content of humanist history coincided in their aims. In this endeavor Bruni's successor in the chancellorship and as historian of Florence, Poggio Bracciolini, was to play a crucial role.

Chapter Five

Poggio Bracciolini and the *Historia fiorentina*

A humanist, and particularly a Florentine humanist, working in the field of historical writing during the second half of the Quattrocento, had before him a model especially well suited to his needs. Bruni's *Historiae Florentini populi*, structurally solid and thematically coherent, drawing formally on that classical historian who stood foremost in the minds of fifteenth-century writers, presented Florentine history in terms which a fellow citizen could find vital and convincing. The gargantuan task of creating live contemporary history out of the classical models seemed largely accomplished, and a mid-century historian ostensibly needed only to apply to his own material the techniques developed by Bruni in order to create a history at once humanistic and contemporary.

It is somewhat astonishing, therefore, that Poggio, who clearly considered his work to be a continuation of the *Historiae*,[1] deliberately conceived his *Historia fiorentina* in terms that implied an historical form different from that which Bruni had used. The difference emerges clearly in Poggio's opening sentence: "I shall write of those wars which the Florentine people fought with the Visconti family and with others during the previous century, of the beginnings and various conditions of our city down to the first war with the Archbishop, then of the origins of the Visconti family, how

---

[1] Poggio knew that Leonardo did not consider the *Historiae* to be a finished work. There is evidence that contemporaries thought Poggio had begun where Bruni had stopped (see Vespasiano da Bisticci, *Vite di uomini illustri* [Milan, 1951], p. 295). Machiavelli's association of the two works has already been noted in chap. i.

In addition to this direct evidence, the fact that the first printed edition of Poggio's history is bound together with Acciaiuoli's translation of the *Historiae Florentini populi* should be taken into consideration. This edition was first published at Venice in 1476. The first printed edition published at Florence appeared in 1492.

capable it was and how in men and dominions it was more powerful than all the other princes of Italy." [2]

Poggio reveals here a narrower scope than Bruni. Instead of describing the whole range of deeds of the Florentine people down to his own day, he has selected a series of wars waged within a specific field of operations and within precise chronological limits. Since these chronological limits include the last fifty years covered by the *Historiae Florentini populi*, Poggio has been forced to rewrite and reformulate a period already dealt with by Bruni. The most striking indication of Poggio's departure from Bruni's model, however, lies in the use made of classical antquity. Bruni's history bears the imprint of the author's close acquaintance with Livy's *Ab urbe condita*. By contrast, Poggio's opening sentence indicates an unmistakable affinity to the introduction to Sallust's *Bellum Jugurthinum*, a work which a humanist historian writing of a single series of wars could hardly have ignored.[3]

The narrative style of the *Historia fiorentina* resembles the introductory sentence in differing formally and thematically from the *Historiae Florentini populi*. Yet it cannot be concluded that these works bear no likeness to each other. On the contrary, the historical ideas in Poggio's *Historia* are quite similar to Bruni's. For both humanists the substance of history is fundamentally intangible and can be narrated with didactic effect. In addition, Poggio not only presents a synoptical picture of the political and psychological dimensions of history but has actually probed more deeply into the ramifications of this picture to bring out aspects of the past which Bruni ignores.

One of the most obvious indications of Poggio's coherent presentation is the thoroughness with which political factors are interrelated in the *Historia fiorentina*. This relationship is most conspicuous in the connection between foreign and domestic affairs, which also

[2] "Ea scripturus bella, quae Florentinus populus cum Vicecomitum familia, quaeve cum ceteris ad haec usque tempora paulo centum amplius annos vario marte gessit, operae pretium fore putavi, initia, variumque urbis nostrae statum usque ad primum cum Archiepiscopo bellum recensere paucis, tum adiicere eius familiae primordia, quae pollens potensque viris, et imperio prae caeteris Italiae principibus fuit" (*Historia*, 193A–194A). There is no formal preface to the work, but Jacopo did write a dedicatory letter to Federigo da Montefeltro in which the theme of history as "celebratio virorum illustrium" is stressed. "Mihi vero ut primum per aetatem licuit, ne nostrae Reipublicae, plurimorumque clarorum virorum memoria deperiet" (*Historia*, 192).

[3] Sallust writes, "Bellum scripturus sum quod populus Romanus cum Jugurtha rege Numidarum gessit" (*Bellum Jugurthinum*, V).

constitutes an important aspect of Bruni's political insight. Very early in Poggio's work, when Charles of Calabria is called to the lordship of Florence, the historian explains the domestic change by referring to external pressures.[4] Shortly afterward the effect of war on the internal stability of the state is again mentioned when Poggio describes the panic of the *contadini* within the walls of Florence as the enemy approaches.[5] Poggio also feels, like Bruni, that external quiet can be a prelude to internal troubles.[6]

There is a perceptible difference, however, between the two historians' ways of relating the foreign to the domestic. Poggio, concerned with war and diplomacy, approaches events more exclusively from the perspective of foreign affairs. In all the cases cited above, the external event is the principal subject narrated, and its domestic effect is simply appended to the account. Other examples of this differing emphasis can easily be found. In 1363 Pisa inflicts a serious military reverse upon Florence. Bruni cites this defeat as an illustration of the defects of popular government in the conduct of war,[7] thereby using the pressures created by military events to shed light on the inner workings of the political structure. Poggio uses the defeat as background for the return of Bencio Buondelmonte with a group of exiles. This effect is ignored by Bruni, but Poggio adduces it to show the impact of the return of the exiles on the future conduct of the war.[8] He has found the information not in Bruni but in Bruni's source, Filippo Villani, who presents it in the context of Buondelmonte's personal military significance.[9] Bruni

---

[4] "Diutino etenim bello fessa . . . ad imperium urbis . . . Carolum Calabriae Ducem in decennium evocavit" (197C–198A).

[5] "Turba agrestium in urbe confluens, magnum tumultum ex inspirato excivit, trepidatumque est magis interiori, nequa seditio ex repentino hostium adventu oriretur, quam externo metu" (203A).

[6] "Quieta ab externis bellis civitate, pax in dissensiones domesticas versa est" (242B).

[7] See chap. iii, n. 112.

[8] "Diminutis Florentinorum adverso praelio militibus, cum de supplemento consultarent, exulibus omnibus, qui variis de causis extorres patria erant, Senatus consulto venia data est, si certo tempore propriis sumptibus pro Republica militassent. Ad centum quinquaginta fuere, quorum opera admodum civibus utilis fuit. Exulum ductor fuit Benghius Bondelmontes nobilissimo genere natus, qui defensioni Bargae intentus, comparatis nonnullis praeter eos peditibus, castella omnibus qui custodiae praeerant, incendit." (212B.)

[9] "In Barga era capitano per i Fiorentini Benghi del Tegghia Bondelmonti, a cui i Fiorentini, poichè gl'Inglesi aveano abbandonato Figghine aveano mandati cento cinquanta degli abanditi ch'erano stati in san Minato a monte, i quali doveano certo tempo servire il commune nella guerra alle loro spese, e poi essere ribanditi" (F. Villani, *Cronica*, IX, 75).

is interested in the Florentine defeat only for its domestic significance and Villani only for its military importance, but Poggio
brings out both its military importance and the extent to which it
shows the interrelation between foreign and domestic affairs.

Another instance of Poggio's subordination of domestic to foreign considerations is seen in his handling of the Guelf-Ghibelline
struggle. Bruni introduces this feud in a strictly domestic context,
while describing Tuscan politics.[10] Poggio introduces it while speaking of the origins of the Visconti family and the extent to which the
Milanese house constitutes a threat to Tuscany.[11] The war of Eight
Saints, when Pope Gregory sends orators to stir up dissensions
within Florence, provides still another example. Although Bruni
clearly shows that the war is not going well for Gregory, he narrates this particular action in terms of tensions and unrest within
Florence itself.[12] In contrast, Poggio explains the sending of the
orators purely in terms of Gregory's feeling that he cannot win the
war by force alone.[13] A final instance concerns a revolt in Siena
during Florence's war with Giangaleazzo. Bruni narrates the revolt
in terms of tensions previously existing within the city. Although
he alludes to problems caused by the war, such as a shortage of food,
he does not explicitly relate these problems to the revolt.[14] Poggio,
on the other hand, sees the disturbances within the city as direct

Poggio's sources have been listed in Rubinstein, "Poggio," pp. 17–18. For the
period down to the death of Giangaleazzo he is basically dependent on Bruni. After
this he uses the chronicle of Buoninsegni, either Capponi or Palmieri for the account
of the Pisan war, the *Decades* of Biondo, and Fazio's history of Alphonso of Aragon.
Throughout the book he shows evidence of having used sources beyond Bruni, as here
when he has gone to the Villani chronicles. Other instances of this practice will be
noted in the text as they occur.

[10] Bruni, *Historiae*, I, i, 154.

[11] After mentioning a specific act of aggression on the part of the Archbishop,
Poggio says, "Nam cum in Italia essent sectae duae Guelforum scilicet, et Ghibel-
linorum, posterioris partes Vicecomites sibi tutandas suscipere. De quibus priusquam
ulterius progrediar pauca videntur dicenda." (198B.)

[12] "Per idem tempus octo viris, qui ad curam belli auctoritate publica delecti
fuerant, prorogatum imperium est ad menses sex. Id qui saepius factum erat (nam
idem viri ab initio belli ad illud usque tempus continuaverant), magnam illis apud
multos conflarat invidiam. Et carpebantur iam eorum acta et factionibus oppugna-
bantur. Quae cum audiisset pontifex, ad augendam octo virorum invidiam, oratores
suos Florentiam misit." (Bruni, *Historiae*, II, viii, 550.)

[13] "Gregorius, quod viribus, aut consilio desperabat, assequi astu, calliditateque
se consecuturum putans, Florentiam oratores misit, tentatum si quo modo posset,
quod vi nequiverat, civili fieri dissensione" (237B–C).

[14] "Intra urbem vero Senarum caritas erat annonae, et pestis eodem tempore
populum affligebat; nec eadem voluntas omnium erat civium. Multi bellum contra
vicinos susceptum et mediolanensis adhaerentiam improbabant. Quas ob res seditione
inter cives coorta, deventum est ad arma." (Bruni, *Historiae*, III, x, 74.)

and immediate consequences of the pressures created by the war, without any reference to pre-existing tensions.[15]

Each historian, then, betrays a strong sense of the interrelatedness of political factors, although Poggio concentrates on the ramifications of this relationship in the field of military and diplomatic affairs, the field which constitutes his basic concern. A deeper probing into Poggio's historical ideas reveals another basic similarity between his and Bruni's conceptualization of history: the tendency to narrate historical events in terms of the psychological realities which inform them.

Early in his work Poggio follows the account of a series of military events by an assessment of their psychological effect.[16] Later he begins the war of Eight Saints with a lengthy analysis of Florentine doubts and hesitations.[17] When the war concludes with the Pope's death, Poggio tells how the rumor of his decease affects the spirits both of the Florentines and of Bernarbo Visconti in Milan.[18] The actions through which Giangaleazzo seizes power in Milan are prefaced by an account of the fears and suspicions that have prompted them.[19] During a subsequent war with Florence, the Milanese leader tries to destroy a bridge over the Po by means of a flotilla of burning ships. Ignoring the sensual aspect of the burning fleet and even the failure of the tactic, Poggio describes the impact of the spectacle on those who see it.[20] He narrates the effect of a major Florentine defeat during this same war not in strategic language but exclusively in terms of the states of mind which characterize the various combatants — the Germans, the Milanese, the Emperor Robert, and finally the Florentines.[21]

Nor does Poggio's concern with psychological states diminish when he is no longer using Bruni as a source. He narrates the factors contributing to the Pisan war in psychological terms, using this means of presentation as a vehicle for relating the various specific causes of the war.[22] In this later section of the work diplomatic

15 "Cum gravi premerentur Senenses bello, seditione orta inter cives" (259D).
16 "Magnum haec tanta belli moles, tam diversis excitata locis terrorem incussit" (202A).
17 221C–222A.
18 Of the Florentines he says, "Mentes hominum excitarunt" (241A), and of Bernarbo, "Bernabovis animum maxime in iram . . . incendit" (242A–B).
19 246A.
20 "Magnus terror ex hoc apparatu Mantuano incesset" (275C).
21 283A–284D.
22 296D–298A. His source here is probably Matteo Palmieri's *De captivitate Pisarum liber*, vol. IX, part 1, of *RR.II.SS.*, ed. G. Scaramella (Città di Castello,

events are consistently presented in a psychological context,[23] and
military maneuvers are given the same psychological significance
with which they have been endowed in earlier books.[24] Finally,
Poggio's attempts at historical generalization invoke psychological
categories.[25]

The foregoing examples show clearly that Poggio understood the
significance of psychological elements in history in much the same
way as Bruni did. In the *Historia fiorentina* psychological states
are consistently narrated in terms of their effects and are used as
a means of relating historical events to one another. In addition,
Poggio, like Bruni, seems to use the psychological element of history as a means for expressing the reality of change. In short, the
later historian has achieved a meaningful transformation of this
insight from a context in which it serves as an exhortation to civic
responsibility and commitment into one which helps to explicate
the political realities behind military and diplomatic events.[26]

In certain cases Poggio has even managed to penetrate more
deeply than Bruni the relationship between general psychological
states and the particular events which manifest them. In the realm
of military affairs, the clearest example of this penetration is found
in Poggio's account of a personal combat between two Frenchmen
and two Florentines outside the walls of Bologna in 1376. Bruni's

---

1904). Palmieri also presents the war in psychological terms but does not relate
these factors to the specific causes of the war.

[23] After Florentine ambassadors are rebuffed by Ladislaus, "magnam timorem
Florentinis antea incusserat apparatus regis incerti erga se animi suspicio" (307C).
Later, after telling how Filippo Maria has broken certain clauses of the treaty and
has tried to excuse himself, Poggio goes on to say that this action creates doubts
and suspicion in the minds of the Florentines. He then proceeds to treat a series of
events which, in connection with this suspicion, lead to war (320C–324C).

[24] For example, he summarizes the state of affairs after a military operation:
"Dum haec inter spem metumque agitatur" (336A).

[25] "Erectis omnium ducis adventu ad pugnam animis" (349A), and "Adversam
populo Florentino martem fore cum plures arbitrarentur plusque timoris quam spei
inesset" (409A). Compare the first example with Poggio's source, Flavio Biondo,
who assesses this same series of events in the following manner: "Quam tamen
causam ne ipsos ad maturandam resistendam excitaret in aperte contentionis tempora
reservavit quin etiam ne fines in foedere ascriptos transgredi videretur oblata occasione fori livii occupandi" (F. Biondo, *Historiarum ab inclinatione Romanorum imperii decades* [Venice, 1483], 279v; hereafter *Decades*).

[26] Baudi di Vesme, who is unusual in praising Poggio above his fellow humanist
historians, including Bruni, still faults him for lack of a vital political interest (C.
Baudi di Vesme, *Brevi considerazioni sulla storiografia fiorentina e sul pensiero
politico nel XV secolo* [Turin, 1953], p. 9). From the preceding analysis it is clear
that Poggio's political interests are quite strong and that what is lacking is a certain
type of republican commitment.

account does not contain an explicit comment on the significance of the event. He attributes the Florentine victory to the *virtus* of one of the combatants and concludes his description by noting simply that the victors returned to Bologna with great praise.[27] Poggio narrates the encounter even more briefly than Bruni, giving no cause at all for the Florentine victory.[28] He devotes his attention rather to showing the value of the combat in defending the city, for because of it the Bolognese take heart and their commander can develop better tactics for the city's defense.[29] Bruni, for whose historical conceptions and interests the personal combat has little significance, devotes more space to direct narrative than to analysis; Poggio, even though the military event is more strictly within his scope, narrrates the event as briefly as possible in order to analyze its significance within his general presentation of military history.

In diplomatic affairs Poggio not only has managed to penetrate more deeply than Bruni the connections between psychological states and specific events but has achieved a clearer articulation of the states themselves. Poggio explains diplomatic events principally in terms of two basic motivational categories, the first of which, desire, is considerably more important than the second, indignation or outrage. The conduct of Florence's enemies is unfailingly explained by desire for power, which moves not only Ladislaus of Naples and all the members of the Visconti family but even a treacherous condottiere in Florence's own hire.[30] Poggio's consistent partisanship is seen clearly in the fact that he never imputes such motives to the Florentines, whose foreign policy seems designed only to protect their own liberty.[31] Avarice is also a strong motivational

---

[27] "Magna cum laude" (Bruni, *Historiae*, II, viii, 542–544).

[28] "Biffolus Britonem adversarium ex equo deiicet, inde pedestri marte ad terram prostratum superat. Legato victi vitam postulanti donat. Idem et Guidonis decus fuit; nam superatum Gallum concessa vita tamquam victoriae munus Legato largitur." (234B.)

[29] "Ita insolentia hostium repressa et Florentinorum animi in spem erecti. Hoc duellum Rodolphi secutum est prudens responsum." (234B.)

[30] Giovanni Visconti is moved to war, "ambitiosum et dominandi cupidum" (198A–B). His successor, Bernarbo, is similarly motivated, though here Poggio is willing to acknowledge the influence of factional zeal: "Tum cupido immoderata dominandi, tum etiam Ghibellinarum partium favor" (209C). Giangaleazzo begins his wars for the same reasons: "Huius ambitio nimia et imperandi libido bellum contra Florentinos excivit" (245A). Filippo Maria, in turn, is motivated "ampliandi imperii cupidus" (319B). Of Ladislaus, Poggio says, "Erat regis animus elatus imperandi cupiditate" (306D). Finally, Roberto Malatesta, the treacherous *condottiere*, fails to serve the commune because "fallici spe ductus imperio urbis inhiabat" (212A).

[31] They are, for instance, induced to fight the Pope only "pro libertate . . . et

factor in the *Historia fiorentina*, although it usually applies to lesser figures, and particularly to condottieri.[32]

Desire is for Poggio a basic human trait, present to such a degree in all diplomatic events that none can really be understood without taking it into account. Indignation, the second basic feeling used to explain diplomatic affairs, is somewhat more subtle. Both individuals and groups can be moved to action by indignation or outrage and, governed by these feelings, can act in such a way that their deeds do not reflect pure self-interested desire. Both Florentines and their enemies can be swayed by such impulses.[33] Related to this feeling is the motive of revenge, which assumes a certain importance in the *Historia fiorentina*, though not as much as in Bruni's work.[34] A

---

pro salute patriae" (223A–B). Similarly, the Florentines undertake the Giangaleazzo war "pro libertate" (245A). Furthermore, Florence is ever anxious to avoid war. After recovering some booty seized by the Genoese, Florence disbands its ships, "ne cum Genuensi aliqua belli causa oriretur" (268C). When Florence does become involved in a war which is clearly aggressive, Poggio still does not suggest cupidity as a motive. He lists the motivations for the Florentine attack on Pisa, which leads to the capture of that city, as follows: first the Florentines' feeling that it is a just war because they have bought the city from Gabriello Visconti; second, their shame at having lost the fortress; third, the former hatred of the Pisans against the Florentines; and last, the fact that the two cities are on opposite sides of the Guelf-Ghibelline struggle (297A). These are all psychological factors, of course, but greed and ambition are conspicuously absent from the list.

[32] Hawkwood ravages Bolognese territory "praedae cupidus" (218D), and he is induced to come over to the Florentines "pollicitationibus tum pecuniis allectus" (237A). The betrayers of San Miniato are "praemiorum spe corrupti" (254B). Amadeus of Savoy joins an alliance against Filippo Maria, "enim innata avaritia pecuniae et stipendii recipiundi causa foederi ascriptus" (345D). The Duke of Armagnac is similarly motivated (260A).

[33] An example occurs very early in the book, when Florence decides on war "indignatione tam improbi responsi" of the Milanese ruler to its ambassadors (202C). In the war of Eight Saints indignation is a strong factor on both sides. The Pope in excommunicating the Florentines is motivated by indignation at their actions: "Hinc indignatio Pontificis se delusum existimantis iraque in Florentinos incensa est" (228C). The papal indignation constitutes a continuing theme in the narrative of the war. For example, Poggio narrates the failure of a papal mission in terms of Gregory's increasing indignation: "Reversis Romam Legatis, quaeque egerant expositis, irritatus Pontifex cui minime eiusmodi consilium cessisset, quotidie indignationis animi edebat signa" (238C). Among those opposing the Pope this feeling is also an important consideration. Both the failure of the siege of Bologna and the expulsion of the Britons from Cesena are explained by the indignation of the people — in the first case, at the arrogance of the legates ("quorum insolentiam, avaritiam, fastidium, arrogantiam, superbiam" [235B]), and in the second case, at the outrageous conduct of the mercenaries ("Britones Cesenam ingressi, tamquam in urbe ex hostibus vi capta, omnia sacra, profanaque pro libidine diripuit" [235C]).

[34] One of Gregory's military expeditions is clearly motivated by revenge. "Ad has Florentinorum ulsciscendas iniurias Pontifex Ramundum nepotem contra eos cum parte exercitus per agrum Senensem maritimum ire jussit" (239A). After a naval attack has failed, Giangaleazzo presses a land attack, "cum acceptum dedecus

significant indication of its reduced importance is the fact that Poggio never uses it to explain diplomatic maneuvers.

Poggio, then, interprets diplomatic history in terms of the prosecution of one's self-interest. Obviously biased in Florence's favor, he considers that city to be defending its liberty, while the other states of Italy are motivated by cupidity in the conduct of their foreign policy. Self-interest, however, does not explain every event in the sphere of foreign affairs, and Poggio makes it clear that in certain situations a state or an individual may be moved by indignation at another's outrageous conduct.

Like Bruni, Poggio is analytical in his treatment of motivation, but in a somewhat different way. Bruni analyzes motives either to show how they have confused and contradicted the true interests of the party in question or to discover the circumstances which have determined the predominance of one motive over another. Poggio's motivational categories are more rigid than Bruni's. This difference makes it less important to show why a particular motive predominates, for major decisions are almost always governed by desire to pursue one's self-interest. Instead of following Bruni, the mid-century historian seeks to describe the influence of specific events on the quality of this basic motive. Thus he is observing his usual practice of bringing out the relationship of psychological states to concrete events.

The manner in which Poggio treats Giovanni Visconti's ambition during his war with Florence illustrates the historian's attempt at this sort of analysis. He consistently explains the war by Visconti's desire for power and additional territory. Giovanni's greed persists throughout the struggle, but its intensity rises or falls according to the vicissitudes of precise historical events. The war begins after Visconti's purchase of Bologna, a specific acquisition which inflames his natural greed.[35] Similarly, the Archbishop becomes willing to make peace — that is, his cupidity diminishes in intensity — when he sees that he has no further chance of success.[36] The fortuitous accession of Genoa to his dominions in turn increases his cupidity and makes him ready to continue the war. So interested is Poggio in

---

ulscisci in animo haberet" (276D). Florence, allowing itself to be drawn into military operations motivated by the desire to avenge a previous defeat, sends troops against Pietro di Balneo "ut acceptas iniurias ulsciscerentur" (295A).

[35] 198A–B.
[36] 207B.

following the rise and fall in the intensity of Visconti's greed that he narrates the Archbishop's death as a cessation of desire.[37]

Poggio conspicuously avoids interpreting the vicissitudes of the war in terms of concrete alterations in the relative power of the two states. Neither Bologna nor Genoa is treated as an increment to the actual strength of Giovanni Visconti. The historian deals with the Pisan war in the same fashion. When the Pisans receive a subsidy from Milan, Poggio focuses not on the additional capacity for resisting Florence made possible by the Milanese help but on the change in the quality of the Pisan desire for war.[38] He assesses the significance of Giangaleazzo's ducal title in the same way.[39]

It is clear from these examples that in both diplomatic and military operations Poggio expresses the reality of historical change in strictly psychological terms. Like Bruni, he gives the psychological aspect of the narrative a real and vital function in conveying the very essence of the historical process. Bruni, however, usually narrates this process simply as the transformation of one psychological state into another [40] or as the spread of an attitude through different social groups.[41] Poggio, by focusing on the quality of the psychological state and treating the effect of specific events on this quality, successfully encompasses concrete events and nonpsychological factors within his presentation of historical change without sacrificing his perception of this change as ultimately psychological. The heightened emphasis on the more tangible dimensions of history which Poggio's approach permits him is of considerable importance in understanding his contribution to humanist historiography and will be discussed more fully in Chapter Six.

The *Historia fiorentina*, then, shows that its creator has conceptualized the political dimensions of history in such a way that events may be coherently related to one another. One should not allow the greater singleness of purpose with which Bruni explores the ramifications of his own conceptualization to obscure the presence of such a vision in Poggio's work. Its existence is clear not only in his accounts of military and diplomatic events but even in his

[37] "Mors peropportuna inanes curas illius et dominandi appetitum diremit" (209A).

[38] "Auxit animos reddidit cupidiores" (212D).

[39] "Aucta dignitate et cupiditas quoque dominandi crevit" (272C).

[40] As in the case of the Sicilian Vespers or the expulsion of Walter of Brienne, where he uses the phrase "odio superante metum."

[41] For example, the spread of unrest through the classes of Florentine society during the disturbances of 1378.

treatment of historical problems which lie outside his scope, such as the relative strength of tyrannies and republics.

Poggio's preference for a republic is not uncritical, for he sees the same sorts of problems in this form of government that Bruni sees. A republic is, first of all, more prone to factional strife. Republican Verona, for instance, cannot regain its liberty from Milan because of the internal dissensions arising from the strength of the old republican factions, while Padua can rely on its unity in support of the Carrara to recover its independence.[42] Another problem intrinsic to a republic is the ignorance and cowardice of the people, to which Poggio explicitly alludes on two separate occasions. When the people decide on war with Lucca, he says, "Nevertheless, as often happens, the better part was overruled by the larger." [43] At the very end of the work, in denouncing the decision to call back Sforza to protect Florence, he castigates the same want of judgment on the part of the common citizen.[44]

Tyrannies, on the other hand, are weakened by the rulers' inability to get valid counsel. One of the first events noted in the Visconti war is the beheading of a Brescian noble who has suggested that the war is unwise. Poggio comments, "In addition to being tyrannical this act set a bad example, for a good man showed by his fall how dangerous it is to give good counsel to tyrants and princes." [45] In like fashion the sedition which breaks out in Milan after the death of Giangaleazzo is explained by the fact that counselors of the adolescent duke look to their own selfish interests rather than the public good.[46]

As a comparison of republican and tyrannical government, the *Historia* lacks not a critical spirit but an exploration of the inner working of institutions. Bruni devotes considerable attention to the

---

[42] "Sed nulla ibi aut seditio aut desidia Francisci virtute quae hostium consilia praeverterat reperta est" (258B). Poggio explicitly considers factional strife to be as horrible as does Bruni ("quae pestis omni externo bello perniciosior est" [242B]), but he sees it as a weakness of princes as well as of republics. Many of Filippo Maria's problems, for instance, are due to internal dissension. See Filippo's difficulties in seizing Genoa (321C) or the problems raised by the Guelf-Ghibelline struggle in Brescia (240D).

[43] "Tamen ut saepissime contingit, melior pars a maiori superata est" (260B).

[44] "Ignotum esse populorum voluntatem semper ad peiora mobilem et ut plurimum fortunam respicientem, praesertim ubi ingruat fames quae omnem timorem abjicere ex animis consueverit" (409A–B).

[45] "Mali exempli res, et plus quam tyrannica: docuit suo damno vir bonus quanto cum periculo dentur tyrannis ac principibus sana consilia" (207C).

[46] 292B.

psychological effects of institutions and locates the power of a republic in its ability to mobilize the psychological energies of its citizenry. This sort of analysis clearly lies outside Poggio's diplomatic and military scope, and he cannot be expected to deal with it. Hence the *Historia* contains no suggestion of the way in which institutions function. The absence of such questioning should not blind the reader to the analytical judgments it does contain. The value of republican institutions is not simply assumed but understood in terms of the conceptual realities which permeate the political aspects of Poggio's work.

The substance of the *Historia fiorentina* cannot, however, be understood entirely in terms of the political and psychological concepts which most closely relate the work to Bruni's history. A second essential element is a series of moral judgments on the events of Florentine history. Here moral categories are invoked which, although they may in some circumstances be related to political considerations, are ultimately uncritical, justified by implicit assumptions which are not directly related to any political consideration. Two such judgments will illustrate this element in the *Historia* and associate it with the analytical aspect of the work.

The historian's judgment on perfidious conduct is not always consistent. On the one hand, he sees clearly that it is often self-defeating. The manner in which Giangaleazzo has acquired his lands, for instance,[47] makes it almost impossible for his sons to keep them after his death, for the powers from whom he has taken the lands strive all the more vigorously to recover them. Giangaleazzo's successor also experiences the foolishness and inefficacy of trickery. Again, the decisive factor causing Venice to ally with Florence is Filippo Maria's attempted poisoning of the condottiere Carmignola, an act which shows the Venetians that Milan is interested in war and induces them to take measures for their own protection.[48] In this case the deception fails to attain its purpose not because of the moral outrage it evokes but because of the sharper insight it provides into the true intentions of the deceiver. This is like the case of Giangaleazzo, where the important factor is again not moral indignation but simply the existence of dispossessed powers anxious to recover their own. Like Bruni, however, Poggio considers deception a useful military tactic, and his narrative is full of examples of

[47] "Per vim dolumve de alienis" (290C).
[48] 338B.

successful tricks which result in the taking of a town or the winning of a battle.[49]

Poggio, then, judges perfidy and deceit by their practical effects, which in turn are analytically interpreted within his historical ideas. Faithless acts in a military context are usually strategically valid, while such acts in the diplomatic sphere generally are not. Here Poggio's history is didactic, showing the student how to discriminate between specific acts of dissimulation in terms of a synoptical view relating historical events to one another. All of Poggio's observations within this field do not, however, reflect political considerations. Some of his comments (all pertaining to one particular type of perfidy) are definitely moralistic, judging faithless acts to be bad regardless of their historical context.

When Giangaleazzo tries to bribe the Duke of Armagnac into leaving Florence's service and the Frenchman summarily refuses the offer, Poggio gives the following reason: "For everyone must keep faith, and especially princes." [50] This is not the only occasion in the *Historia* when the responsibility of princes to keep their pledges is stressed. When the Pope refuses to keep his part of a treaty, Poggio says, "Not only does it particularly behoove his exalted station to keep faith, but it is even shameful for private citizens not to do so. It seems dishonorable and detestable for citizens, who claim liberty, but even more so among princes, to violate their oaths, to show contempt for religion by not keeping their word, and willfully to put aside their honor for their own comfort." [51]

---

[49] The fortress of Mt. Viviano is taken by a ruse (203C); reinforcements are sneaked into Scaparia (205B); Miniato is taken by an elaborate trick (217C–218A); the English mercenaries seize the castle at Mt. Giorgio through the betrayal of a priest (234A); and deception is an important tactic in the Giangaleazzo war (see 258A–B). In later parts of the work the value of trickery in battle comes to be emphasized. Ladislaus enters Rome through a complicated trick by which he induces the Pope to attack Picena in order to draw off the Papal forces from Rome itself (315B–D). Even the great Carmignola is defeated in battle by a trick involving an ambush (372A–373A). The Venetians win a naval battle by the simulation of flight, followed by a vigorous attack on the Genoese formation, now broken by the pursuit (373C–D). None of these incidents weakens in any practical way the position of the deceiver, and none calls forth any expression of disapproval from Poggio.

[50] "Tum omnibus tum maxime principibus fidem servandam esse" (260C).

[51] "Quod ne dum in tanta dignitate cuius maxime interest servare fidem, sed in privato etiam viro culpandum foret, cum turpissimum videatur et detestandum tum in civitatibus, quae libertatem asserunt tum maxime in principibus, non servari pacta jusjurandum, religionem contemni violari fidem datam, omnia pro arbitrio et voluntate fide posthabita pro commode habere" (293C).

The historian's comment on the betrayal of Florentine merchants by Ladislaus is even more severe.[52]

All the instances in which Poggio takes a decidedly moralistic stance against perfidious conduct concern nonrepublican powers. The historian's condemnation is much more severe when applied to princes than to private persons or republics. His attention to the conduct of tyrants in the *Historia* is clear evidence that he wishes his history to have didactic and moral value for them as well as for citizens of a republic — an attention which represents a definite expansion in scope over the *Historiae Florentini populi*. Bruni is interested in princes only insofar as their actions affect the foreign policy of a republic, insofar as their weaknesses make it easier for a republic to deal wtih them. Poggio goes beyond this concern, suggesting moral rules which deal directly with the conduct of tyrants even when this conduct does not teach a republic how to manage its relations with princes.[53]

More important than the concern to impose a wider didactic value on his work is the manner in which Poggio introduces this value into the narrative. He does not try to create an historical conceptualization which would endow the actions of princes with moral significance. Rather, he superimposes upon an historical narrative constructed in terms of a causal complex similar to Bruni's a moral judgment of a type that Bruni regularly avoids.[54] Poggio's means of broadening the relevance of his narrative weakens the rigor of his analysis and demonstrates the limits of his creativity, since he

[52] "Scelestum facinus, non solum nomine regio indignum sed pirata etiam nequissime quorum est in rapinis quoque promissam fidem servare" (316C).

[53] Notice that he does not say princes are more faithless; this would be useful knowledge for a republic. Instead he limits himself to saying that faithlessness is more reprehensible in princes, a statement of interest only to a prince. Poggio's concern with the moral conduct of princes could be related to two factors in his own life: his long service under a prince in the papal court, and the establishment of the Medici domination during his own service in the Florentine chancery. It would be difficult if not impossible to establish the direct relationship between these biographical factors and Poggio's broader historical interests, nor is it of great importance in assessing his historiography.

[54] Poggio could not easily find examples of this type of judgment in his nearest classical model, Sallust, whose condemnations of Jugurtha's perfidy occur in the context of the moral decay of Republican Rome, a decay which the success of this perfidy reveals. (When the Numidian leaves the city of Rome, he says, "Urbem venalem et mature perituram, si emptorem invenerit" [*Bellum Jugurthinum*, XXXV].) Sallust does, however, comment explicitly on Jugurtha's evil character, and if Poggio has a classical model — he hardly needs one, for the Villani chronicles are full of this type of moral judgment — it is probably to be found here.

seems to have been unable to develop analytical tools independent of Bruni's. Nevertheless, it is important to note that in spite of the negative aspects of his procedure he has succeeded in extending the scope of history beyond Bruni's narrow focus.

Thus the first type of moralistic judgment shows Poggio's desire to broaden the applicability and relevance of the narrative to include people outside the Florentine republican tradition. A second type reveals his desire to deepen and intensify the moral value of his history for those within the tradition. In assessing the psychological vigor and toughness of a citizen body, Poggio usually follows Bruni in relating this quality directly to specific policies designed to take advantage of it. When describing the siege of Signa, he dwells first on the bravery of the women and the stamina of the men, but he goes on to show how the defensive tactics of the military commander take into account the popular mood.[55]

On one occasion, however, when giving an example of this willingness to bear hardships, Poggio digresses to make an explicitly moralistic comment to his own contemporaries. Speaking of the Florentine effort in the war with Giangaleazzo, he describes the financial sacrifices and the money raised in taxes during the war,[56] and then he says, "But today that city is so reduced that, when it needs twenty or thirty thousand florins, it either must borrow or impose an extraordinary tax, which is a bad and unjust way of collecting money. The city must do this because of those who put their private interests over the public good and who claim for themselves the disasters of others and in this way avoid all burden of taxation." [57]

Two of the themes in this statement are also found in Bruni's

[55] 274C–D.

[56] One of the themes Poggio carries over from Bruni is the stress on the amount of money Florence is able and willing to spend in order to defend itself against its enemies. Very early in the narrative he points out that Florence has taken the larger burden in the alliance against Giovanni Visconti, marvelling at the "vectigalibus . . . magnam pecuniam vim" which Florence has collected to prosecute the war (207B). He continually refers to the Florentines' effort in superlative terms. Later on in the war against the Archbishop they collect a force "summa diligentia" (213C). Taxes are imposed to finance the war with Pope Gregory "summo studio" (239C). Similar terms are used to describe the war against Giangaleazzo (282C) and, later, the war against Filippo Maria (427A).

[57] "At hodie eo redacta civitas est, cum viginti aut triginta aureorum millia cogenda sunt, aut versura comparetur pecunia aut ad extraordinaria tributa recurrant, quod iniquum est pessimumque exigendae pecuniae genus at abominandum atque ab his excitatum quibus potior est res privata, quam publica, quique opes sibi vendicant per aliorum calamitatem, ipsi omni eiusmodi tributi onere expertes" (282B–C).

Historiae: the emphasis on the financial aspects of the war and the suggestion of a harmful tendency to place private over public interests. But Bruni conspicuously avoids any attempt to compare the specific quality of a psychological factor in one age with that of another and to evoke from this comparison a moralistic condemnation of his own time. The theme of the moral inferiority of contemporaries, present in such classical authors as Livy, Tacitus, and Cicero, forms one of Sallust's central concerns. This comment of Poggio's, which is not duplicated in the work, is another example of his indebtedness to Sallust. It also indicates his willingness to append extraneous considerations to his coherent view of history, taken from Bruni, in order to broaden and deepen the didactic value of the narrative by specific application.

Poggio's condemnation of perfidy among princes and his unfavorable comparison of fifteenth-century Florence with the Florence of earlier times constitute an important element which he has added to the historical conceptions found in Bruni's work. Poggio also wants history to celebrate illustrious men and condemn evil ones. While this desire is related to the moralistic element, it is broader, for a specific person or deed may be celebrated without focusing on any particular moral injunction. The substance of the narrative reflects the element of *celebratio* in several ways. The historian describes the honors paid to successful condottieri,[58] as well as victory celebrations after arduous and honorable military campaigns.[59] Conversely, he is quick to give examples of the dishonor of those who have not performed their duties well.[60]

---

[58] He mentions the magnificent funeral of Farnese, together with his statue placed in the Duomo (211A–B); Bruni simply states that he is given a public funeral (II, viii, 474). Further on Poggio mentions the funeral honors accorded Manno Donati, specifically saying that they are given him because of his great deeds ("ob eius res et pace et bello egregie gestas" [219A]); Bruni mentions only the death, not the funeral (II, v, 506). On still another occasion Poggio notes the honors paid the Sienese condottiere Giovanni Ubaldini on his death (257A), while Bruni mentions only the death and not the funeral (III, x, 114). Both Bruni (III, ix, 194) and Poggio (271B–C) mention the funeral of Hawkwood, but only the latter speaks of the fresco in the Duomo.

[59] For instance, he narrates the displaying of the chains captured from the Pisan harbor (210D). In this case Bruni, interested in the event since it reflects on a people instead of a single individual, gives a full account (II, viii, 470), which Poggio has virtually copied. On another occasion Poggio describes in considerable detail the victory celebrations after the capture of Pisa (306A).

[60] In one significant case near the beginning of the work, Poggio recounts without explanation the punishment of a commander who gives up his castle under unspecified threats from the enemy (201D–202A), pointing out that this execution is strictly exemplary in purpose ("quo caeteri a simili facinore deterrerentur").

Poggio's desire to make his history more explicitly relevant to his contemporaries leads him to connect with the present some elements in the narrative which have no obvious moral significance. Bruni, it will be remembered, does this only in the case of constitutional changes which have persevered down to the fifteenth century.[61] Poggio follows Bruni in noting the institutions which have lasted [62] but goes beyond his predecessor in describing the early buildings of Florence which could still be seen in the Quattrocento.[63] He even mentions that the annual horse race commemorates the fall of Pisa in 1406.[64]

The importance Poggio attaches to connecting past with contemporary events can be illuminated by comparing the respective reactions of Bruni and Poggio to ostensibly miraculous happenings. Even though Bruni's sources contain an eyewitness account of the miraculous announcement of the Florentine victory at Campaldino, he does not rely on this evidence but shows that the event is comprehensible in terms of his own reconstruction of the historical process. Poggio's account of the miraculous announcement of the death of Gregory XI is similar to this in presenting no evidence from eyewitnesses.[65] Poggio, however, does not adopt Bruni's method of verification. Instead, he maintains that the legend is quite credible because he knows of a similar occurrence that took place

---

Bruni doesn't mention the incident at all, subsuming it under the heading of "other castles" whose capture he alludes to (II, vii, 360). Matteo Villani narrates it in full (II, 6), explaining that the custodian is young and inexperienced and has been tricked by the enemy into giving his brother as a hostage. For Poggio, however, the punishment of the man has exemplary importance, which can only be obscured by a full recital of all the mitigating circumstances. In a later incident during the war of Eight Saints, when a condottiere in the pay of Florence deserts, his picture is hung upside down, "ut moris est eorum qui fidem frangunt" (237A–B). Bruni narrates the hanging of the picture without specifying why it is inverted but giving a full account of how the mercenary is induced to desert (II, viii, 52). Still later Poggio describes as follows the public disgrace of the would-be betrayer of San Giovanni in Val d'Arno during the wars with Giangaleazzo: "Rei proditionis exilio mulctati, publiceque in foro ad ignominiam sceleris depicti" (256B). Bruni virtually ignores the incident, saying that the troops entered the Val d'Arno expecting to have a town betrayed to them but that they were disappointed (III, x, 110).

[61] See his comments on the institution of the priors (I, ii, 362).

[62] "Hoc ordo, licet varie et numero dignitate immutatus, ad hanc diem perseverat" (197A–B).

[63] 195A–B.

[64] 306A.

[65] The event is in the *Historia* (240D–241A) but is ignored by Bruni (II, viii, 554). Poggio's source is D. Buoninsegni's *Historia fiorentina* (Florence, 1581), pp. 594–595. Buoninsegni describes efforts to find how the voice originated and then tells how confirmation of the report came to Florence. In narrating the incident thus, he more closely resembles Villani than either of the humanists.

while he was at the papal court. The incident represents a further example of Poggio's feeling that the reality of the narrative is enhanced by direct contemporary references, and also of his sense that the relevance to present-day problems implicit in the analytical element of his historical view is not sufficiently clear and needs to be stressed by other elements.

A further indication of Poggio's unwillingness to relate all the events of the narrative to one another in terms of his psychological analysis is the greater role played by chance and fortune in determining action. The *Historia*, considerably shorter than the *Historiae Florentini populi*, contains many more abstract references to the power of fortune, though, like Bruni, Poggio tends to emphasize its importance in military affairs.[66] There are also in the work several events, again generally military, in which the deciding factor is said to be chance.[67] Nor are the situations in which fortune has been the decisive force of small importance. Poggio underlines, for instance, the significance that the fall of San Giovanni in Val d'Arno would have had in weakening Florence's strategic position in Tuscany.[68] Finally, in addition to those events which the historian explains by the intervention of fortune, there are important occurrences where the causality is obviously contingent.[69]

As one would expect, these fortuitous events are seen to have didactic value. For instance, Poggio draws a general lesson from Ladislaus' death, saying, "But the fates, by whom human plans are often interrupted, intervened." [70] After showing the threat

[66] "Fortunae arbitrium quae plurimum in bellis posset" (262A); "ita incerto gestum marte, ut eos qui ante ferme pro victis habebantur, victoria secuta sit" (310A); "cum praesertim rerum humanarum et maxime bellorum dominam constet esse fortunam cuius est eludere nostras cogitationes" (319A [from an oration]); "fortunae quae plurimum in bello potest" (410A); and "fortunae quae in rebus humanis maxime dominatur" (367B).

[67] The failure of the attempt to trick San Giovanni in Val d'Arno into surrender is referred to as "ea fortuna" (256B). Speaking of Florence's unfortunate choice in hiring the Duke of Armagnac as military commander, Poggio says, "Erat futura superior admodum eo bello florentini respublica, nisi eorum consiliis fortuna obstitisset" (260A). Although the Emperor Robert's force could easily have been defeated after his first rash charge is broken, "Roberti fortuna paucis exceptis exercitum servavit" (283A). After mentioning several factors which make the siege of a city by the Milanese difficult, the historian says, "Interea juxta Benacum fortuna paulum Venetis favit" (401A).

[68] "Nam si ea successisset fraus, facile futurum erat ut hostis Aretio potiretur" (256B).

[69] The death of Giovanni Visconti, for instance, is responsible for the cessation of the war: "Ex quo quies Italiae paulum est a bellis data" (209A).

[70] "Sed fatis volentibus quibus hominum consilia saepius interrumpuntur" (316D).

posed to Florence by the successes of Piccinino, the historian makes a similar comment before describing the manner in which Florence is saved.[71] In addition to these explicit comments there are several narrated instances where men learn the power of fortune from events.[72]

The suggestion that human plans are of little avail in the face of fortune seems to contrast rather strongly with the value placed on *consilia* throughout the work. The existence of a conceptualized picture of historical events would seem to imply the value of intelligent planning, and Bruni himself describes military operations in terms of the superiority of plans over brute force. Poggio, too, in those sections of the *Historia* devoted to the narration of military maneuvers, praises well-considered tactics with great frequency and deplores rash military actions based on pure strength in arms or on mere passion.[73]

The efficacy of *consilia* in military operations is, in fact, a theme stressed throughout the work. The Emperor Robert is beaten by Giangaleazzo's superior tactics even though the Italian is outnumbered.[74] The theme is present also in those later sections where Poggio is not relying on Bruni for his material. Describing the war with Filippo Maria, he relates arguments in the Milanese camp over whether to attack the Florentines at once. Here again the advantage of using *consilia* instead of trying the fortunes of war is

[71] "Sed raro fortunam sequuntur hominum consilia, paucique illius beneficio utuntur. Dum Nicholaus humiliora petit fortuna rei bene gerenda de manibus elapsa est." (408B).

[72] This is one of the effects of the fall of Pisa to Florence. "Haec tanta fortunae commutatio nonnullorum flexit animos ad contemplandam vanam et parum fidem rerum humanarum sortem" (303D). The cardinal invokes a similar sentiment in advising the Duke of Milan to accept a peace with Florence on adverse terms: "Utile procul dubio fore adversae fortunae cedere, cuius arbitrio humanae res regi viderentur; non in eodem statu semper omnia futura" (344B).

[73] He particularly emphasizes this in narrating the defeat of the Duke of Armagnac, whose rashness is contrasted with the prudence of Hawkwood. First Poggio characterizes the French character ("noverat enim Gallorum naturam pronam ad certamen esse, saepiusque impetu quodam praecipiti, quam ratione ad pugnandum ferri" [262A]) and then Armagnac's own considerations ("at ille plus viribus, quam consilio fretus" [262B]). After describing the defeat the historian comments, "Plus momenti in belli victoria consilium praebere quam vires" (263A). Turning then to Hawkwood's successful attempt to extricate himself from the difficult position into which the rash action and subsequent defeat of Armagnac have placed him, Poggio describes the thinking of Hawkwood, "Magis astu quam viribus utendum ratus" (263C). To underline his point he explicates the lesson to be drawn from the English condottiere's success: "Docuit plus ingenium in bellis, quam vires posse" (264B).

[74] 282D.

stressed.[75] In the same war an army is trapped when the condottiere advances "imprudently, relying more on boldness than plans." [76]

The presence in Poggio's work of these two opposing views of the importance of human effort and planning raises again the problem of the exact relationship between the conceptualized picture of history which can be extrapolated from Poggio's *Historia* and its moralistic and traditional aspect. These two elements are not different tools of analysis, applied to different sections of the work or even to different types of historical events. On the contrary, they reflect two levels of interpretation, each fully present within the same event. The defeat of Armagnac and escape of Hawkwood, which calls forth Poggio's most elaborate defense of the value of intelligent tactical planning, also includes one of his more explicit comments on the power of fortune.[77]

The existence of two levels of interpretation within the presentation of a single event is clearest in Poggio's treatment of the war of Eight Saints and the Ciompi crisis which follows the war. Though such an internal event as the Ciompi revolt lies beyond the historian's scope, it is too important to be completely ignored, and he devotes three periods to his assessment of it. In his account Poggio narrates, as opinions of the contemporaries of the Ciompi, two quite different interpretations of the significance of the revolt. He may have taken this technique, by which he avoids making his own choice, from the classical historians,[78] or he may have devised it himself, but he certainly did not find it in Bruni, whose historical concepts exclude such ambiguity. In the first place — and this interpretation will be discussed at some length — Poggio suggests that the revolt is a punishment for previous conduct. "Many thought that it arose from divine judgment, by which both the authors of the impious war and the city which had been the enemy of the Pope were punished." [79] His concern for developing the theme of divine retribution is also manifest in the remark with which he concludes his account of the war with the Pope: "It is well worth mentioning that, whether the war was just or unjust, the eight who had charge of it all died

---

[75] 350B–351B.

[76] "Maioris audaciae quam consilii . . . incautius progressus" (382D).

[77] "Fortunae arbitrium, quae plurimum in bellis posset" (262A).

[78] See Tacitus, *Annales,* I, 9–10.

[79] "Ferebatur a multis id divino judicio fieri, quo civitas hostis Pontificum et belli impii auctores plecterentur" (242C).

within a short time after its cessation and most of their progeny perished." [80]

Poggio's suspicion of the war's evil nature sheds considerable light on some of his basic concerns in narrating the beginning of the conflict. In analyzing the causes of the war he is very careful to show that Florence is fighting for its liberty and that this goal justifies its resistance to the Pope. He stresses this by explicit statement at the end of Book I [81] and again at the beginning of Book II. [82] Finally, he includes an oration which, though the model for it in the *Historiae Florentini populi* emphasizes the virtues of good government, deals with the abstract value of liberty. [83]

Counterpoised to the Florentine action in defense of its liberty is the Pope's greed and irrational conduct. The historian stresses that the war is completely unprovoked, occasioned only by Florentine vulnerability after a bad harvest. [84] Florence's defiance of the interdict is justified by the unmerited injuries the city has suffered at the hands of the Pope. [85] In the course of the narrative of the opening of the war many points relevant to Poggio's psychological concepts are found, in particular the importance of indignation on both sides and the folly of outrageous conduct, which only stiffens resistance.

It is clear, however, that Poggio's account of the war cannot be understood simply as a coherent exposition of these psychological concepts. A significant portion of the narrative is not related to the causal complex but is designed to explore the war insofar as it manifests unanalyzed moral categories. Poggio's answers on the moralistic level are, to be sure, neither simple nor unambiguous. The war is good insofar as it represents the defense of liberty, which is a virtue, and it is rewarded by victory. It is evil insofar as it represents disobedience to the church and a defiance of religious authority, which are not virtues, and it is punished, perhaps, by the death of the leaders and the outbreak of dissensions at home. [86]

---

[80] "Illud vero animadversum memoratu dignum, seu justum, seu injustum cum Gregorio fuerit, Octoviros, qui bello gerendo praefuerunt, parvum infra tempus post illius mortem defunctos esse omnes, genusque eorum maiori ex parte deletum" (243A).

[81] "Quibus rebus permoti omnes una mente ad tuendam libertatem" (220D).

[82] "Bellumne adversus Pontificis legatos pro libertate suscipiendum esset" (223A).

[83] 224A–226A.

[84] 220B.

[85] "Non enim de religione sed perfidia iniuriisque Pastorum Ecclesiae certamen esse" (239D).

[86] Poggio's qualms about the morality of this war may not easily be dismissed

Poggio's second interpretation of the Ciompi revolt, expressed through another contemporary opinion, ignores the possibility of divine retribution and reflects only the analytical dimension of the *Historia*. "Others maintain that it is the nature and custom of republics to be vexed with civil dissension and that it is hardly surprising that the same thing which once occurred among the greatest of republics should happen in Florence." [87] This theme, which is an important part of Bruni's understanding of the republican form of government, constitutes a significant part of Poggio's historical view and finds expression in other parts of the *Historia*. The weakness from internal discord which pertains to republics has already been discussed as one of Poggio's minor themes in connection with his explanation of Verona's inability to recover its liberty after the death of Giangaleazzo. Poggio also connects it with basic psychological characteristics.[88] Thus the second opinion which Poggio imputes to contemporaries can be seen to be a summary of Bruni's interpretation of the crisis.

The foregoing analysis reveals a deep ambiguity in the relationship between the levels of inquiry in Poggio's work. The *Historia fiorentina*, while it shows an energetic application of analytical tools to the search for answers to deeply felt questions — it constitutes "la vera storia" in the Crocean sense of this term — is fundamentally an incoherent work. Its political and moral dimensions, although both are fully present throughout the narrative, are not interdependent and do not illuminate each other.

The effect of this fragmentation of the intangible dimensions of Poggio's historical view is to force the attention of the narrator back to tangible, specific events. Though not of intrinsic significance, these events constitute the only vehicle by means of which the intangible elements, which are ultimately of greater concern to the humanist historian, can be interrelated. The heightened attention to concrete phenomena has already been noted in relation

as hypocrisy. His biographer makes a great issue of Poggio's sincere religiosity (Walser, *Poggius*, p. 135), and V. Rossi in reviewing Walser considers the establishment of genuine religious conviction in Poggio to be one of Walser's chief contributions (*Giornale storico della letteratura italiana*, 70 [1917], 312–317).

87 "Alii rerumpublicarum mores, naturamque asserebant, ut civili quandoque dissidio vexentur, neque mirandum esse id Florentinam urbem passam, quod maximis quondam rebuspublicis accidisset" (242C).

88 See, for instance, his comments on those who oppose the alliance with Bernarbo against the Pope: "Quibus mos est publicam rem in privatam vertere, quique aliorum laudi invidentes, omnia perditum iri quam sana consilia sequi malunt, quorum ipsi non sint auctores" (223D–224A).

to the analytical side of Poggio's historical view. In his treatment of both the military and diplomatic aspects of history he concentrates on those specific events which manifest psychological factors.[89] On the second, more traditional level of historical interpretation, Poggio underlines the relevance of the moralistic elements of his work to specific segments of his audience and offers as examples the actions and lives of specific men rather than abstractly stated modes of behavior.

Poggio's emphasis on specific facts, as compared with Bruni, has an even deeper effect on the *Historia*. Particular historical characters stand out more forcefully and have a greater influence on events. For Bruni, the character of Gregory XI is of small importance in explaining the war of Eight Saints. He emphasizes instead the Florentines' indignation, which is gradually introduced and tied to no specific cause.[90] Poggio, on the other hand, ties the war closely to the intense passions and greed of the Pope.

Even Giangaleazzo, who is Bruni's strongest personality, is more forcefully and broadly portrayed in the *Historia fiorentina*. Poggio more frequently illustrates his cleverness with concrete examples.[91] While Bruni seems interested only in those aspects of Giangaleazzo's personality which are politically significant, Poggio brings out such other characteristics as his liberality and his patronage of art and culture.[92] Bruni, who could hardly have been indifferent to a ruler's active patronage, does not consider this a politically relevant fact and tends to ignore it. Poggio alludes to patronage not only here but later on in describing Carlo Malatesta.[93]

In dealing with personalities throughout the book, Poggio pays

[89] See, for instance, his account of the personal combat discussed earlier in the treatment of motivations (above, at note 29).

[90] First he mentions the suspicions of Florence over the growing power of the legate (II, viii, 510); then the Florentines' rage at his attempt to starve them out (II, viii, 512); and finally their indignation and fear concerning the revolt in Prato. The personality of the Pope is not an issue, either here at the opening of the war or at any time during its conduct.

[91] See the account of Giangaleazzo's seizure of power in Milan, which emphasizes the humility of his pose, including his dressing poorly in order to convince Bernarbo of his lack of pretensions (245B) and his pandering to the multitude by pretending piety (247B). Poggio gives a specific illustration of Giangaleazzo's cleverness by showing him responding in person to a Florentine delegation (271A–272B).

[92] "Sed ea laudanda prae ceteris est virtus, quod omnium doctrinarum, artiumque vires eximies, ad se tamquam egregiorum hominum receptaculum vocavit, summoque in honore habuit" (290D–291A).

[93] "Studiis praeterea litterarum deditissimus et disserendi cum viris doctrina et ingenio praestantibus, quibus admodum utebatur cupidus" (331D–332A).

attention to nonpolitical factors which tend to make the individual stand out on his own. The historian frequently refers to a person's lineage without giving it the political significance with which Bruni endows the lineage of Walter of Brienne.[94] He also considers a man's cultural ideals to lie within the scope of the narrative. Of Federigo da Montefeltro he says, "For in addition to his eloquence and humanity, he was endowed by nature with many good qualities of mind and body."[95]

This is not to say that the historical characters in Poggio's narrative give the impression of having been empirically drawn, for such important men as the Visconti, Ladislaus, and Gregory XI are seen to be motivated by one predominant passion — greed for power — and endowed with one major strength — cleverness. It is to say that the personalities, however much they seem to be drawn from unanalyzed motivational categories, have a more vital place in the *Historia fiorentina* than in Bruni's history, and that this increased importance can be understood in terms of the problems facing Poggio in bringing together into a single work the disparate parts of his historical understanding. Now that the nature of this understanding has been outlined, the problems encountered by the historian in expressing his ideas must be more fully considered.

[94] Of Giovanni Ubaldini, the Sienese condottiere, Poggio says, "Vir nobilitate gentis clarus" (257A); of Carmignola, "Dux belli suae aetatis praecipius et obscuris ortus parentibus propria virtute ad maximam gloriam et imperium evectus" (367C); of Palla Strozzi, "Equestris ordinis vir insignis" (382C); of Angelo Acciaiuoli, "Equestris ordinis civem amplissimum" (430A); and finally, of Jacopo Piccinino, "Nicolai filius, paterni nominis gloria et rebus gestis clarus, florenti aetate juvenis" (431B).

[95] "Nam praeter eloquentiam suam ac humanitatem plurimas corporis animique dotes egregias a natura tributas" (428B).

Chapter Six
Narrative Technique in the *Historia fiorentina*

Poggio has been most often thought of as the fierce polemicist and satirist or the witty author of the *Facetiae*. Symonds, for instance, presents a ferocious individual who, though by no means an ascetic himself, terrorizes kings and prelates alike with his sharp tongue and threats of abuse and mercilessly lampoons the decadent clergy of the fifteenth century.[1] Even Poggio's contemporary, Vespasiano da Bisticci, seems more fascinated by the youthful wit than by the aging chancellor. But it was the aging chancellor who wrote the *Historia fiorentina*, where neither invective nor satire is found, and it would be dangerous to seek there for the literary values found in his earlier works.[2]

Of more interest than the literary side of the *Historia* is the manner in which Poggio organizes his material, so that without sacrificing clarity he draws the reader's attention to the significance of the events narrated. In developing this structure the historian faced several problems which had not troubled Bruni. Poggio's grasp of the intangible dimension of history is fragmented and ambiguous, comprehending both analytical and moralistic aspects. The

---

[1] Symonds, *Renaissance in Italy*, vol. II, *The Revival of Learning*, pp. 168–177.

[2] Rubinstein has rightly observed the literary differences between Poggio and his sources (Rubinstein, "Poggio," p. 14). Poggio seldom corrects the information found in these sources, trying instead to narrate events in a smoother, more elegant form, whether he is drawing on a vernacular chronicle, on Bruni, or on Flavio Biondo. Rubinstein suggests that the mid-century humanist is seeking to develop an historical style which embodies the canons of brevity and rapidity that characterize the stylistic theory both of antiquity and of the Quattrocento.
This literary aspect has been seen by previous scholars, but it is usually mentioned as a prelude to a condemnation of Poggio for not sharing Bruni's political concerns (see, for instance, Rossi, *Il Quattrocento*, p. 172). Except for Rubinstein, only one of the recent students of Poggio has pointed to this aspect as a significant contribution to historiography (see Baudi di Vesme, *Brevi considerazioni*, pp. 8–9, where he praises Poggio above Bruni for the former's "sviluppo più organicamente compatto più razionale e un interesse individualistica").

separate elements of this dimension cannot always be conveyed in the same way. Moreover, the effect of this fragmentation forces attention to the tangible events and creates further tensions which must be resolved before a smooth and cogent narrative is achieved. Finally, Poggio had a more complex set of models for imitation. Bruni could use Livy more or less consistently, gradually modifying the Roman historian's technique to suit the nature of his own historical insights. Poggio had to consider not only the classical histories but also his own humanist sources: Biondo, Palmieri, and Bruni himself.

In the first two books of the *Historia*, Poggio develops the basic structure he will use to organize events throughout the work. The information in these books is derived from several sources — the Villani chronicles and Buoninsegni, as well as Bruni — and here Poggio is most successful in creating an independent style through imitation of classical models. Eschewing the Livian annalistic form, which the hundred-year span of the *Historia* would have permitted him to adopt, he evolves a more supple instrument most closely related to the structure Sallust had given to both of his monographs.

Sallust's narrative technique has been brilliantly analyzed by Sir Ronald Syme in the second of his books on Roman historians.[3] Syme underlines the significance of Sallust's deliberate refusal to abide by annalistic boundaries in ordering his narrative. He could have structured his works in this way, for his principal subjects are military events, which could easily have been ordered annually by names of consuls or by the alternation of summers and winters.[4] By refusing to adopt this scheme, Sallust has incurred the criticism that his narrative is unclear, his chronology defective, and his sense of the meaning of temporal dimensions lacking.

Though the works of Sallust do betray minor chronological mistakes, Syme makes it clear that these errors do not deeply flaw his presentation. On the contrary, his technique allows an increased attention to broader themes and a concentrated interest which fully compensate for these minor drawbacks. Within a rough chronological form, Sallust generally seeks to narrate in terms of important themes, which he closely relates to the specific events of the narrative. In addition, he relies heavily on digressions which break the

---

[3] Syme, *Sallust*.
[4] Syme (*Sallust*, p. 142) points out that this last device would have been of special appeal to such an admirer of Thucydides as Sallust.

narrative order, venturing from the event under consideration into psychology, dramatic effects, or extravagant language. He is also adept at narrating two simultaneous sets of action.[5]

Syme's generalizations can be illustrated from specific passages in Sallust's works. One example will suffice to show the way in which he avoids using the annual consular election as a schematic dividing point. In narrating the year 109 B.C., Sallust ignores the election itself, introducing the new consuls only when they are involved in some important action which is explicitly related to previously narrated events.[6] In this way a clear chronology of events is maintained, not by attaching these events to a fixed point but by relating them to one another.

Sallust's practice of digressing from events in the interest of bringing out specific themes can be seen in his account of another occurrence in the same year. A tribune has brought a suit against those who have been bribed by Jugurtha. The commons support the suit, according to Sallust, rather from hatred of the nobles than from love of country, and the investigation is carried on with unusual severity. After narrating this specific event Sallust passes on to discuss the beginning of parties and factions at Rome after the Carthaginian wars, explaining that these arise because of basic human desires and passions. There follows a section describing the pernicious effects that the parties have on the republic, illustrated by the concrete example of the fate of the Gracchi. Having drawn out the moral significance of the specific political event he has been relating, Sallust abruptly ends the digression by stating that he will return to his subject.[7]

Sallust's general mode of organizing his material can be seen in two military events during the war with Jugurtha. After telling of a battle between Jugurtha and Metellus in which the Romans are victorious, Sallust pauses to make some general observations on the fact that a battle affects the brave and the cowardly in different ways. He then narrates the effect of the defeat on Jugurtha, who simply fades away to gather another army. This action of Jugurtha's, in turn, forces a new strategy on Metellus, who decides to avoid

[5] Syme, *Sallust*, pp. 189, 79–80, 86, 148.

[6] "Post Auli foedus exercitusque nostri foedam fugam Metellus et Silanus consules designati provincias inter se partiverant Metelloque Numidia evenerat, acri viro et quamquam adverso populi partium fama aequabili et inviolata" (Sallust, *Bellum Jugurthinum*, XLIII, 1).

[7] *Bellum Jugurthinum*, XL–XLII.

pitched battles in the future and to devote himself to ravaging Numidian territory. The narrative then turns to the effect of Metellus' new strategy in forcing Jugurtha to devise fresh tactics for combating it. Only after discussing the full ramifications of the battle in this military sphere does the historian turn to deal with the effect of its report at Rome, describing the honors awarded to Metellus and showing how these provide incentive without destroying the Roman general's caution.[8] Sallust has managed here to relate all the individual events to one another in terms of either psychological effects or strategic considerations. He has succeeded in narrating three separate strands of action — the Roman camp, Jugurtha's army, and the Roman Senate — without sacrificing attention to the intangible dimensions of his historical understanding.[9]

Turning now to the *Historia fiorentina* and keeping in mind Sallust's mode of organization, one can see that Poggio has taken more from the Roman historian than the simple introductory sentence (noted in Chapter Five). Poggio's narrative would be confused indeed if it depended only on annalistic lines for its organization. The first two books, for instance, cover the thirty-six year period from 1350 to 1386, yet the passage of one year into another is noted on only eight occasions.[10] The contrast with Bruni is striking. The earlier Florentine historian marks two thirds of the years he covers, while in the *Historia fiorentina* only one fourth are explicitly indicated.

Instead of relying on arbitrary temporal divisions, Poggio struc-

---

[8] *Bellum Jugurthinum*, LII–LV.

[9] A second military incident, the siege of Thala, provides another example of Sallust's narrative technique (*Bellum Jugurthinum*, LXXV–LXXX). The historian first describes the siege itself, stressing the difficulties the strategic location of the town presents, together with the arduous and ingenious efforts of Metellus to take it. When the town is finally taken, Sallust transfers the attention of the reader to another field of activity, Lepcis, where internal revolt is threatening the Roman position. He does this by means of a period that relates the two fields in a manner which, while conceptually loose, is stylistically smooth, for the subject of the narrative continues to be a town: "Sed pariter cum capta Thala legati ex oppido Lepci ad Metellum venerant, oratores uti, praesidium praevectumque eo mitteret" (*Bellum Jugurthinum*, LXXVII, 1). Briefly sketching the internal troubles in Lepcis, the historian launches into a digression on the town's origins and its geographical position, and he finally tells an anecdote, connected with Lepcis, which has emulative value as an example of love of country. Only then, with an explicit statement acknowledging the fact of the digression, does he return to Jugurtha's actions taken in response to the loss of Thala and leading to a new battle. Here again one can see Sallust's use of the digression within a coherently narrated series of events, maintaining order through unity of place and subject.

[10] For 1354, 1362, 1364, 1369, 1370, 1371, 1375, and 1378.

tures the *Historia* around specific events, related to one another by a common relevance to his large historical themes. The manner in which he implements this technique is strongly reminiscent of the *Bellum Jugurthinum*. After the introductory period setting forth the scope of the work, he opens the narrative with a brief summary of past events in Florentine history down to the beginning of the Visconti wars. This summary is an obvious device for prefacing the work. Sallust employs it in his two monographs, and both he and Poggio present more than a superficial account of the past events.

Poggio uses this brief section to suggest through his account of specific events some of the intangible elements which will emerge as significant throughout the work. An example taken from institutional history demonstrates this well, even though that sort of history lies outside his scope. After relating the physical founding of Florence and describing its first buildings, the historian turns to consider its constitutional growth. He fixes on four important stages of growth: the division of the city into sections with a consul over each, the importation of a foreign *podestà* to adjudicate disputes, the creation of the captains of the people, and, finally, the establishment of the priorate. This development is not, however, chronicled as an unrelated series of events. Each change is narrated with full attention to its specific import and presented so that it illuminates themes which constitute part of Poggio's historical conceptualization.

The division of the city is prefaced by the remark, "So that the city might be supported by the strength of its citizens . . ."[11] It has already been noted that the growth of Florence into the predominant Tuscan power and the causes of this growth are important concerns for Bruni in the *Historiae Florentini populi*. Poggio devotes much space in the orations which precede the first Visconti war to bringing out precisely this historical process.[12] Here in the prefatory digression he incorporates the general growth of Florence into the narrative structure in connection with a specific event, without any explicit, abstract statement. In explaining the second constitutional change — the importation of a *podestà* — Poggio

---

[11] "Suffulta civibus ac viribus urbe" (196B).

[12] "Sedem hostium suorum et tanquam fomentum malorum omnium delendam esse, nullam esse in Italia praeter Florentiam Guelforum spem praesidiumque, a qua omnis eorum protectio defensioque oriretur. Hanc solam urbem obstare fortunis suis, quae satis dubiae essent nisi eius civitatis vires deprimerentur." (200B–C).

further explores the relation of Florence's power to its institutions, introducing the notions of justice and factional strife.[13]

When Poggio passes on to the third change, he penetrates more deeply the issue of internal discord by imputing blame to one of the factions. In this manner he suggests the Guelf-Florentine partisanship which will characterize the *Historia*.[14] Finally, introducing the creation of the priorate, Poggio drops the question of blame to dwell on the debilitating effects of factional strife and the necessity for institutional checks on it, themes which seem to have been carried over from Bruni's history.[15]

In this very brief section of the introduction to the main body of the work, Poggio has managed to suggest several of the intangible dimensions which he sees pertaining to the reality of internal affairs. He has done this without abstract digressions or lengthy explanations of causality. The entire section uses only a little over a hundred words, and the four changes are described and given significance in the space of three periods.

The beginning of the actual account of the Visconti wars provides an example of the way in which Poggio ties digressions into the narrative. His work is not a history of Florence and Milan but a history of the Florentine people at war. Hence, while a summary of previous Florentine history unrelated to the body of the narrative is justifiable, such a summary of Milanese history is not. Consequently, he explicitly connects the Visconti Archbishop's acquisition of Bologna, an event occurring within the hundred-year scope of the *Historia*, with the previous account of early Florentine history.[16] The acquisition gives Poggio the opportunity to summarize previous Milanese history, and, after promising such a summary, he goes into the origins of the Visconti family, its growth in power, and the threat it poses to Florence. Like Sallust, he uses the digression

---

[13] "Cum vero tum precibus tum factione civium parum justitiae loci esset, hominumque plus quam legum imperia possent externum magistratum quem Potestatem appellarunt ut jus populi redderet accersiverunt" (197A).

[14] "Paulo postque nobilium exagitati injuriis Capitaneum sibi populus et duodecim seniores ac vexilliferos viginti, quorum consilio respublica administraretur instituunt" (197A).

[15] "Diversis deinde bellis civilibus, partim fatigatis partim pulsis civibus ac multorum direptis factionum culpa bonis, Priores artium qui rempublicam regerent anno Christi secundo et octuagessimo post mille ducentos creati sunt" (197A).

[16] "Hic status erat rerum Florentini populi tum armis foris tum domi seditionibus inquieti usque ad annos mille trecentos quinquaginta cum Johannes Vicecomes Archiepiscopus Mediolanensis suae urbis multarumque praeterea imperio potitus a Jacobo Pepulo Bononiam C. C. millibus emit" (198A).

to introduce moral considerations [17] and then picks up the narrative exactly where he had left it.[18]

The two powers whose conflict will dominate the *Historia* have now been properly introduced. Poggio organizes the events of their conflict by dividing them into two general spheres of action, military and diplomatic. He shifts back and forth between them in order to provide interest through *variatio* and also to explore the relation between the events in each sphere. In the case of the first war between Florence and the Visconti, he begins with a series of diplomatic interchanges and orations which bring out the cause of the war (Visconti's greed, recently inflamed by the acquisition of Bologna) and the way in which the Archbishop searches for pretexts to mask the satisfying of his greed. The war ends abruptly with his death, which the historian dates in 1354.[19]

The Archbishop's death is the first event to be dated since the beginning of the war, and it constitutes a typical example of Poggio's handling of such chronological indications in the first two books of the *Historia*. These indications are not imposed arbitrarily to mark off regular intervals of time but are used to identify and underline significant events which substantially change either the military or the diplomatic situation. Poggio's ability to relate specific events to substantial change, of which this use of dates is a fine example, constitutes one of the most imaginative and fruitful elements of his narrative technique, and he maintains the practice in continuing the account after 1354. The second phase of the Visconti war begins when Bernarbo, after his accession to power, foments trouble for Florence by inciting Pisa. After Poggio tells of both the military and diplomatic aspects of Bernarbo's aggressive policy, he gives the date of another specific act, the seizure of Petrabona, which starts the war.[20] The ensuing conflict with Pisa covers two years and is narrated without explicit temporal orientation until peace is made in 1364.[21]

In quick succession Poggio has recounted a set of wars between Florence and two different members of the Visconti family. Now

---

[17] In this case, by means of the previously noted account of the origins of the Guelf-Ghibelline feud.

[18] "Occupata Bononia . . . occasione movendi Florentinis belli . . . sumpta" (199C).

[19] 209A.

[20] 210B.

[21] 215C.

he turns to a war in which Florence becomes involved on a wider scale with both the Holy Roman Emperor and the Church. The manner in which he makes the transition to an essentially different historical situation further illuminates his narrative technique by showing his ability to use superficial spatial (as well as temporal) indications in order to underline significant change. Because of its importance the transitional passage is quoted in full:

"When the chief of the Ghibelline faction at Pisa, Giovanni Agnello, who with the aid and advice of Bernarbo had seized control of the city while peace was being sought at Pescia, came to Lucca after peace had been established to see the Emperor Charles IV, who had himself come back into Italy at the request of Pope Urban, by chance Agnello broke his neck in a fall, and the Pisans, as soon as they heard a rumor of this, arose in revolt and sent his faction into exile, whereupon Pietro Gambacurta, of the opposing faction, assumed control of the city. At Lucca on behalf of the Emperor was the Patriarch of Aquila, a German, who, taking control in the Emperor's name of San Miniato, which had given itself freely to Charles, attacked hostilely some nearby Florentine places with the intention of compelling the Florentines, as indeed happened, to buy peace from the Emperor, which they did for the sum of 50,000 florins when the Emperor, who had gone to the Pope in Rome, returned to Lucca." [22]

The transition is made by means of two complex periods, one concluding the previous war and the second introducing the new war. The two periods have nothing in common but two points: each describes action which takes place in Lucca and each describes action which takes place before the Emperor. Lucca and the

---

[22] "Confecta pace, Johannes Agnellus Pisanus Ghibellinae factionis princeps, qui Bernabovis auxilio, consilioque, dum Pisciae de pace ageretur, urbis tyrannidem occuparat, haud multo post cum Lucam ad Carolum Quartum Imperatorem Urbani Pontificis exhortatione in Italiam reversum venisset, casuque quodam prolapsus coxam fregisset, in exilium a civibus, tumultu populi excitato, ut primum rumor Pisas delatus est, agitur, Petrusque Gambacurta diversarum partium in patriam suorum favore receptus Reipublicae gubernationem suscepti. Lucae pro Imperatore erat Patriarcha Aquileiensis, natione Germanus, qui oppidum Miniate, quod se Carolo sponte dederat, Imperii nomine occupans, vicina Florentinorum loca novo bello hostiliter invasit, ea mente, ut Florentinos, sicuti postmodum accidit, ad redimendam ab Imperatore pacem impelleret; quae paulo post cum Imperator, qui Romam ad Pontificem ierat, Lucam rediisset, datis Imperatori aureorum millibus quinquaginta, secuta est." (215D–216B.) The translation has sought to reproduce the actual structure of the Latin periods at the expense of proper English form. This manner of articulating the parts of the narrative, while reminiscent of Sallust (see note 9 above), is clumsy and grossly inferior to the narrative technique of the Roman historian.

Emperor are relevant neither to anything which happened in the Pisan war nor to anything which will transpire in the subsequent war. The historian has, however, used these concrete and specific elements to connect the two wars, themselves narrated as conceptualized historical events.[23] In his mode of articulating the transition between the two events one finds the same reliance on specific phenomena which characterizes his manner of interpolating digressions.

Having made the transition, Poggio proceeds to narrate the war over San Miniato, beginning with such military events as the Florentine siege and the inhabitants' resistance under the urging of Bernarbo. The historian then passes to the diplomatic sphere with a description of Florence's search for allies. After the diplomatic situation is established, he returns to military affairs, recounting the fall of San Miniato. Since this is the focal point of the war, the date is given.[24] Finally Poggio outlines the diplomatic maneuvers leading to the peace, which is also dated.[25] The book concludes with a brief summary — hardly more than a list of commanders — of a Papal-Milanese war, providing a background for the events of the second book, which treats the war of Eight Saints.

The second book, though it deals with a single war larger in

[23] Poggio's attention to tangible factors like geography, which is ostensibly of little significance in understanding any of the intangible elements found in the *Historia*, is constant in these first books. Occasionally his interest in considerations of place has a deeper significance. In the war with Giovanni Visconti with which the narrative opens, the historian carefully traces the Milanese route as the army changes camp (203B–C). The importance of this emerges when the Milanese forces are later forced into a trap in a valley. Further on in the work Poggio meticulously traces the respective routes of Hawkwood and the Duke of Armagnac as they come to meet each other, and here again the tactical significance of the routes is clear (260C–261A).

There are occasions, however, when the significance of such a discussion is less obvious. For instance, in the first war with Bernarbo, Poggio follows a foraging expedition of Britons in great detail as it passes through Pistoia and Prato and into the Valombrosa. He continues to trace its route as it passes down the Mugello toward the sea, continues (though beaten by a band of Germans) through Fiesole to Florence, crosses the Arno and descends into Siena through the Val d'Arne to Arezzo and Cortona, and finally goes back through Siena and into Pisa (213A–C). In spite of the wealth of geographical detail, Poggio makes no observations on the duration of the expedition, its purpose, its success, or its effect. The narration has no ostensible relation to the issues in the war with Pisa, then in progress, except that it begins and ends in that city.

Other examples of this concern for geographical detail are found in this section: see the account of the route of British mercenaries during the war of Eight Saints (233B–C), which also makes no mention of duration. In later sections wars are frequently narrated as troop movements (see 390B–391B and 431A–B).

[24] 218B.

[25] 219B.

scope than any of those included in the first book, is organized along similar lines. Chronological indications are found only at the beginning of the war [26] and at the conclusion of peace.[27] Military and diplomatic themes are developed alternately and interrelated. The book concludes with a brief summary of the years between the end of the war and the accession to power of Giangaleazzo, who will dominate the next book.

Poggio, then, demonstrates from the very start of his history an ability to order the events of the narrative in a manner independent from the technique of his predecessor. Bruni attempts to narrate the intangible dimension of his historical view directly, forcing this dimension into the mold of annalistic history. Poggio not only dispenses with the annalistic division but abandons the attempt to express intangible factors directly. In the *Historia fiorentina* these factors are narrated only in connection with the individual events which illustrate them and give them specific meaning. Poggio's achievement in developing this narrative technique harks back to the Roman historian, Sallust, and, like Sallust, Poggio sacrifices a certain amount of chronological precision. Within the historical periods narrated it is often difficult to locate events exactly in time. Rough chronological order is nevertheless maintained, and the confusion that does arise is more than vindicated by the augmented attention to larger historical constructions and by the ease with which such constructions are made to carry the historian's basic concepts, whether these are analytical or moralistic in substance.

This technique remains Poggio's basic organizational tool in the final six books of the *Historia fiorentina*. He begins the Giangaleazzo war with a long introductory section, first stating that the peace of Italy has been disturbed by Giangaleazzo. This is followed by a digression on the Visconti's antecedents and actions down to the outbreak of hostilities. After establishing the Milanese leader's basic character and motivations through an account of his previous acts, Poggio describes Florence's alienation of Siena, first through the seizure of Arezzo and then by the acceptance of Montepulciano as a colony. This is the specific occasion for the war, which is explained further through a series of diplomatic interchanges and

[26] "Bellum inde difficile ac periculosum anno quinto ac septuagesimo supra mille trecentos secutum triennio ferme inter Florentinos et praesides Gregorii Pontificis gestum" (221A).

[27] "Ad sextum Kalendas Aprilis anni octavi et septuagesimi supra mille trecentos hora noctis secunda" (240D).

orations, each series followed by military operations appropriate to the given diplomatic situation. Finally, the war itself is introduced and dated.[28] In following the course of the struggle Poggio adopts the same alternation between military and diplomatic affairs which he has observed in the earlier books.

Although the historian organizes this section on Florence's war with Giangaleazzo in basically the same way in which he orders the earlier section, he betrays the influence of his source material more clearly than in Books I and II. Not only is he relying more heavily on Bruni in recounting the war, but he is drawing from a part of the *Historiae Florentini populi* which reflects Bruni's most sophisticated organizational techniques and his most mature historical conceptualization. The chief indication of Bruni's influence on Poggio is the increased use of an annalistic mode of presentation. Fewer than one fourth of the transitions from year to year are marked in the first two books of the *Historia*. In Book III, which covers mainly the period from 1390 to 1401, more than two thirds are so marked.[29] Furthermore, some of the years are introduced with quite minor events which do not support the structure of the war at all.[30]

On closer examination, however, it appears that Poggio has in fact imposed his own form on the war, even while accepting Bruni's more rigorous dating procedure, for Poggio is unwilling to use the technique of moving into a new year without referring to some significant event. Bruni introduces 1393 by saying that nothing worth mentioning has happened, by which he means that nothing worth mentioning has happened abroad, since he does describe some important disturbances occurring within the city of Florence during the year.[31] Poggio, whose concept of narrative structure demands that specific events be associated with dates, avoids the statement that nothing has happened. Instead, he passes directly to domestic affairs in order to keep the annalistic form and narrates the internal

[28] "His itaque initiis nonagesimo post mille trecentos anno cum bellum quod in duodecim annos protractum est, coeptum esset variis vero utrinque praeliis ac rapinis animi irritati belloque intenti essent" (255C–D).

[29] The years 1390, 1391, 1392, 1398, 1399, 1400, 1401. This proportion is identical with that found in Bruni's work taken as a whole, although it has already been seen that Bruni delineates every year in this section on the Giangaleazzo war.

[30] For instance, 1398 is introduced by a minor military action on the part of the count of Poppi (279C); Poggio takes the material from Bruni, who introduces the year by the same event (III, xi, 244). Even here Poggio tries to blur the chronological line by mentioning the change of year at the end of the period in much the same way Bruni makes the transition from 1396 to 1397 (III, xi, 230).

[31] III, xi, 192–194.

sedition as the first thing happening in that year, even though this topic does not properly fall within his scope.[32]

To introduce the other years in the section Poggio has chosen peace treaties, or such important shifts in the diplomatic picture as the fall of Bologna. Thus he does not arbitrarily mark the beginning of the year, as Bruni inevitably does, but uses the annalistic form to give a definite temporal status to an event taking place in a particular year.

A final indication of Poggio's independence from Bruni should be noted. It has been observed that Bruni tends to break the war down into separate sections — two periods of peace in which psychological realities predominate in the narrative, and two periods of war in which strategic and tactical considerations are uppermost. In Poggio's *Historia fiorentina*, however, military and diplomatic events are presented alternately, and tactical and psychological considerations are expressed in the same event. Bruni's practice of alternating tactical and psychological dimensions in the last four books of his work has been seen as an improvement over his previous narrative technique. Paradoxically, Poggio develops the war as a more convincing unity by failing to follow the earlier historian.

Little purpose would be served by describing Poggio's narrative further, for no innovations in technique emerge, a fact hardly surprising considering both the speed with which the work was written and the age of the historian at the time of its composition. His principal source beyond Bruni is the *Decades* of Flavio Biondo. Poggio follows the subject matter of this work quite regularly, often at the expense of clarity, for Biondo is frequently unclear and disorganized. Two examples of Poggio's divergence from Biondo's order will show that even here the Florentine historian has maintained his original structural principles intact.

Biondo introduces the third decade with a long, abstract section on the difficulties of translating vernacular terms and fifteenth-century practices into Latin words and classical forms. To illustrate these difficulties he describes at some length the way in which the meaning of the word "emperor" has changed since Roman times.[33] He goes on to consider changes in military terminology and place names.[34] When he finally does turn to the specific events of the

---

[32] "Pax foris parta seditiones domesticas Florentiae eo qui secutus est anno excitavit" (271B).
[33] Biondo, *Decades*, 254.
[34] Biondo, *Decades*, 254v–255.

narrative, he presents them not for their intrinsic interest but as illustrations of the problems he has abstractly described.[35] In this way concrete data in the *Decades* are subordinated to general considerations.

Poggio reverses Biondo's order. None of his sections opens with an abstract discussion comparable to that found at the beginning of the third decade. Not until he is able to introduce the subject in connection with a specific imperial coronation does he explore the process whereby the imperial title has changed radically in meaning since its origin among the soldiers of republican Rome. Such an occasion arises when Sigismund passes through Tuscany on his way to be crowned by the Pope. Even then Poggio mentions the coronation only after describing the emperor's journey through Italy, explicitly introducing the subject with the statement, "This seems to be the very place, after Sigismund has been mentioned, in which to say a few words about the manner of crowning emperors." [36] Such a statement reveals the historian's acute sense of the demands imposed on him by the narrative structure he has chosen. He feels it necessary to relate all abstract discussions to concrete events falling naturally within the scope of his history. He uses the digression both to castigate the pretensions of the emperors and popes and to endow the passage with contemporary relevance by describing the coronation ceremonies he himself has seen, returning by means of an explicit statement to the narrative — to the exact point at which he had left it.[37]

A second instance of alteration by Poggio of the account in the *Decades* shows his greater concern for interrelating the various parts of the narrative. Biondo stops abruptly in the course of recounting Carmignola's entry into Brescia and, without explanation or explicit justification, begins to describe the city.[38] Poggio, after narrating the entry of Carmignola, also describes the city. The Florentine historian, however, carefully explains the reason for the digression in such a way as to give the reader an indication of the type of description he is about to encounter: "Because this city was defended with great energy and much passion and taken only after a long

---

[35] "Tantas itaque scribendi difficultates quo superemus modo sequentia demonstrabunt" (Biondo, *Decades*, 256).

[36] "Locus ipse postulare videtur, posteaquam Sigismundi mentio incidit, ut paucis de hoc novo Imperatoris coronandi moro disseramus" (380B).

[37] "Nunc ad institutum revertamur. Post Sigismundi ex Lucensium agro discessum . . ." (381C).

[38] Biondo, *Decades*, 279v.

siege, it seemed necessary to describe its site in a few words so that it should be clear to the reader how the city was fortified so strongly that it could only be conquered with great difficulties." [39] The description, then, promises tactical overtones, and in comparison with Biondo's brief and basically irrelevant outline Poggio gives the reader an adequate understanding of the difficulties of the ensuing struggle, difficulties ranging from the size of the city to the disposition of its various factions. Though most of this information can be found somewhere in Biondo's work, Poggio sets it all down together in response to clearly defined questions which arise from the narrative structure itself.

To summarize the nature of Poggio's organizational principles, he adopts a technique somewhat more flexible than Bruni's. Abandoning the annalistic form, he organizes events around military and diplomatic categories in such a way that he can concentrate on whole wars as historical constructs. He utilizes specific facts to move between these constructs and to digress within them in order to bring out both his historical analysis and his moralizing judgments. His mode of presentation is strongly influenced by Sallust.

Turning to the orations in the *Historia fiorentina*, it is not surprising to find that Poggio has generally followed Bruni's practice. The orations are constructed along classical lines, preserving the tripartite structure found both in Bruni's *Historiae* and in the Roman models. Many of them are very reminiscent of Bruni in exploiting, according to classical form, the relation between moral and practical considerations. The Florentine attempt to justify to the King of France the seizure of Pisa is an excellent example of this usage.[40] The orators begin by stressing the moral position of the Florentines, who, having legitimately purchased the city from its former ruler, consider it to be theirs by right.[41] The traditional hatred of the Pisans for the Florentines is rehearsed, after which the oration turns to the practical features of the situation, stressing the difficulties the King would encounter by intervening. In conclusion, the Florentine legate returns to moral considerations by mentioning the traditional friendship between Florence and France. The oration made to the defeated Pisans also combines moral and practical

[39] "Huius urbis quoniam summis viribus maximoque odio defensa et expugnata longiori obsidione fuit necessarium videtur situm paucis describere, ut quae urbem tam munitam tam validam difficultas expugnandi fuerit legentibus constet" (340D).

[40] 300D–301B.

[41] "Emptionem optimo jure factam, pecuniam persolutam" (300D).

ideas, dwelling on the extent to which Florence has sought to defend its own liberty in attacking the city but including suggestions that the victory was due to divine favor.[42]

The orations in Poggio's history occasionally provide commentary on the narrative, bringing out historical realities which would otherwise remain implicit in the events. Both Visconti's oration to the Tuscan Ghibellines [43] and the later Milanese mission to the Pisans [44] describe the strategic position of Florence, a position which has been briefly narrated and which constitutes the underlying cause for the war. Giovanni Ricci, suggesting to the Florentine signoria necessary preparations for the threatening war with Giangaleazzo, reviews the events leading to the war, explicitly interpreting them as revelations of Giangaleazzo's hostile intentions.[45] All of these events have been previously narrated, and Giangaleazzo's intentions have been implied, but the oration serves to underscore and explicate them.[46]

Poggio also writes dialogue orations, paired speeches which deal with separate aspects of the same problem. It has been noted that when Bruni uses this technique he frequently devotes one speech of the pair to an exposition of the moral ramifications of a proposed action, while in the other he treats the practical issues involved. Many of Poggio's dialogues are constructed in like manner. For example, the papal orators, seeking to stir up internal troubles in Florence, tell the populace that the war is being used by the rulers of the city to hold the citizens in servitude.[47] The Florentine reply ignores this charge, stressing the moral fact that Florence has always been faithful to the Pope and does not deserve this sort of treat-

---

[42] 303A–304B. This oration is taken from either Palmieri or Capponi. Poggio neglects to render the reply of the Pisans. Other examples of such a commingling of factors can be found in Cosimo dei Medici's speech before the Venetians, where he asks for payment of Sforza's salary on the ground that nothing is more reprehensible than faithlessness and also because of the possibility that Sforza will desert to the Milanese if he is not paid (388D–389A). A further example can be found in one of the few nondiplomatic orations. This is a speech before the Florentine signoria seeking to persuade the people to accept an alliance with Bernarbo against the Pope. It begins with an abstract praise of liberty and proceeds from this moral consideration to take up the practical strengths of such an alliance, including the weakness of the Pope in Italy due to the hatred his pride and vainglory have instilled in the hearts of his subjects (224A–226A).

[43] 200B–201B.

[44] 205A–205B.

[45] 252A–253D.

[46] In like manner Paolo Guinigi's speech to the Sienese requesting help against Florence serves to underline Florentine aggressions in Tuscany (360D–361B).

[47] 237C–238B.

ment.[48] Another instance of this form is found in the dialogue between Florence and Venice when Florence is seeking help against Milan. The Florentines try to show that when Filippo Maria has beaten their city he will turn on Venice, and that consequently the Serenissima in its own best interests should enter into an alliance against Visconti.[49] The brief Venetian reply declines the alliance solely on the moral ground that the city cannot break faith by dissolving its longstanding agreement with Filippo Maria.[50]

The most sophisticated of the paired orations involves an argument within the Florentine signoria over the advisability of a war with Lucca. Poggio is as concerned with this question as Bruni is, and he is just as opposed to the war.[51] Rainaldo Albizzi delivers the speech in favor of attacking Lucca, making three practical points: Guinigi hates Florence, Lucca occupies a strategic position, and the war will be an easy one. He seeks to prove his points, however, by an uncritical use of Guinigi's status as a tyrant. The Lucchese leader hates Florence because tyrants hate republics, which will cause him to make use of his strategic position to embarrass the city by fomenting revolt in Pisa. It will be easy to beat him, however, because tyrants are hated by their subjects and therefore the Lucchese will not support him.[52]

In the second part of the dialogue Niccolò Uzzano defends the position that Florence should not initiate the war by elaborating a single moral principle: a just peace is to be preferred to an unjust and aggressive war. He explains this ideal, however, in a manner which provides an exact contrast to Albizzi's oration, for he brings a great number of specific practical considerations to bear on this general moral problem. He dwells on the present state of exhaustion in which Florence finds itself; he mentions the unpopular high points to the ambiguities of the diplomatic situation. If we attack Lucca unjustly, he says, we shall certainly invite the intervention

---

[48] 328B–C.

[49] 333D–334B.

[50] 334B–C.

[51] "Nam tunc ambigebat tanto desiderio confecta pace Florentinis quietem ab armis longinquam fore, eosque adversos ab omni bellorum strepitu in otio quieturos, sed aut fatis ita jubentibus, aut civium quibus Reipublicae damna questui erant libidine novis calamitatibus aditus est patefactus et qui enixius quam reliqui pacem appetiverant, bellorum sumptus improbantes, quique praeterita pericula tum varias fortunae vices horrere debebant, inconsulto impetu, minimeque justo incoepto ad bellum Lucense haudquaquam necessarium biennio fere praeter omnium spem prosilere" (353C). Poggio's pro-Medici sympathies are most apparent in this section, where he specifically places the blame for the war on the Albizzi faction.

[52] 354D–356D.

of some other power into Tuscan affairs.[53] In its analysis of moral categories in terms of political realities this speech of Poggio's need bow to none of Bruni's.

Poggio, however, does not consistently devote dialogue orations to the interweaving of moral and practical strands of argument. In some cases both speeches are frankly and uncritically moralistic. An example of this sort is found early in the work, when the Florentines complain to the Milanese commander about what they consider to be unprovoked aggression. The orator from Florence notes the lack of a just cause for the war and the fact that the city has sought in no way to offend the Archbishop.[54] The commander replies not with any practical consideration but with the statement that Florence is guilty of unjust government.[55] A diplomatic interchange between Florence and King Ladislaus proceeds along similar lines. Again the Florentines complain that Ladislaus has no just cause for the war and seek to remind him of Florence's past favors, which are deserving of gratitude. The King replies by simply expressing his interest in maintaining the peace of Italy.[56]

Orations of this nature are clearly less valuable in filling out the narrative than the more complex type previously discussed. They can only be understood in relation to the unanalytical element of Poggio's historical vision, that element which devotes itself to the elaboration of implicit moral ideals as part of the didactic value of history. One finds a similar concern to embellish moral categories in Poggio's single orations. For example, the oration of the Florentine legates to Gregory XI, which Rubinstein has shown to be taken from Bruni's *Historiae Florentini populi*,[57] is, in spite of superficial similarities, quite different from the one which Bruni presents. Bruni's speech emphasizes the necessity of good government, saying that it is the mismanagement of the Pope's legates which has caused his states to revolt and that in supporting these states Florence is really serving the Pope's interests. By contrast, the oration in the taxes which will be necessary to prosecute the war; and finally, he *Historia fiorentina* takes on the nature of a panegyric to liberty, describing the problems involved in defending it, tracing the long

[53] 356D–360B.

[54] 202A–B.

[55] "Non enim aequum esse bonos et bene de Republica meritos cives urbe per factionem inimicorum pelli" (202B–C).

[56] 307D–308B. The interchange between Ladislaus and the Sienese, which follows shortly, is similarly devoid of practical arguments (308C–309B).

[57] Rubinstein, "Poggio," p. 16.

history of Florentine liberty, and maintaining that in defense of this freedom Florence is resisting the Pope.[58] Both Bruni and Poggio are committed to the ideal of liberty, but at least in this oration Poggio is more concerned with extolling its virtues than with showing how it constitutes a valid and practicable historical reality. In a similarly uncritical identification of liberty with moral good, Poggio has the Pisans plead not to be sold to Milan on the ground that no one should lose his liberty in such a manner.[59]

As a final observation on Poggio's use of orations, it must be acknowledged that he seeks to integrate them more convincingly into the narrative than does Bruni. The very first oration in the work serves as an excellent example. This is a brief statement by Giovanni Visconti to the Ghibelline leaders of Tuscany and Emilia, maintaining that he is attacking Florence chiefly because it is the leading Guelf power in Tuscany. This oration is related to the narrative in several ways. In the first place, in showing that the Florentine hegemony is a factor in the war, it explicates the significance of previously narrated Florentine actions. This use of orations is, of course, common to both Poggio and Bruni and has already been discussed. Secondly, the speech itself is a concrete illustration of a subsequent suggestion by Poggio that the Archbishop's move to help the Ghibellines is only a pretext masking his own ambition.[60] Finally, the oration as an historical event in itself is given a definite effect in the context of other historical events: it convinces the Ghibellines to act.[61] The fact that Poggio's orations are more closely connected to the narrative than are Bruni's does not compensate for their frequent analytical deficiencies; here Poggio's narrative technique suffers in comparison with his predecessor's.

In describing battles, on the other hand, Poggio has developed an instrument which incorporates both the analytical and moralizing dimensions of his historical vision into a single form. In addition to many simple foraging expeditions and minor raids, there are ten major battles set out in the *Historia*, including two naval engagements and two sieges.

The first major battle in the work, fought in 1364, is between

[58] 229B–233A.

[59] 279A.

[60] The Archbishop says in the orations, "Hanc solam urbem obstare fortunis suis" (200C).

[61] "Eiusmodi hortationibus incensi omnes, Archiepiscopi consilia sequenda decrevere" (201B).

the Florentine troops under Malatesta and the Pisans under Hawkwood.[62] Poggio begins his account of the battle by noting the situation which precipitates it. The Florentines, seeing that the enemy camp has relaxed its discipline, hope to catch their opponents unawares. The Pisan condottiere, however, corrects this laxity before the battle begins. Next the historian proceeds to a description of the Florentine battle lines. The battle itself is introduced by an abstract statement to the effect that it is long and hard fought, which is explained by the mental states of the two sides: the Pisans are elated after an earlier victory, and the Florentines are eager to avenge their recent defeat. Poggio describes the combat itself in a single period and, without stating what causes the Pisan defeat, concludes the fighting by saying simply that after an hour's vigorous combat the enemy line breaks. The aftermath of the battle is described in three aspects: first, the casualty statistics are given; secondly, its strategic significance is suggested by considering the question whether to proceed to an immediate attack on the city of Pisa; finally, descriptions are given of the honors awarded to the victorious Malatesta and the celebrations within Florence. The battle ·is obviously narrated in accordance with the humanistic canons for this form, noted in Chapter Four.[63]

In recounting military events, Poggio is clearly concerned with analyzing their significance within the political and psychological themes that are part of his historical vision. This concern is shown in the previously described battle by his interest in the mental states of the opposing sides and by his attention to the strategic significance of the battle.

In other battles recounted in the *Historia*, Poggio's interest in analytical narration can be seen in the means that he uses to orient the battle in terms of a precise time. In no case does he mention a time or date for a battle without explicating the relevance of the specific chronological indication. For instance, in narrating the battle between Armagnac and the Milanese,[64] the historian mentions that it takes place at noon and in the middle of the summer. The midday summer heat is shown to be a decisive factor in wearing down the French troops and defeating their attempt to charge a great distance on foot.[65] On another occasion, when a Florentine

62 214B–215B.
63 See chap. iv at n. 121.
64 262A–263A.
65 "Aetatis tempus erat et increbuerat aestus" (262B).

army attempting to relieve the siege of Zaganara is defeated,[66] Poggio mentions that the Florentines meet the enemy at daybreak. This is given immediate tactical significance by showing how the besieging army is taken by surprise — some are eating, others are cleaning up, and most are unarmed.[67] Finally, in relating a battle between Piccinino and the Florentines, the historian provides both the Roman dating (the third of the Kalends of July) and the Christian dating (the feast of Peter and Paul).[68] This, too, is given immediate tactical significance by showing Niccolò's hope that the Florentine troops will be lax because of the feast day.

The same attention to tactical significance is seen in Poggio's geographical indications. Describing Hawkwood's retreat after the Duke of Armagnac has been defeated, he begins by saying that the English mercenary captain pitches his camp near Cremona; the location is immediately followed by a tactical description of the field, creek, and hedges which separate him from the enemy forces.[69] In recounting the battle between Piccinino and the Florentines, the fact that the Florentines are camped in the middle of a four-mile plain is noted, and then it is observed that therefore the dust of the advancing army can be seen afar off. A surprise attack such as Piccinino has in mind is thus almost impossible to execute successfully.[70]

Poggio's attention to analysis is reflected not only in the way in which he relates battles to specific times and places but in the explicit tactical lessons he frequently draws from them. In commenting on Armagnac's defeat at the hands of the Milanese, he says that it proves counsel to be more valuable than pure strength in war.[71] In describing the Florentine relief expedition to Zaganara, he comments explicitly on the dangers of relying on fortune in war.[72]

One aspect of Poggio's technique in narrating military affairs, which constitutes a very small part of Bruni's narrative, is his attention to exemplary conduct. In the previously described battle be-

[66] 330C–332A.
[67] 331A–B.
[68] 412C–415A.
[69] 263C.
[70] 413B.
[71] "Suoque docuit exemplo plus momenti in belli victoria consilium praebere, quam vires" (263A). A similar lesson is drawn from Hawkwood's subsequent escape (265B).
[72] "Cuius prudentia admodum desiderata est cum neque loco neque tempore rem fortunae commisisset" (331C).

tween the Pisans and Florentines, much of the space devoted to summing up the results of the conflict deals with the honors bestowed on the victors. This concern with the narration of glory is clearly part of the moralistic dimension of Poggio's historical view, and, in keeping with his general narrative practice, he seeks to narrate single battles in such a way that they manifest both the moralistic and analytical dimensions.

A final aspect of Poggio's battle narratives needs some elaboration. In describing the actual physical clash of the engagement, he avoids to a great degree any suggestion of sensual experience. He depicts the actual combat of the Pisan battle in the following manner: "The clamor grew on both sides and swords flashed; with great force and bitter combat the battle was fought at close quarters and foot to foot." [73] In this description only one sensual element is found, the flashing of swords, and the verb used here can also mean any sort of rough, uneven movement. Furthermore, there is in Poggio's description of battles no attempt to seize upon any detail and vitalize it through an evocation of its sensual dimensions so that it will leave an indelible impression on the reader. [74]

Poggio's refusal of detail, his decision to exclude sensual elements from the narrative, has already been noted in Bruni's historical writing. The later historian, also like Bruni, declines to include physical features in his descriptions of persons. He, too, tends to conceptualize in his descriptions of buildings and objects, mentioning size but not color, geometrical shape but not texture. Geography is described only to the extent that tactical considerations render it necessary.

This is not to say that the humanists have no sense of the value of significant details. On rare occasions both Bruni and Poggio elicit such details with a sure hand. For example, Bruni, drawing on a collection of miscellaneous anecdotes in Villani, includes the following passage after his account of the fall of the great banking houses in 1345: "While the city was preoccupied with these cares, a wolf entered through the Porta Collina at midday and ran through the city. He wandered around a great deal in the section across the Arno. When the clamor which hunters make followed him, he left

---

[73] "Clamor ingens utrinque increbuerat, utrinque gladii micabant, summa vi asperoque marte cominus collato pede certabatur" (214C–D).

[74] The lack of sensual elements in his account of Giangaleazzo's burning ships at Mantua has already been noted (see chap. v at n. 20).

by the other gate and was caught outside the Porta Pisana. On the same day the sign of the people, sculpted over the door of the Palazzo della Signoria, fell down of its own accord." [75] Poggio uses the wolf motif for a different effect. Hawkwood, at one point in his retreat from the Milanese, receives a caged wolf from the opposing condottiere, to whom Hawkwood replies that wolves are known for their ability to escape from traps.[76] Hawkwood proceeds, of course, to do just that.

In spite of an occasional use of concrete detail, given vitality and substance in sensual terms, humanist historians in general are too much interested in the conceptual elements of history to give much thought to its tangible dimension. Even the most specific events remain little more than illustrations of either causal principles or moral categories. The events take on no reality in themselves. In Bruni's history this lack is not so conspicuous, for he undertakes to narrate intangible realities directly in terms of such generalizations as *suspicio*. Relying on fixed chronological periods to provide the structure for the events of the narrative, he avoids the necessity of focusing attention on concrete phenomena. Poggio, however, seeks to evolve a narrative technique which can express his view of the intangible dimension of history in and through specific events. Here the lifelessness of these events is more noticeable, and it militates decidedly against the effectiveness of his technique.

In conclusion, Poggio, while acquiring a coherent historical understanding, weakens the rigor of his analysis by the addition of a moralizing element. By seeking to combine both of these elements in one narrative, he has, nevertheless, developed a style at once more supple than Bruni's and more aptly designed to relate the specific events of history to the general values and insights found by the humanists in such events. In the process, however, the humanist inattention to concrete detail emerges with still greater clarity.

Poggio rewrote only the last fifty years of Bruni's history. The next historian of Florence, Bartolommeo della Scala, was suffi-

___

[75] "Solicita ob eam rem civitate, lupus, medio die, porta Collina ingressus, per urbem decurrit. Peragrata maxima trans Arnum parte cum clamor, venantium more, illum prosequeretur, tandem, egressus alia porta via pisana oppressus est. Eadem quoque die signa populi ad publicas aedes supra portam sculpta sua cecidere." (II, vii, 328.)

[76] 263E–264A.

ciently dissatisfied with the work of his predecessors that he decided to start again from the beginning, writing a comprehensive history of Florence from its origins, using new analytical tools and new narrative techniques in an attempt finally to produce a humanist history of Florence which would bear comparison with the great histories of Rome.

Chapter Seven
Bartolommeo della Scala and the *Historia Florentinorum*

In that small part of his proposed work which Scala was able to finish before his death, he betrays an explicit emotional commitment to the subject of his narrative which sharply distinguishes the *Historia Florentinorum* from the histories of Bruni and Poggio.[1] This personal involvement emerges in the first chapter, when Scala talks of the barbarian invasions of Italy after the decline of the

[1] The observation made in chap. i that little modern scholarship has been devoted to Scala needs elaboration here. Excellent studies of particular aspects of Scala's life and thought are certainly available, and Rubinstein's work on the dating and sources of the *Historia Florentinorum* has been an invaluable aid in the preparation of this chapter. Parronchi's study of Scala's epigraphs for his own palace should also be mentioned ("The Language of Humanism and of Sculpture," *Journal of the Warburg and Courtauld Institutes*, 27 [1964], 108–136), although that scholar seems a little too willing to accept without question Scala's mediocrity.

What is lacking is a general assessment of Scala's place in the intellectual history of the fifteenth century – a deficiency which the present chapter is not designed to fill. The Florentine State Archives possess a number of Scala's letters, and the National Library at Florence has several of his works in manuscript. The material is thus available for a reassessment of his contribution, but to attempt such a project would certainly be out of place in a study of the tradition of humanist historiography in Florence.

In fact, certain problems which arise in connection with Scala make it inadvisable to attempt a thoroughgoing discussion even of his contribution to historical writing. The lack of biographical information, for instance, makes generalizations about his chancellorship dangerous (see chap. i, n. 16). The foremost of these problems, however, arises from the fact that Scala was certainly influenced by humanist historians not in the Florentine tradition. He used Platina and Flavio Biondo as sources for the *Historia* and was probably acquainted with other humanist historians such as Valla and those of the Venetian school.

It is by no means inconceivable that the peculiarities of the *Historia* can be partly explained by Scala's exposure to these other historians, and any serious discussion of his historical technique would have to explore this possibility in some depth. That Scala was influenced by non-Florentine historians, however, does not affect the fact that his history reveals certain problems within the tradition of Florentine humanist historiography, and it is upon these problems that this chapter will focus. To attempt more would be to distort the scope of this book and lose sight of the very development that I am seeking to expose.

Empire in the west. "I can scarcely write this without feeling great grief as such slaughter, such ruin, such conflagration, and so many overturned cities come into my mind" [2] — for who can restrain his tears when he sees such a noble land reduced to such degradation and begging in vain for help? [3] Scala expresses his solicitude again when describing Totila's devastation of Florence. Calling upon fifteenth-century Florentines to avoid a similar disaster, he voices his shame at having to describe his own city in such a fallen state.[4] This time a note of pessimism and impotence finds its way into Scala's comment, as he wonders whether his contemporaries have any real control over the forces which he sees threatening the existence of his city.[5]

This personal element cannot be explained by simple patriotism, by Scala's feelings for the city in which he had achieved such political and cultural recognition. It can only be fully understood as a part of his general approach to the task of historical writing. He begins the Proèmio to the *Historia Florentinorum* by complaining about the thanklessness of writing history: "Great indeed seems the labor and small the reward in writing history. Indeed, where the mere exposition of events is one's task, wherever one errs he is blamed, and whatever praise is forthcoming, the reader gives to the sources." [6] This is not a sentiment unfamiliar to students of humanist historiography, since Bruni had voiced a similar disappointment about the rewards of writing history when he translated Plutarch into Latin.[7] Like Bruni, Scala bemoans the fact that an

---

[2] "Quod ego vix queo sine igenti dolore meminisse cum tot cladium tot ruinarum tot incensarum eversarum ac desolatarum urbium venit in mentem" (Scala, *Historia Florentinorum*, p. 20).

[3] "Nam quis etiam lachrimas continere queat miserabilesque singulius cui sit ante oculos Italia Regina quondam et domina provinciarum exterarumque omnium regionum lugubri iam ac lacero indumento obsita squalida miseriesque frustra questibus suorum acclamans auxilium" (p. 20).

[4] "Taedet jam me pudetque rerum nostrarum; multum addit ad scribendi laborem tristitia animi maerorque quidam incomparabilis, qui per tot tantasque Italiae ruinas etsi per longissima intervalla gradientem pene conficiunt: verum tamen enitendum est" (p. 39).

[5] "Utinam falsa jamjam augurer quam vereor ne rursum in vos ipsi armetis eos qui e possessione dulcissimae atque omnium clarissimae Patriae vos ejiciant, dum ita inter vos adeo atque impie uter tandem imperet latius, obstinatissime decernitis, quamquam in vestra forsitan non est manu, ut mitius jam agatis cum Italia, quam ita vastatis, diripitis, incenditis, et ruinae novae exponitis" (p. 40).

[6] "Multi profecto laboris at gloriae non multae videtur esse historiam scribere. Quippe ubi praeter rerum meram explicationem nihil sit tuum, at si quid insit errati, facile te arguant legentes, laudem vero ab auctoribus ad res libenter transferent." (p. 1.)

[7] See chap. iv at note 35.

historian has no opportunity to be creative; [8] also like Bruni he clearly sees his own role as an important one. Further on in the Proèmio he says, "What, however, can be considered a more difficult task of writing than to undertake laboriously the effort of finding things either which do not exist in a place where they can be readily found, since they are far from our memory and knowledge, or which are found to be disorganized, with no order of time, place, things, or persons, almost neglected, and certainly confused by some uncertain narrative exposition?" [9]

In his Proèmio Scala introduces his commitment to Florence only after dwelling at some length on the obstacles to accurate research and a clear presentation of materials. Maintaining that the affairs of his own city are as worthy of mention as those of Rome itself, although they have suffered from inadequate historians,[10] he shows how his work will be more effectively didactic because Florentine readers will be directly concerned with its subject matter.[11] The close relationship between Scala's personal commitments and his goal of accurate and thorough historical writing emerges clearly in the preface to the *Historia Florentinorum*.

The body of the work betrays both Scala's concern for the significance of his material and his desire to avoid the simple chronicling of facts. For example, when he finishes his account of Charlemagne's reconstruction of Florence, he briefly turns his attention to events between the death of Charlemagne and the accession of the Ottonian emperors.[12] His account is, in fact, little more than a list of the emperors who reigned in this interval, but when he

---

[8] "Caeteris in artibus ad hoc, quamtum velis valet arbitrium, atque evagari tibi tuo modo licet, si quid novi adferas amirantur, saepe etiam cum alii invenerint. Tu sive ea quid expoliveris sive tradideris scriptis tuis paulo elegantius, solidam ipsi gloriam retuleris." (p. 1.)

[9] "Ad laborem autem scribendi si reperiendarum quoque rerum difficilior opera accesserit, quae vel non extent unde sumas, quae a nostra memoria et cognitione recesserunt, vel quae notata reperias ordinem non servent ullum, neque modum temporis, loci, rerum personarum, aut neglecta penitus, aut certe quae confusa quae incerta ratione scribendi, quid excogitari potest negotiosius?" (pp. 1–2).

[10] "Nostrae, arbitror, res magnae sane ac memorabiles fuerunt, sed aut injuria temporum, aut hominum nostrorum negligentia, antiquiora praesertim maiori ex parte periere" (p. 2).

[11] "Fit autem natura, ut amet sua magis quisque quam aliena, quae quamvis et ipsa studiose leguntur, praesertim scripta decenter, ut est genus humanum natura cognoscendi avidum, tamen plus esse in his momenti, quae plus amamus, solet, sive de virtute, sive de vitiis habenda oratio sit" (p. 2). "Atque illud in historia primum est; quidquid agas, sive id publicum sive privatum, rerum omnium suppeditabit, exempla, quidque melius factu sit, quod etiam supra res humanas invenirem laboriosissimum, percommode ostendet" (p. 2–3).

[12] Pages 52–54.

comes to the end of the passage he makes clear to his reader that he does not consider the section to be devoid of significance: "It may indeed seem that we have recounted at excessive length the line of the Emperors. Some will perhaps think that these things which we are telling are quite superfluous. We have, however, seen that in this line the succession of Charlemagne was not left barren. At the same time, if we recognize that the order among the Roman Emperors was changed, passing from the Romans to the Greeks, then to the French, and finally to the Germans, it will not have been by chance but because of many things which have befallen in the narrative that Otto, the first King of the Germans, was Emperor of the Romans in Germany, having been awarded the honor by the Roman people." [13] Scala intends to shed light on a political aspect of his history by discussing the emperors; because he is not sure that he can make that point clear within the narrative, he provides an explanation at the end of the section.

Just as Scala's sense of the importance of his undertaking has a direct effect on his presentation of events, so his emphasis on accuracy and a clear presentation of facts bears fruit in the composition of the *Historia*. At the very beginning of the first book, he expresses his awareness of the difficulties of dealing with early history, where the sources have more the nature of fables than of true accounts.[14] Further on, he apologizes again for setting down fabulous stories about the founding of Fiesole, explaining that these tales are supported by some excellent authors and some Greek historians.[15] His insistence on using all possible sources on a given point is perhaps most clearly seen in his account of Charlemagne's relationship to Florence. As sources on this matter Scala mentions Bruni, Petrarch, Donato Acciaiuoli, Sozomeno, and Platina. Then he turns to narrate Villani's version, "whom we have followed most of all in this part, not neglecting, however, anything to be found among other writers which might explain the series of events more carefully." [16] Even

---

[13] "Verum longius fieret modo si ordinem Imperatorum recenseamus. Nam et haec quae attingimus erunt fortasse qui supervacanea reputent. Nobis vero Caroli successionem non usquequaque jejunam reliquisse visum est, simul non ab re forte fuerit propter multa quae incident in narrationem, si variatum esse Imperatoribus Romanis cognoverimus, ut a Romanis ad Graecos, inde ad Gallos, ab his rursum ad Germanos translatum, quanquam Otho Germanorum Rex primus, deferente cum honorem populo Romano et Imperator in Germania Romanorum fuit." (pp. 54–55.)

[14] "Verum quae jam de civitatis primordiis nominisque diversitate traduntur, ea varia sunt et inanibus pleraque fabulis quam historiae similiora" (p. 3).

[15] "Nonulli nobiles auctores dicunt . . . ut historiae Graecorum tradunt" (p. 4).

[16] "Quem nos hac in parte potissimum sequimur non neglectis tamen si qua

though Villani makes minor errors, Scala finds him to be generally correct, and in any case the humanist thinks it wrong to denounce the errors of others for his own glory.

In this way Scala follows the standard humanist practice of using one basic source at a time,[17] but he gives the impression of having criticized all the available sources in order to find the most accurate one. The historian does not always follow this practice, however. In the first book he gives several accounts of the founding of both Florence and Fiesole, together with several explanations of how Florence got its name, without explicitly choosing the best. Later in the same book he presents without critical comparison two conflicting reports of a battle between Radagasus and Stilicho.[18] Furthermore, on at least one occasion he criticizes his sources from his own conception of historical reality.[19]

What is striking about Scala's work is not, however, the sophisticated criticism of his sources. Such sophistication is no more characteristic of the *Historia Florentinorum*, written at the end of the fifteenth century, than of the *Historiae Florentini populi*, begun in the first years of that century. What does impress the reader is the frequency of Scala's references to his sources. No humanist is more modest in claiming his own achievement; none is more consistent in acknowledging his use of other writers. No work of humanist history contains less direct narrative; virtually all important events in the *Historia Florentinorum* are narrated explicitly as the accounts of previous historians. This fact alone is sufficient to show that Scala took seriously his own description of the historian's chief task: the collection, selection, and organization of facts found in the works of others.

The reader is struck not only by the frequency of Scala's appeals to authority but also by the nature of the data he supports by these appeals. Previous humanists refer to their sources to support inter-

---

et apud alios quoque scriptores reperiantur, etiam rei gestae seriem explicat curiosius" (p. 43).

17 For instance, at the beginning of Book IV he expresses his relief that he can now use Bruni as a major source: "Iam vero lenior multo afflat aura et lintrem Leonardus Aretinus sublevat regitque iter" (p. 114).

18 Page 22.

19 Recounting the miraculous rescue of a child from a lion at the end of Book III, Scala supports the credibility of this story by saying that he has heard from respectable men who have been long in Africa that lions can act in that way. As final evidence, Scala mentions (p. 113) that Aristotle also admits this as a possible way for lions to act. Villani, explaining the incident, says that it is due either to divine will or to the extraordinarily gentle temper of the lion (G. Villani, *Crònica*, VI, 70).

pretations that they themselves do not care to defend explicitly,[20] or to establish the accuracy of events directly related to their political interests.[21] In Scala's history, by contrast, these appeals almost always refer to tangible details — to buildings, geography, personal anecdotes and characterizations, in short, to the physical aspect of the material.

The historian's use of supporting evidence to establish the physical dimensions of Florentine history can be easily illustrated from the first book of the *Historia Florentinorum*. He cites Livy as evidence that Florence did indeed build aqueducts in imitation of Rome,[22] quotes authority to give weight to the theory that the temple of Mars in Florence was named after that on the Capitoline Hill,[23] and defends the validity of a relic by citing versions of its provenance drawn from various writers.[24] In the same section Scala cites Giovanni Villani as a source on the care of Florence's early buildings[25] and establishes Totila's destruction of Florence by reference to several authors.[26] He mentions Biondo and Sabellicus as sources for the personality of Attila[27] and explicitly uses Procopius on Totila, with supplementary evidence drawn from Dante.[28] His interest in physical evidence is further illustrated by his citation of an inscription on the cathedral wall to substantiate his story about Brunelleschi's construction of the dome,[29] and by his use of the discovery of bones in strategic places to prove the sack of Florence by Totila.[30] By far the greater number of his references to authority in Book I are used to prove the validity of facts about entities that are essentially tangible — people, buildings, relics.

This concern on Scala's part for establishing the veracity of tangible events and things[31] reflects the basic orientation of his work around concrete phenomena. The most succinct description of his theme, offering a comparison with both Bruni and Poggio, occurs

---

[20] See Poggio's interpretation of the Ciompi revolt.
[21] See Bruni's concern with the dating of constitutional changes in Florence.
[22] Page 7.
[23] Page 8.
[24] Page 10.
[25] Page 10.
[26] "Ut plerique asserunt scriptores" (p. 11).
[27] Page 26.
[28] Page 30.
[29] Page 24.
[30] Page 36.
[31] The concern continues in later books. In Book II (p. 58) he cites Biondo to show that the emperors are given three crowns.

at the point in the first book where he describes his subject as "our deeds on land and sea since the founding of the city." [32] This is of course intended as a generalized statement. Yet Scala differs from his predecessors in introducing into his statement a definite geographical orientation. By contrast with this, both Bruni's statement of a political theme and Poggio's promise to write of a certain group of wars represent abstractions, suggesting historical constructions and avoiding references to place.

The importance of concrete phenomena as the substance of Scala's narrative emerges even more clearly when he describes later in this same section the activities of the Florentines between the founding of the city and the birth of Christ. Since there are no direct sources, the historian is forced to reconstruct the period in terms of his own view of historical reality. He does this in the following terms: "And so in the seventy or, as Palmieri would have it, eighty-eight years between the founding of the city and the advent of our Savior, while all peoples flourished in peace, those who founded the city, free from other cares, embellished the state by private construction and the ornamentation of public buildings." [33] When Bruni opens the second book of the *Historiae* with a description of Florence's first activities, he focuses on its acquisition of liberty and consequent political vitality at home and abroad.[34] Poggio, too, narrates the growth of the Florentine state in constitutional terms.[35] All three historians use the term *civitas* to describe the subject of their narratives, but only Scala directly and explicitly gives this term physical dimensions.

The subject of Scala's narrative — Florence and its inhabitants — is not an abstraction but a concrete physical entity.[36] Its foundation and growth are described in terms of its buildings and physical attributes. Although Poggio shows a heightened interest in the

[32] "Res nostras terra marique a condita urbe gestas" (p. 19).

[33] "Igitur septuaginta sive ut Palmerio placet octo et octoginta, qui inter conditem urbem et Salvatoris ad nos adventum cessere annis, dum pace omnes fere gentes fruuntur, qui urbem condiderunt, vacui curis quibusque caeteris intentique privatis extruendis atque ornandis aedificiis, civitatem illustravere" (p. 19).

[34] "Post Federici obitum, cuius de nefando scelere supra diximus, florentinus populus, iam pridem illorum qui rempublicam occuparant superbiam saevitiamque exosus, capessere gubernacula rerum ac tueri libertatem perrexit, civitatemque totam omnemque eius statum populari arbitrio continere" (Bruni, *Historiae*, I, ii, 160).

[35] Poggio, *Historia*, 196B–197B.

[36] Scala's concern with the concrete embodiment of abstractions is not limited to the *Historia*. Parronchi, "The Language," has shown how Scala commissioned the decorations of his palace by Bertoldo di Giovanni as illustrations of his own epigraphs.

tangible dimension of history, the historical Florentine state remains for him an abstraction, to be analyzed and grasped in terms of certain political and psychological realities. Scala is the first among Florentine humanist historians to focus his investigation on the physical aspect of history in such a way that this aspect becomes the very substance of his narrative. He writes the history of a visible city, which must be given concrete form before it can acquire any other dimension.

Scala's interest in the physical dimension of his subject also leads him to introduce into the narrative sensual details which earlier humanists largely avoid. When he speaks of the derivation of the name of Florence from flowers which grew in the city, he alludes to the odor of the lilies.[37] He evokes the sense of sight in mentioning the corpses which Totila had thrown into the cisterns.[38] Describing a battle, Scala is not content with an abstract statement about the clamor, but singles out the howling of the women as a graphic illustration of this.[39] The elicitation of visual values can be seen when he presents the Guelf-Ghibelline feud in terms of the pink and white lilies used as insignia,[40] or when he describes the porphyry columns given by the Pisans to Florence.[41] An even more striking example is his narration of an eclipse of the sun, where he explicitly deals with its visual effect, saying, "The stars appeared to men at midday just as they do in the dark of night." [42]

It cannot be denied that Scala is interested in amusing and pleasing his reader. Not only does he express this interest in his Proèmio,[43] but in the same place he acknowledges that even patriotic history is more gladly read when it is written well.[44] On occasion he apologizes for the roughness and inelegance of his presentation, blaming the state of his sources.[45] Furthermore, the inclusion of poetry and legendary material in the narrative should probably be understood in the light of Scala's desire to entertain his reader.

Scala's desire to amuse the reader, however, is not a sufficient

---

[37] Page 5.
[38] Page 35.
[39] "Mulieres passim ululantes exaudiri" (p. 13).
[40] Page 101.
[41] Page 64.
[42] "E medio die stellae, ut obscura in nocte apparuerunt mortalibus" (p. 93).
[43] "Ut iter hinc mihi quoque si qua possim, ad juvandum genus humanum parem" (p. 3).
[44] "Praesertim scripta decenter" (p. 2).
[45] See p. 17.

explanation for his attention to tangible details in the *Historia Florentinorum*. The explicit sense of the significance of his work suggests the presence of a deeper meaning in this concreteness. Upon a closer examination of the manner in which the historian uses his tangible facts, it appears that far from taking the place of a conceptual analysis of historical events, the concrete events in the *Historia Florentinorum* are used precisely to convey that analysis.

Scala frequently uses tangible objects as introductions to political and constitutional developments. His first allusion to constitutional practice in Florence — the introduction of Roman magistrates — occurs only after he has fully outlined the foundation and construction of the city's walls and buildings.[46] He describes the consequences of the fall of Fiesole and the incorporation of its inhabitants into the population of Florence first in terms of the necessity of enlarging the city. Only after enumerating the new buildings and connecting them with ruins familiar to his own contemporaries does the historian mention the constitutional changes brought about by the new situation.[47] Later on, Scala begins his account of the manner in which the city wages war by a description of the Carroccio, together with various symbols of power and places of assembly.[48]

In a similar fashion the historian associates the religious history of Florence with its physical manifestations. The conversion of the Florentines to Christianity is first mentioned in connection with the decorations on the baptistery, and it is only in the course of describing these ornaments that the transformation of the pagan temple of Mars into a Christian baptistery is noted.[49] Further on, narrating the actual conversion, he again refers to the baptistery before going on to describe the miracles of St. Zenobius.[50]

[46] Page 18.
[47] Page 56.
[48] Pages 72–73. On rare occasions he reverses the order, mentioning the constitutional innovation before the objects associated with it. When dealing with the institution of captains of the people and the division of the city into sections in order to limit the power of the nobles, he mentions the building of the Palazzo della Signoria only after a full recitation of the new institutions. The construction of the palace, however, is explicitly associated with the political significance of these constitutional forms: "Ita veriti ne quando vel totus simul Senatus aut populus ab infensissima nobilitate opprimi consultando quiret, de aedificanda curia primum actum. Locus ad aedem Apollinaris delectus illic." (p. 99.)
[49] Page 9.
[50] Page 20.

Scala relates concrete objects to intangible aspects of history in a more than superficial manner. Such objects are frequently analyzed and explained in terms of strategic or other considerations which remind one of the approach of earlier humanist historians. When Scala describes the aqueducts which Florence built in imitation of Rome, he includes a discussion of the terrain around Florence, showing why the aqueducts were necessary.[51] Further on, he explains the building of towers within the city walls by the prevailing civic discord among the factions.[52] The best example of Scala's understanding of the connection between tangible and analytical dimensions in history, however, is found in his treatment of the rise of Totila and the capture and sack of Florence at the hands of this barbarian leader. In this section of the narrative many of the analytical tools and historical presuppositions which characterize the histories of both Poggio and Bruni can be found, together with Scala's distinctive mode of structuring the account around tangible phenomena. Because of its importance this passage will be analyzed at some length.

Scala begins the section on Totila with a simple and direct statement of the significant event that he is about to narrate. "Totila, however, of whom we shall now speak, destroyed Florence." [53] The rest of Book I — approximately ten pages — is devoted to this event, and Scala significantly begins his account neither with the political or diplomatic background of the sack nor with the military events leading up to it, but with a characterization of the person of Totila, bringing out his importance by a list of particular deeds and moral traits: "This is that Totila, King of the Goths and scourge of God, the memory alone of whose name can bring terror to mortal men. He it is who razed Rome to its foundations, who destroyed and burned all of Italy and afterwards overturned this wretched city and leveled it to the ground. A wild leader, savage, unrelenting, contemptuous of men and gods, energetic, astute, clever in mind and swift of hand, wondrously prudent in military affairs." [54]

---

[51] Page 7. Compare with Bruni, *Historiae*, I, i, 62.

[52] Page 68.

[53] "Totila autem, de quo jam dicemus, Florentiam evertit" (p. 28).

[54] "Is Totila ille est Gothorum Rex flagellum Dei, cuius sola nominis memoris incutere terrorem potest mortalibus. Hic est, inquam, qui Romam eruit a fundamentis, qui evertit incenditque Italiam, atque hanc urbem, postquam miserabiliter diripuit solo aequavit, ferus dux, immitis, inexorabilis, hominum deorumque contemptor, caeterum impiget, argutus, solers animo simul manuque promptus, et militari prudentia admirandus." (pp. 28–29.)

While maintaining the humanist reticence about physical descriptions of people, Scala pictures the Goth as very important, defined by his acts, and as devious, unprincipled, and extremely clever, defined by his personal traits. After this presentation the historian describes the political situation which makes Totila dangerous, showing that the vices of Justinian's men in Italy after Belisarius' departure have turned the people against the emperor.[55] After listing specific injustices and explicitly stating the importance of this popular discontent in giving opportunity to Totila,[56] Scala begins to narrate the Goth's military successes by naming the regions through which he passes victoriously prior to his arrival before the gates of Florence.

Now Scala, drawing on Procopius, relates how the Goths are driven away from Florence by Justinian's relief army and that, except for a chance event (which he pauses to describe), they would have been destroyed. Having narrated Totila's temporary discomfiture, Scala criticizes and refines his account, using Dante's report of a portent which drives the Goths away. He supports Dante in turn with Seneca's assurance that such things do indeed happen.[57] Before narrating Totila's final assault on Florence, Scala pauses to deal with the question whether the Goth totally destroyed the city and left it desolate for Charlemagne to rebuild three hundred years later.[58] The historian decides that Totila did completely overturn Florence, basing his opinion on the popular reverence for Charlemagne felt by the Florentines of the Quattrocento and deducing that some historical event must have inspired this reverence.[59] In fact, he places the ensuing account of the fall of Florence in the context of an attempt to show how the fifteenth-century feeling toward Charlemagne arose.[60]

Continuing his organization of this passage around the person of Totila, Scala begins his narrative of the final siege with an analysis of Totila's personal motivations in attacking Florence (he wishes

---

[55] "Hi autem avari, incontinentes, pigri raptores, imbelles, contentiosi, atque ardentes in cupiditatibus odia in se populorum concitaverunt" (p. 29).

[56] "Per hanc igitur occasionem rerum perperam administratarum Totila bellum aggressus" (p. 29).

[57] Page 30.

[58] Scala, in deciding that Totila has destroyed Florence, is not relying on Procopius, who does not mention it, but on Villani, who takes it from Malespini, where Attila and Totila are combined into one man.

[59] Page 31.

[60] "Si modo diligentius ut res esse gesta traditur aperiamus" (p. 31).

to avenge the Florentine defeat of the Visigoths), together with the strategic considerations inducing him to undertake the siege (Florence's situation on the plain seems to him easy to assault). The section concludes with a characterization of his state of mind.[61] Totila's strategic reasoning is not sound, however, and, after failing in an attempt to take the city by force, he devises a stratagem for tricking Florence into surrender.

Scala states Totila's stratagem abstractly before presenting the oration by which the Goth hopes to induce the leaders of Florence to give over the city of their own accord.[62] In the course of this oration Scala stresses the oppression of Justinian's administrators by having Totila promise to bring back the just days of Theodoric. The oration finished, the historian turns to the reactions of the Florentines, describing their reasons for accepting Totila's proposition in terms which emphasize the vicissitudes of fortune and their basic distrust of the Goth.[63]

According to Scala, Totila, once inside the city, seeks by doing favors for the Florentines to persuade them that he may be trusted. First he intervenes on their side in the war with Pistoia. He further softens them with his oratory, the effectiveness of which Scala pointedly underlines.[64] Having shown how Totila has apparently become trusted and liked by the Florentines, Scala turns to describe the Goth's actions in his own interests. He secretly brings his own soldiers within the walls of the city; he murders some of the leading citizens and throws their bodies into a cistern. This cistern Scala describes in considerable detail,[65] and the reason for his attention soon becomes clear, for the crisis which results in the sack of the city arises in the following manner: "The water at that time was stagnant and scarcely moving. When the multitude of corpses had grown into a sort of gory mass, it oozed into the Arno in the appearance of a heap of butchered flesh. When certain people noticed this, since they suspected at once, they ran to arms." [66] But

[61] "Itaque aggressus ingenti animo inferebat bellum" (p. 32).

[62] "Ita omissa obsidione ostentat amicitiam et principes civitatis allicit ad colloquia nec venisse se hostem asserit Florentinorum" (p. 32).

[63] "Neminem tanta unquam prudentia fuisse ut futurarum rerum vicissitudines varietatesque cunctas posset prospicere. Satis esse eum prudentem, qui praesentes casus callide animadverterit utiliterque administraverit." (p. 33.) Compare Poggio, *Historia*, 344B, where he gives similar motivations for the Florentines in seeking peace with Milan.

[64] "Cuius erat Totila insignis artifex" (p. 34).

[65] Page 35.

[66] "Stagnabat per id tempus aqua illic modo vix fluebat. Cum tamen multitu-

it is too late. The soldiers already in the city let in their comrades, and Florence is sacked with great slaughter. Scala describes the buildings destroyed and those saved, concluding his account by dating the event in 548.

This passage contains several themes, historical preconceptions, and analytical tools which seem similar to those found in the histories of Bruni and Poggio (and which will shortly be searched out in the whole body of Scala's history). The passage is most significant, however, for the way in which Scala presents the event. Despite considerable analytical interest, the event under consideration involves on the one hand a specific individual, depicted with strong personal traits, and on the other the walls and buildings which constitute the city of Florence, the destruction of which is described with greater care than Scala has used in describing the attitudes of the inhabitants of the city. Moreover, the precipitating event of the sack is a physical fact presented in strongly sensual terms — the sight of a mass of rotting flesh floating in the Arno — which crystallizes both the previous suspicions of the Florentines and the previous preparation of Totila into a final battle, leading to the destruction of the city.[67] The sight of the corpses is not meaningful in itself; it assumes the power to precipitate a crisis only in connection with the attitudes, motivations, and political realities already noted.

Scala's method of presenting change stands in marked contrast to that found in Bruni's *Historiae*. In Scala's work there is little emphasis on psychological change. He makes the reader understand that the Florentines' suspicions are never completely allayed. From the beginning he makes it clear that the leaders of the city accept Totila's blandishments only because, faced with superior force, they hope that time will bring a change in the Goth's fortunes. Placed against the constant suspicion and hostility of the Florentines is the unchanging, vengeful attitude of the Goth. To-

---

dine jam cadaverum excrevisset unda in cruoris speciem effluxisse in arnum fertur, idque carnificinae modum fecit. Nam cum id quidam advertissent quod erant illico suspicati conclamaverunt arma." (p. 35.)

[67] In a striking reversal of standard humanist practice, Scala makes his account more vivid and more directly sensual than either of his vernacular sources. Villani, *Crònica*, II, 1, says, "E così ne fece morire un grande quantità, che niente se ne sentiva nella città di Firenze, se non che all'uscita della città ove si scuoprivano i detti acquidocci, ovvera gora, e rientravana in Arno, si vedea tutta l'aqua rossa e sanguinosa." Malespini, *Istoria fiorentina*, chap. 22, says that the deed would have been discovered "se non che quell'acqua di quel ramo d'arno incominciò a diventare rossa per lo molto sangue di quegli uomini dicollati e morti."

tila never contemplates making a true ally of Florence but acts always in terms of the personal character set out for him by Scala at the beginning of the section. What changes an atmosphere of mutual suspicion into one of active warfare is a tangible event, which immediately crystallizes suspicion into action.

So also the effect of this transformation is physical — the destruction of the buildings and walls of the city — and not psychological or political. It can indeed have political consequences, and it has already been noted that the destruction of the city bore psychological consequences for Scala's own time in the form of reverence for the man who restored Florence from the ruins which Totila had made of it. At the basis of these political and psychological consequences, however, lies the physical destruction of the city, a change which is fundamentally and irredeemably tangible and to which Scala devotes his closest attention in the narrative itself.[68]

In spite of the vast difference between Scala and his humanist predecessors, reflected here in his means of representing historical change, his work manifests several ideas and approaches which are similar to those found in the works of Bruni and Poggio. The most important of these is a tendency to interrelate historical events in terms of a coherent set of political factors and psychological realities. First of all, Scala tends to narrate foreign and domestic events in relation to each other. This relationship, not so clearly articulated as in either Bruni's work or Poggio's, is most explicitly stated when Scala says, after narrating a series of wars, "And so, as things were quiet abroad, internal sedition disturbed the peace at home." [69] After briefly discussing this internal strife, he introduces the next war, "At last, excited by external dangers, things quieted down a little at home." [70] A further example is his explanation of an internal change in Aretine polity as the result of the external threat of a Florentine army.[71]

In the realm of domestic history, Scala introduces psychological considerations most noticeably in his treatment of internal discord.

---

[68] The relative similarity between Scala's mode of presenting change here and Livy's mode in his narration of the rape of Lucretia is quite obvious. Both men concentrate on tangible events which crystallize pre-existent and basically unchanging psychological attitudes.

[69] "Foris ita pacatis rebus, domi intestinae seditiones turbaverunt otium" (p. 67).

[70] "Donec excitati externis periculis paulum domi quievere" (p. 68).

[71] "Crevere animi Aretini Guelfis ac tumultu excitato eam partem Gibellinorum, quae in urbe quieta ad eam diem fuerat, ejecerunt" (p. 109). See also his interpretation of the subjugation of Florence by Frederick II (p. 94).

Like Bruni, Scala concentrates on faction in discussing the early political history of Florence, and, again like Bruni, he presents it as a psychological problem. He explains the first outbreak of civic discord in Florence in terms of the states of mind of the noble families.[72] The outbreak of the Guelf-Ghibelline feud in Florence is explained by the indignation of the Amadei.[73] Later on, when Scala comes to assess the reasons behind the failure of an attempt at reconciliation, he blames the intensity of feeling on both sides, illustrating this with specific grievances.[74] He sees the spirit of competition as a possible source of strength for Florence, but, significantly, the only specific example of the beneficial use of competition involves the construction of buildings.[75] Constitutional changes are interpreted as attempts to control this competitive spirit.[76]

Finally, political decisions are often made in the light of psychological factors. Florence delays its foreign activity until the loyalty of its *contadini* can be assured.[77] The Ghibelline faction decides on treachery rather than open assault in order to seize the baptistery, because they fear that the people will be unduly upset by a direct attack.[78] Changes in the political situation also have psychological effects. The historian explains the ouster of Novellus after the battle of Benevento by the fact that popular hatred rises as Novellus' power diminishes.[79]

In the sphere of foreign policy Scala also evidences concern for the psychological aspect of events. He describes the conflict between Florence and Fiesole as psychological.[80] The enmity between these two cities is further explained, in the course of an oration, by the

[72] "Nam cum essent ea tempestate civitatis facile principes pollerentque praeter caeteros divitiis atque anteirent dignitate stimulante animos fortuna quae vix unquam praesenti rerum statu conquiescit" (p. 67).

[73] "Ea vero perciti indignitate Amidei quod spretos se Bondelmonte despectosque putarent" (p. 87).

[74] Pages 146–147.

[75] Immediately after the founding of the city the Senate organizes the construction of new buildings in such a way that the competition between private citizens will cause the city to rise more quickly (p. 10).

[76] Scala says that when tenure of office is reduced from one year to six months, the change is made because the longer tenure affects the integrity of the magistrates in an adverse manner (p. 77).

[77] After Florence has made sure of this loyalty, "his itaque peractis ad commoda urbis conversae mentes" (p. 84). See also the Florentine reasons for destroying a rebel town (p. 74).

[78] Page 95.

[79] "Iam vero plebs respicere res novas videbatur et Novelli impotentior dominatus odiosus erat" (p. 142).

[80] "Studio multo maiore quam viribus, atque in tenui fortuna haud tenuis tamen animorum ferocia obstinatioque permansit" (p. 11).

fact that Fiesloans have acquired a harsh temperament from living on a mountain, while Florence's location on a plain has given its inhabitants a more gentle disposition.[81] The war which breaks out between Florence and Pisa surprises the historian because Florence and Pisa have always been so friendly.[82] Furthermore, he explains the Florentines' willingness to enter the war against such a formidable foe by their outrage at new Pisan indignities.[83] As the scope of the war widens, the historian maintains his attention to psychological factors, noting the ardor of Florence's quarrel with the Sienese and its indignation against the Pistoians.[84]

Battles also are described in terms of the psychological realities which inform them. In the first battle in the war between Fiesole and Florence, Scala notes both the motivations of the Fiesolans [85] and the psychological state of Florence.[86] In this same battle he notes the psychological effect on the Florentines of Bishop Zenobius' presence.[87] Tactical considerations are narrated in psychological contexts,[88] and the effect of a battle is depicted in psychological terms.[89]

Scala approaches the problem of divine intervention in historical events from a psychological viewpoint. This approach is clearest in the Florentine oration to the Fiesolans after the capture of their city. The Florentine orator suggests that Fiesole has fallen by divine will, for the patron saint of Fiesole could have come to the city's aid, had it been God's wish. In describing how the saint could

---

[81] Page 15.

[82] "Quorum fuerat tanta coniunctio quondam animorum" (p. 84).

[83] "Tamen rei indignitas et iustae irae animos fecerunt" (p. 89).

[84] Page 102.

[85] "Fesulanis autem re cognita repugnare primum et tutari urbis maenia venit in mentem" (p. 13).

[86] "Florentiae quoque in principio non nihil trepidatum constat" (p. 13).

[87] "Animos atque ardorem excitavisse" (p. 22).

[88] After defeating Prato in battle, the Pistoians, "qua quidem elati victoria," decide to pursue the losers (p. 66). After a Florentine victory, since it is midsummer and the Florentines certainly have the occasion to follow up the victory, "itaque magnus Gibellines Senensesque invaserat terror" (p. 118). In response to this terror Manfred sends Jordanus so that, "amoto obsidionis metu," the Sienese will attack the enemy. "Quod Gibellini cum rescissent nihil magis versabant animis quam ut Guelfos extraherent in praelium" (p. 119). Scala also explains a Florentine victory by the hope which arises from their faith in the justice of the Florentine cause (p. 90). Villani credits the victory to the judgment of God on the pride of the Pisans (G. Villani, *Cr̀onica*, VI, 31).

[89] See p. 129, where Scala narrates the effect of the news of Montaperti at Rome: "maximum timorem incussere"; and p. 141, where he narrates the effect of Benevento in psychological terms: "Secundum eam victoriam omnes per Italiam Guelfi respirare coeperunt."

have acted, however, the Florentine evokes psychological factors. "He could have excited you and admonished you to emulate your ancestors so that, if you would not go armed on the feast day, you would at least exercise more caution. He could have stirred up against the invaders the mob which filled your city and fields just before the attack . . . He could have given us another idea and not made us so anxious to attack you on this day." [90] On other occasions in the work divine portents are presented as psychological effects. Conrad lifts the siege of Milan because he is terrified by a vision of St. Ambrose.[91] Finally, the portents accompanying Charles of Anjou's appearance in Italy are described in terms of their psychological effect.[92]

From these observations it is apparent that in war, diplomatic relations, and internal political affairs Scala concentrates on psychological elements both as causal factors and as effects of major events. Motivations are considered in analyzing decisions,[93] and the quality of feelings and attitudes is adduced to analyze the political realities of a given situation. Despite the fact that this political and psychological element does not comprehend the whole substance of Scala's narrative, it is an important historical concern for him and suggests a similarity between his work and that of Bruni and Poggio.

The section in which Scala recounts Totila's destruction of Florence contains two more elements which suggest similarities with previous humanist histories: attention to strategic considerations (in explaining why Totila thought Florence might be vulnerable to attack), and emphasis on the importance of fortune in determining historical events. Scala describes military events with atten-

90 "Potuit enim excitare vos atque admonere veterum aemulationem ut si non armati die festo tamen magis cauti fueritis. Potuit externam multitudinem qua urbs agerque vester completus paulo ante fuit, irritare in invasores . . . Potuit tandem et nobis dare aliam mentem . . . nec injicere in animos nostros hunc tantum hodie furorem vindicandi." (pp. 15–16.)

91 Page 58.

92 "Per eos vero dies crinita fulserat excitaveratque omnes mortales ad rerum futurarum exspectationem" (p. 139).

93 The most thorough analysis of motivations in this context is found in Scala's narration of Conradin's descent into Italy. He first assesses the motives of Henry of Castile in urging the young Hohenstaufen to make the journey, pointing out Henry's interests in the matter; next the historian turns to the elements in Conradin's own motivations — his youth and his previous inactivity. Then Scala deals with the negative factors influencing Conradin, mainly the opposition of his mother. Finally he concludes with a sentence summing up the most powerful reasons for making the journey: "Vicit tandem studiosa Henrici diligensque incitatio spesque quaedam iniecta permagna recuperandi Italici regni" (p. 153).

tion to strategic and tactical considerations in other parts of the *Historia* as well as here. He places a series of events beginning with the taking of Prato in the context of Florence's strategic goal of expanding into its *contado*,[94] and he begins his account of the Pisan war by mentioning Pisa's sea power as a strategic advantage.[95] Referring to Villani's suggestion that a war between Pisa and Florence begins over a minor ceremonial dispute, he states that the war has more serious origins in Frederick's alliance with Pisa and the advantages Pisa thinks it can derive from this alliance.[96]

Scala also recognizes the virtues of well-considered military tactics as opposed to rash action. Prato loses a battle when it selects an ill-advised site for the battlefield.[97] At Montaperti the German mercenaries attack rashly, depending solely on the shock value of a surprise attack, and are destroyed to a man.[98] In the same battle the Florentines are so confident of an easy victory that they fail to fortify the camp properly and are vulnerable to the unexpected Sienese assault.[99] Finally, Scala disparages the haste and rashness of Novellus' flight from Florence after the defeat of Manfred.[100]

The value of plans and thoughtful attention to tactics is limited, however, by the power of fortune to influence events. This — the last element to be considered in the passage on the sack of Florence — is also to be found in other parts of the *Historia*. Scala's first explicit reference to the power of fortune is a comment on a defeat suffered by the Goths. They would certainly have won a victory, he says, "had not fortune mocked the virtue of the victors, as it often does." [101] In addition to this, there are explicit references to the power of fortune in orations throughout the work.[102] Although in dealing with problems of his own time Scala notes the helplessness of men in the face of fortune,[103] he does not become fatalistic.

94 Page 64.
95 Page 63.
96 Page 85.
97 Page 66.
98 Page 118.
99 Page 126. Bruni doesn't mention this unpreparedness as a factor (*Historiae*, I, ii, 212–220).
100 Page 145.
101 "Nisi fortuna, quod saepe solet, victorum virtuti illusisset" (p. 25).
102 See the oration advocating an attack on Siena: "Tam varii sunt rerum eventus, praesertim bellicarum ut etiam sibi diligentius consulueris, facile a vero tamen saepius aberres ac diversi a spe fiant rerum exitus" (p. 121).
103 He says in the introduction to Book II, when warning the contemporary rulers of Florence about the danger from foreign intervention, "Quanquam in vestra

There is a suggestion that man has a responsibility to use to his own advantage what fortune has given him. The Pisans, advocating the destruction of Florence after its defeat at Montaperti, say, "For we shall implore the help of fortune in vain if we reject through prudence or laziness that which it has freely bestowed upon us." [104]

Intangible elements of a less analytical nature, constituting implicit assumptions on Scala's part, also find their way into his presentation of Florentine history, just as they do into Poggio's. Scala betrays the same feeling that keeping faith is an absolute moral imperative, although he does not restrict his injunction to princes. In fact, his most specific comments are directed at Florence itself. At one point he says that to break faith is "alien to the customs and dignity of the Florentine people." [105] Scala is also concerned to celebrate in his history the glory and honor both of the city of Florence and of its inhabitants and servants. He notes victory festivals at Florence [106] and public honors awarded to its heroes on their death.[107] He narrates the minting of gold coins not as an economic fact but as a means of increasing the fame of Florence.[108] Finally, his descriptions of people tend to emphasize the quality of the individual's character rather than to assess his competence or the nature of his contribution to the city.[109]

In spite of Scala's tendency to represent both change and sta-

---

forsitan non est manu ut mitius iam agatis cum Italia quam ita vastatis, diripitis, incenditis et ruinae novae exponitis. Sed erratorum fortasse veterum fato quodam inevitabile justissimo scelerum ultore humanorum, pene haud immerite repetuntur. Sed vos quo vestra fortuna feret." (p. 40.) Rubinstein, "Bartolomeo Scala's Historia," p. 59, makes much of this passage.

104 "Frustra enim fortunae opem . . . implorabimus si quae ipsa ultro obtulerit per prudentiam atque ignaviam repudiaverimus" (p. 134). The battle of Montaperti, to which the Pisans are referring, has already been explicitly placed by Scala in the context of a fortuituous event. He says, while referring to it, "Ita fortuna rebus in nostris lusit perpetuo ludo, quae tunc demum negare videtur cum miscet suo arbitratu cuncta ac minime intelligenda mortalibus res cunctas mortalium administrat, quod vel his temporibus maxime patuit" (p. 115).

105 "A populi Florentini consuetudine et dignitate alienum" (p. 124).

106 Pages 23, 109, and 118.

107 See the account of the funeral of Brunelleschi (p. 104).

108 "Ea res vero fecit ut civitatis fama ad extremos quoque facilius penetrarit" (p. 104).

109 Pliny is called "certe gravis auctor" (p. 6); Charlemagne, "Carolus . . . Pipini Filius cognomento magnus Gallorum Rex Romanorum Imperator" (p. 11); Bishop Romulus is noted for being "ingenti fama sanctitatis" (p. 12); Brunelleschi is called "magno ingenio architectus" (p. 23), and Carlo Marsuppini "clarus poeta" (p. 24); Dante and Bruni are each called, "gravissimus auctor" (p. 43). Brunetto Latini is characterized simply as "gravem virum" (p. 115).

bility in history by means of concrete events and in spite of his consistent references to physical objects in portraying Florentine history, the intangible dimension of his work is readily apparent. It is defined by an analysis of events in terms of a coherent understanding of interrelated psychological and political factors and also by a less analytical group of implicit assumptions and attitudes. The presentation of a narrative so diversified in its essential composition involves structural problems even more complex than those besetting Poggio. No definitive analysis of Scala's narrative techniques is possible because of the uncompleted state of the *Historia Florentinorum*. There is every reason to believe that Poggio did nearly all he intended and left at his death a reasonably finished work, which was in turn given final form by his son. Scala, however, who completed a mere four out of a projected twenty books and stopped writing in mid-sentence, certainly did not leave the manuscript in a final, polished form. In spite of this important qualification, several organizational practices in the work are employed with sufficient consistency and sophistication to provide an insight into the way in which Scala sought to solve the structural problems implicit in his history.

The most obvious aspect of the *Historia*'s organization is Scala's refusal to develop the narrative along clear chronological lines. There seems to be no coherent principle for dating events. Seven times he dates important occurrences,[110] but on two occasions he dates very minor wars.[111] Twice he mentions the simple passing of a century.[112] These are the only dates in the work, and it is clear that they occur far too infrequently to provide any organizational structure.

Even more significant than the relative absence of dates is Scala's willingness to depart completely from a chronological order of events to follow something — usually a physical object but not always — forward in time from the point at which it is introduced. When first he comes to mention the Duomo, for instance, he digresses to follow its history down to the construction of the dome

---

[110] The founding of Fiesole (p. 4); the founding of Florence (p. 10); the accession of Constantine (p. 20); the birth of St. Zenobius (p. 20); the sack of Rome (p. 24); the destruction of Florence by Totila (p. 38); the battle of Montaperti (p. 129).

[111] The Pisan war (p. 89) and the Volterran war (p. 109).

[112] Pages 55 and 63. The latter date, 1100, is associated with Florence's expansion into the *contado*.

by Brunelleschi, showing how it has attained the form by which it is known to his own contemporaries.[113] He sometimes moves both forward and backward chronologically in describing his subject matter. When he first mentions Poggibonsi, the historian begins his account by saying that some ruins of the castle still remain; he then turns back to discuss Poggibonsi's early history before narrating the siege which had originally drawn his attention to the town.[114] Quite unimportant things, such as streets, also provide an occasion for breaking the chronological order. Recounting the flight of the Ghibellines from Florence after the defeat of Manfred at Benevento, Scala notes that the street over which they pass is still called Via Ghibellina. This observation is followed by a digression which suggests another possible source for the name.[115] Sometimes these digressions are simply contemporary references which do not effectively break the narrative order; when Scala tells of the founding of Venice, for instance, he includes a brief clause remarking on the power of that city in his own day.[116]

The subordination of chronological order to the portrayal of change or permanence in physical objects, seen in the context of Scala's attention to such concrete phenomena throughout his narrative, is a further indication of the extent to which he has grounded his representation of Florentine history in concrete, tangible realities and specific historical events. The historian has, however, developed no consistent method for relating the intangible, conceptualized dimension of his historical approach to this foundation. Instead, he relies on several different techniques, adapting them to the specific problems with which he is faced.

The simplest way of relating the tangible and intangible parts of his work is by explicit statement. Scala's use of this technique in drawing out the significance of his list of emperors after Charlemagne has already been noted. The most obvious cases of explicit commentary used to clarify the didactic value and conceptual significance of the work are his introductions to each book. Book I is introduced by the general Proèmio, which has already been discussed. At the beginning of Book II, while lamenting the collapse of Italy during the barbarian invasions, the historian suggests that lessons may be drawn from this collapse for the conduct of present-

113 Page 24.
114 Page 105.
115 Page 111.
116 Page 27.

day affairs. He opens Book III with an essay on the problems of discussing the early history of a city, outlining his expository method, which includes not only the use of all available sources but an attempt to clarify and elucidate his account by means of orations.[117] The preface to Book IV, beginning with an expression of relief that he can at last follow Bruni's diligent history, concludes with a commentary on the revival of arts and letters in his own day. The introduction to Book V he connects more closely with the narrative, explicitly discussing the causes for Conradin's descent into Italy.

Within the narrative itself, Scala frequently explicates the meaning of a series of events, not trying to draw a lesson or illustrate a principle but simply interrelating events by a direct statement which either introduces or concludes his account. For instance, a general statement to the effect that Florence is engaged in attacking the tyrants of its *contado* introduces the narrative of several specific wars, relating them to one another and thus giving them a more general significance.[118] Again, he introduces a particular siege with the strategic explanation that Florence is about to eject the Ubaldini family from the Mugello.[119]

At other times Scala includes a general observation in order to summarize a series of narrated events. After preliminary orations, which point up the causes of the Pisan war, and a discussion of the strategic advantages of each side, he dates the beginning of the conflict, names the Florentine leader, and, in the same period, places this first Pisan war in the context of all those that follow it down to the surrender of Pisan liberty in 1406.[120] Not all his summaries attempt to place events in such a large frame, however. After his long narrative of the deliberations before Montaperti, Scala includes, as Bruni does not, a simple summary statement of the decision which emerges from these discussions.[121] Although

117 "Oratione etiam illustranda duxi" (p. 76).

118 "Annus erat millesimus fere ac centesimus Christianae salutis quo Gothi in Asia et Hierosolymis gloriosissime bellantur, cum Florentini multo facti potentiores bella cum finitimis multifariam gerebant, pulsisque de locis etiam munitioribus tyrannis regulisque, qui permulti in Etruria tunc erant, fines porrigebant" (p. 63).

119 "Florentini autem per eam occasionem dum in Apulia bellum geritur, Ubaldinos, ea inter Gibellinos clara potensque familia fuit, Mugello eiiciunt" (p. 102).

120 "Praetor erat urbis Odopetrus Gregorius, et annus Christi millesimus ducentesimus et vigesimus secundus, cum primum Pisanis illata sunt Florentinorum arma, vertebatur, quae deinde supra modum supraque fidem utrumque populum ad finem usque libertatis alterius varia fortuna vexavere" (p. 89).

121 "Ita decretum populum fit ut ad Arbiam copiae confestim admoveantur" (p. 125).

his use of language is not uniformly precise, he can effectively employ the connective powers of Latin syntax to convey the relationship between events without explicit statement. He prefaces the Frankish intervention into Italian affairs by an account of shifts in papal diplomacy from Byzantium to the Franks, introducing the actual descent of Charles Martel with the simple but meaningful connective "sic." [122]

At his best, Scala has developed a narrative style that ties his analytical judgments and historical reconstructions to precise events in a manner which draws the attention of the reader to the significance of the events being narrated and at the same time uses the events to give concrete meaning to these judgments and reconstructions. Such a passage appears in Book II, where Scala discusses a domestic disturbance of the late twelfth century.[123] He begins the account by assessing the general nature of the events he is about to narrate: "After foreign affairs had been settled, internal sedition disturbed the peace at home." [124] From this statement he passes on to note two fires that are raising havoc at the time.[125]

Next comes a complex period which introduces the basic elements of the disturbance, the origins of which are explained by discussing the Uberti family, which leads the uprising. In his discussion the historian notes the excessive wealth and dignity of the Uberti, explaining that their position causes them to chafe under the rule of the consuls and excites the envy of the other noble families. The Uberti in turn, by means of much largesse, win the sympathies of the lower orders. Scala carefully relates all the elements of the dispute, showing how the situation — the excessive influence of the Uberti — creates certain states of mind, which in turn create a new situation — the division of the city into factions. Having explained more or less abstractly this division, Scala describes it in more precise terms.[126] He then pauses to declare that the real mo-

122 Pages 40–41. The connective "sic" can be used without clarity or precision to indicate a simple continuation or transition, but here it seems to convey the precise causal sense of the result of a previously narrated series of happenings.
123 It occurred in 1177, although Scala himself does not date it.
124 "Foris ita pacatis rebus, domi intestinae seditiones turbaverunt otium" (p. 67).
125 The technique of including such facts as fires or celestial phenomena to stress the importance of a period of time was used by Bruni: see his introduction to the year 1340 (*Historiae*, II, vi, 262).
126 "Ea res continuo duas in partes civitatem distraxit, plerisque de nobilitate superbiam Ubertorum potentiamque accusantibus, et apud multitudinem, quae ob crebras largitiones Ubertorum fere tota erat, odii semper novas causas vestigantibus, quo plebis animos ab illorum studiis averterent" (p. 67).

tives of the Uberti are to rule the city in their own interests and that they are not in any way in favor of the popular party.

After explaining the background of the dispute, Scala begins his account of the period of active strife by exposing the Uberti's tactic of seizing the consulship, "the only bulwark of law and civil peace." [127] Describing in general terms the tactics of the Uberti,[128] Scala begins to withdraw from the event to prepare for narrating the next section (a series of wars) first by giving the duration of the disturbance and finally by tying it down to some sort of physical object. To do this, he notes that after these disturbances many of the noble families build towers over their homes in order to protect themselves.[129] This passage, by its use of periodic structure to bind together analytical and descriptive elements, by its analysis of events in terms of psychological and political factors, and finally by its portrayal of change in physical terms, shows Scala's narrative technique at its best.

Scala makes use of orations to express his themes in much the same way as do Bruni and Poggio. This technique, in fact, shows the least change during the century and remains the most consistent point of similarity with the humanists' classical models.

The speech of the Florentine commander to the defeated Fiesolans is an excellent example of Scala's orations. The speaker begins by rehearsing the long history of friendly relations and intermarriages between the Florentines and the Fiesolans, stressing that Florence feels no lasting enmity toward its neighbors and has no wish to destroy them. From this general protestation of good will, the speech turns to consider the practical issues involved, maintaining that the struggle is purely a political one, concerned with locating the seat of the combined power of Florence and Fiesole. After pointing out the advantages of this combined power and digressing briefly to deal with the state of mind of each of the combatants, the oration concludes by dwelling on the physical aspect of the Fiesolan defeat — the fact that its citizens must now leave the harsh mountain top to dwell in the fertile fields of the Florentines.[130] In the extent to which practical and spiritual factors are considered within the same

[127] "Unicum jam legum et civilis otii propugnaculum" (p. 67).

[128] "Ubertorum tandem huc omnes tendere conatus, ut soli consulatibus caeterisque reipublicae fungerentur honoribus" (p. 68).

[129] Page 68.

[130] "Et vos partiae caritatem ab his montanis asperitatibus, ab his devictis maenibus ad fertiliores campos ad maenia nostra transferatis, quae non minus vestra post hac futura sunt" (p. 16).

oration and are applied to the same event, in the analysis of themes which recur in the narrative itself (such as the psychological observations), and in the reference to physical change, this oration not only expresses some of Scala's most obvious historical ideas but also demonstrates his ability to adapt this classical form to his own use.

There are few full-fledged battles recounted in the *Historia*. Scala's brief account of the battle of Châlons gives some indication that in military narratives as well as orations his general technique is similar to that of his humanist predecessors and is related to classical models. He begins by showing Attila's strategic considerations in offering battle (auspices have predicted that he will lose but that the enemy chief will fall). Then the battle itself is narrated in general terms but with enough detail to describe the stages by which Attila is defeated, including his last desperate stand on a hill. Finally, after recording the Hun's defeat, Scala describes the results of the battle in terms of geographical movement, noting his source for these results.[131]

In conclusion, Scala's achievement as an historian seems to have been consistently underrated. His is not, as Gervinus would have it, a book shamefully useless to any culture with political concerns.[132] It contains deep political interests, analyzed according to historical preconceptions quite similar to those which can be found in both Bruni's *Historiae Florentini populi* and Poggio's *Historia fiorentina*. Nor is Fueter justified in suggesting that the variety of material included in the narrative constitutes a regression to the medieval chronicles.[133] Scala selects his materials with less rigor than Bruni, to be sure, but he has a wider conception of Florentine history, one which includes the tangible aspects of the city. The *civitas* of which Scala writes is not only an abstraction but a concrete entity of walls, buildings, and persons.

In spite of these important qualities, it cannot be denied that the *Historia Florentinorum* is somewhat lacking in interest. Scala's history can, in fact, be charged with the same deficiencies that were found in Poggio's *Historia fiorentina*. The closer the humanist his-

---

131 "Et aliis quidem ex praelio a Tholosanis, ut scribit Antonius Sabellicus, campis rediisse in Galliam placet, aliis traduxisse copias in Dalmatiam et venisse demum in Pannoniam, illisque cum comparasset exercitum, de invadenda Italia cepisse consilium" (p. 26).

132 See chap. i at note 80.

133 Fueter, *Geschichte*, p. 25.

torians come to the representation of concrete events, the more apparent becomes their inability to portray this dimension of history forcefully. Scala, like Poggio and Bruni before him, seldom describes an event in such a way that an indelible impression is left in the reader's mind. The image of rotting corpses in the Arno, which precipitates the destruction of Florence by Totila, is an exception, for although Scala is more concerned with sensory data than his humanist predecessors, he seldom writes with such vividness. The delight in the senses for their own sake which characterizes so much of classical literature and which is even to be found in the vernacular chronicles is a quality to which the humanist historians seem quite insensitive, and, as the analytical concepts of these writers come more and more to be expressed through tangible phenomena, this insensitivity becomes an increasingly serious obstacle to the creation of moving, effective, and truly didactic history.

Epilogue

I shall conclude with some general observations suggested by these researches. While the complexities of Florentine political life make it unwise to relate politics to trends in historiography, the foregoing chapters clearly reveal that intellectuals throughout the Quattrocento share certain basic conceptions of political reality. The group of ideas and attitudes which Hans Baron has identified as civic humanism — the rational analysis of politics, the concern for moral and spiritual vigor, the republican commitment — can neither be dismissed as shallow rhetoric nor understood as a temporary response to a fleeting danger. These attitudes permeate the life work of Leonardo Bruni. For Poggio and Scala they provide an analytical structure capable of presenting both nonpsychological dimensions of history and nonrepublican political commitments.

In fact, the very survival of civic humanism during the Quattrocento suggests that perhaps the analytical side of Machiavelli's contribution has been overemphasized. A close reading of his account of Walter of Brienne in the *Istorie fiorentine*, for instance, shows clearly that his basic interpretation is taken directly from Bruni's *Historiae*. The difference between Machiavelli and Bruni in this example is not analytical but rhetorical. Machiavelli successfully incorporates sensory elements and provides a more convincing picture of the event, while Bruni's account is wholly devoid of references to sensory objects. If this difference obtains throughout Machiavelli's history, then his true accomplishment takes on a somewhat different complexion, especially in view of Scala's failure to develop an effective appeal to the senses.

At least insofar as the writing of history is concerned, the place of rhetoric in Renaissance humanism is one that merits respect. Rhetoric cannot be equated with frivolous decoration and meaningless ornament. All the major rhetorical techniques of these historians are adopted in response to basic conceptual problems, and they help the historians to present new perceptions of historical reality and new areas of moral sensitivity.

If the rhetorical and intellectual sides of humanist historiography cannot be easily separated, neither can facile generalizations be safely made about the humanists' use of their classical models. Sometimes, to be sure, fifteenth-century scholars are little more than slavish imitators of the Romans — humanist historical theory being a case in point. But Bruni's causal analyses certainly represent an imaginative blending of classical — chiefly Polybian — ideas with contemporary ways of thinking. On another level of imitation, his development of the annalistic form shows his capacity to transform a classical mode into one which serves his own purposes.

Rhetorical history has been revealed in this study to be a valid form of historical writing. "Wie es eigentlich gewesen" is not the only premise on which an honest and compelling representation of the past can be based. The inculcation of moral and spiritual values, the elegant inspiration of the reader to right conduct, these goals do not preclude among Quattrocento historians an historical tradition of lasting value as well as immediate impact.

Appendixes   Bibliography   Index

Appendix A

Dating of Poggio's *Historia fiorentina*

There has never been much dispute about the dating of the *Historia fiorentina*. Poggio began the work after he became first chancellor in 1453 and worked on it mainly after he had gone into semiretirement in 1457. P. Christoni, "Del tempo in cui P. Bracciolini scrisse le storie fiorentine," *Studi storici*, 6 (1897), 117–122, has devoted an unnecessary amount of space to internal evidence which ultimately proves irrelevant. The most nearly conclusive indication of the date of composition is found in the dedicatory letter of Poggio's son, who says that his father wrote the history after returning to Florence to accept the chancellorship: "Poggius enim ingravescente aetate tanquam emeritis impetrata in patriam revertisset, ut memoriae tantae urbis consuleret, inter privata, publicaeque negotia, commentaria rerum Florentinarum a primo bello cum Johanne Mediolanensi Archiepiscope, usque ad pacem cum Alphonso per Nicolaum Pontificem factam morte praeventus reliquit" (*Historia fiorentina*, ed. G. Recanati, vol. XX, *RR.II.SS.*, ed. Muratori [1731], col. 192; hereafter Poggio, *Historia*). This statement establishes that Poggio began the work while still active in the chancery and that he was unable to bring it to completion. Since he wrote both the *De miseria humanae conditionis* and his version of Lucan's *Asino* immediately after returning to Florence, the *terminus ante quem* of 1455 suggested by Christoni seems eminently reasonable, and the latest scholar to write on the subject has seen fit to accept this date (N. Rubinstein, "Poggio Bracciolini: Cancelliere e storico di Firenze," *Atti e Memorie dell'Accademia Petrarca di Lettere, Arte, e Scienze di Arezzo*, n.s., XXXVII [1965], 8).

The problem here is not one of dating. It is rather one of determining how much of the Recanati edition is in the form in which Poggio left it. The Latin text survives in only three manuscripts. The single illuminated copy of the Latin version is in the Biblioteca Marciana in Venice (cod. 288, 1. 216) and dates from the fifteenth century.

There are two sixteenth-century manuscripts, one in the Biblioteca Laurenziana in Florence (Plutarch 762, cod. 40), and another in the National Library at Naples (U.G. 35, cart. XV). A collation of the first books of both of these shows them to be substantially similar, differing only in minor respects, which can be explained as copying errors. The Venetian manuscript, from which Recanati made his edition, is the earliest; the Neapolitan manuscript seems to be a copy of it (in over 75 per cent of the cases where there are dissimilarities among the three examples, these two agree), and the Florentine manuscript appears to be a remoter copy. These texts all contain the dedicatory letter of Jacopo to Federigo da Montefeltro, translated into Latin. Since there is little external evidence specifying the extent to which Jacopo changed or added to the work left unfinished by his father, it is impossible to be assured in the matter, and there has been considerable dispute since the publication of the Latin version in 1715. Apostolo Zeno, *Dissertazione vossiane* (Venice, 1753), I, 40, says that Jacopo, in addition to dividing the work into books, completed his father's manuscript ("Le diede l'ultima mano"). More recent opinion has tended to de-emphasize the son's role. Christoni ("Del tempo," p. 122) says flatly that Jacopo did not finish his father's work but simply organized it into books and translated it. E. Walser (*Poggius*, p. 310) has no opinion at all. V. Rossi, *Il Quattrocento* (Milan, 1933), p. 172, echoes Zeno's opinion.

The only solid external evidence is Jacopo's statement in the dedicatory letter (*Historia*, col. 192): "Mihi vero . . . nihil fuit potius quam omnia in octo digesta libros." This seems clear enough, but one cannot completely ignore the possibility that Jacopo is playing down his role in the composition of the book in order to increase its stature. It does indeed seem strange that, if Poggio was interrupted in his task by death, he would have brought the account down exactly to the convenient stopping point of 1455. There is, however, no obvious external evidence in the work bespeaking another hand, and, although some books seem more sloppily constructed than others, there is no consistent shift in organizational principles. The issue is not without importance, for Jacopo was considerably more politically committed than his father — he lost his life through implication in the Pazzi conspiracy — and if there were a serious possibility that he wrote any substantial portion of the *Historia*, one would have to discount its political ideas. However, given the complete lack of positive evidence, one is, I think, quite justified in considering the whole work to be Poggio's.

Appendix B

Dating of Scala's *Historia Florentinorum*

Nicolai Rubinstein, "Bartolomeo Scala's Historia Florentinorum," in *Studi di bibliografia e di storia in onore di Tammaro de Marinis* (Verona: Stamperia Valdonega, 1964), IV, 49–59, suggests that Scala worked on the history mainly during the period after the expulsion of the Medici in 1494, when he himself was temporarily deprived of office.

Rubinstein's evidence for dating the work during this period of Scala's life consists of, first, a thinly veiled reference to the invasion of Charles VIII and, second, a theory of the founding of Florence put forward by Poliziano between 1492 and 1494 (see Rubinstein, pp. 49–50). However, some of Rubinstein's own evidence, as he readily admits, suggests an earlier date for the beginning of the work. In the first place, Poliziano mentions Scala's "longum opus et arduum" in a letter to Scala dated December 25, 1493 (Poliziano, *Opera* [Basel, 1553], p. 59; quoted by Rubinstein, p. 49). Since this letter was written well before the invasion of Charles VIII, Scala's references to the invasion cannot be used to show that he wrote the main body of the history after 1494. In the second place, Rubinstein himself has discovered a document from the archives of Pistoia showing that Scala was consulting the chronicle of Sozomeno, an important source for the *Historia Florentinorum*, as early as 1484.

There is also internal evidence to suggest that much of the work was already written when the Medici were driven out of Florence. In the first book Scala, discussing the history of Venice, digresses to stress its importance to his own day: "Indeque factam Venetiarum originem, quae nunc est inter primas Italiae urbes, et quidem tanta potentia ut audeat cum tota fere Italia gente jam decertare armis" (*Historia Florentinorum*, ed. J. Oligero [Rome, 1677], p. 27; this edition is reprinted in *Thesaurus antiquitatum Italiae*, ed. Graevius [Leyden, 1723], vol. VIII, part 1). This would seem to be a comment more relevant to the period following the Ferrarese war in the late 1480's than to the mid-90's. An even more conclusive piece of internal evidence is Scala's reference to the long struggle between Florence and Pisa. Speaking of the beginning of the first war between these cities, he says (*Historia*, p. 89), "Praetor erat urbis Odopetrus Gregorius et annus Christi millesimus ducentesimus et vigesimus secundus, cum primum Pisanis illata sunt Florentinorum arma, vertebatur, quae deinde supra modum supraque fidem utrumque populum ad finem usque libertatis alterius varia fortuna vexavere." Scala would hardly have spoken of Pisa's future loss of liberty in so sanguine a fashion had he known of Pisa's revolt in 1494.

This reference to Pisa occurs in the middle of Book III, while the reference to Venice is found in Book I. If it can be shown that such separated parts of the narrative were conceived before 1494, then the one reference to the French invasion can be considered a later interpolation rather than part of the original work. This interpretation is especially seductive because the reference to Charles occurs not in the narrative itself but in a preface. There is, however, no direct evidence to establish definitely the earlier composition of the work, and it is clear that Scala was working on all books during the period from 1494 until his death in 1497.

Rubinstein (see pp. 57–58) has closely studied the sources used by Scala. His principal source was Giovanni Villani, supplemented by the works of Bruni, Sozomeno, Flavio Biondo, Palmieri and Platina. He also explicitly used Dionysius of Halicarnassus and Plutarch as models in writing of the origins of Florence.

There is no recent biographical work on Scala. The latest book-length biography is D. Manni's *Bartholomaei Scalae Collensis vita* (Florence, 1768). See Rossi, *Il Quattrocento*, p. 401, n. 60, for a bibliography of more recent monographs on Scala.

Appendix C
Uses of the Word *Populus*

The word *populus* is used very seldom by Bruni to mean a general group of men. (It is used in this general sense on the following pages of the *Historiae*: vol. I, book iii, p. 310; II, vii, 346; III, x, 134; and III, xi, 256.) In the *Historiae* the term usually describes men organized into an active, decision-making body, and it contains intimations of many of the important themes associated with Bruni's civic humanism. Bruni, from the beginning of the work, attributes the activities of the commune to the "florentinus populus": "Haec permulta quidem et egregia mirabili felicitate una aestate a florentino populo gesta sunt" (I, ii, 174), and "Ita et foris et domi eo anno populi maiestas exaltata est" (I, ii, 176); the *populus* remains the basic agent in foreign policy throughout (see III, ix, 62, where certain castles outside the city express the desire to give themselves "florentino populo"; and III, x, 110, where the Milanese war "a florentino populo gestum est"). The decision-making function of the *populus* emerges unmistakably in the analysis of Florence's motive for not buying Lucca (II, vi, 224), and it is the *populus* which enters into alliance with other powers (I, iv, 502).

The *populus* is an organized body. Bruni speaks of nobles and plebs as opposing forces in the struggles leading to the creation of the *gonfaloniere*, but when he explains the organizational advantages of the reform for the nonnoble classes, the word *populus* is used: "Si populus una sentiret neminis iniuriam pateretur, privatim inflictas contumelias publice vindicaret" (I, ix, 418). The word is used similarly in connection with the earlier reform which establishes the Thirty-Six (I, ii, 270). The term carries strong connotations of liberty. It is the *populus* which seizes its freedom on the death of Frederick II (I, ii, 160), and the restoration of liberty is paired with the return of the *populus* to power in Pistoia when the historian describes Florence's intentions in attacking the city: "Populumque ac libertatem in ea quoque urbe asserere constituit" (I, ii, 162). The *populus*, in search of its liberty, establishes the Ordinances of Justice (I, iv, 430). Finally, in describing the diplomatic methods of a *populus* Bruni clearly opposes them to those of a tyrant: "Venenis autem et proditionibus uti tirannorum esse, non populorum" (III, ix, 100).

Not only is the *populus* by definition free, but, since the term almost always defines a Florentine body, it tends to be Guelf. Bruni speaks of the "florentinus populus" in opposition to the imperial faction in Tuscany: "Ex hoc iam florentinus populus adversam imperio factionem palam adsciscere visus est, et ad favorem eius plane respicere" (I, ii, 164). Villani uses the term *popolo* in this instance to refer to the elements of the population which support the Guelf leaders (*Crònica*, VI, 43). It is the *populus* which restores the Guelf faction to Arezzo, and the bishop of that city is called "homo diversarium partium et aretini populi inimicus" (I, iii, 382). Many of Bruni's concrete political concerns are expressed, then, in this term, which he uses to describe the scope of the *Historiae*.

Bruni is not, of course, alone in giving these connotations to the term *populus*. Giangaleazzo, for one, forbade the use of the word *popolo* within his dominions as a means of asserting his lordship (see D. Hay, *The Italian Renaissance in its Historical Background* [Cambridge, Eng., 1961], p. 105).

Selected Bibliography

SOURCES CONSULTED

Accolti, B. *De praestantia virorum sui aevi*, in P. *Villani, Liber de civitatis Florentiae famosis civibus*. Florence, 1847.

Ammirato, S. *Istorie fiorentine.* 11 vols. Florence, 1846–1849.

Biondo, F. *Ab inclinatione Romanorum imperii decades tres.* Venice, 1483.

Borghini, V. *Discorsi.* 4 vols. Milan, 1808–1809.

Bracciolini, P. *Epistolae.* Vol. III of *Opera omnia*, ed. Tonelli. Florence, 1832. Reprinted in *Monumenta politica et philosophica rariora*, ed. L. Firpo. Turin: Bottega d'Erasmo, 1964.

—— *Historia fiorentina*, ed. G. Recanati. Venice, 1715.

—— *Historia fiorentina*, ed. G. Recanati. Vol. XX of *Rerum Italicarum Scriptores*, ed. L. Muratori. Milan, 1731.

—— *Istoria fiorentina*, trans. J. Bracciolini. Venice, 1476.

Bruni, L. *Historiarum Florentini populi libri XII.* Vol. XIX, part 3, of *Rerum Italicarum Scriptores*, ed. E. Santini. Città di Castello: Casa editrice S. Lapi, 1934.

—— *Istoria fiorentina*, trans. D. Acciaiuoli. Venice, 1476.

—— *Istoria fiorentina di L. Aretino tradotta in volgare da D. Acciaiuoli*, ed. G. Mancini et al. 3 vols. Florence: Le Monnier, 1855–1860.

—— *Leonardo Bruni Arretini: Epistolarum libri VIII*, ed. L. Mehus. Florence, 1741.

Bruto, G. *De historia laudibus.* Cracow, 1589.

Buoninsegni, D. *Historia fiorentina.* Florence, 1581.

Capponi, N. *Commentari della guerra o dell'acquisto di Pisa.* Vol. XVIII of *Rerum Italicarum Scriptores*, ed. L. Muratori. Milan, 1731.

Cavalcanti, G. *Istorie fiorentine.* Florence, 1838.

Compagni, D. *Crònica.* Vol. IX, part 2, of *Rerum Italicarum Scriptores*, ed. I. del Lungo. Città di Castello: Casa editrice S. Lapi, 1913.

Cortesi, P. *De hominibus doctis*, in P. *Villani, Liber de civitatis Florentiae famosis civibus*. Florence, 1847.

Dati, G. *Istoria di Firenze.* Florence, 1735.

Fazio, B. *De rebus gestis ab Alphonso primo.* Lyons, 1560.

Ficino, M. *Opera.* Basel, n.d.

Fontius, B. *Carmina*, ed. I. Fogel and L. Juhász. Leipzig: B. G. Teubner, 1932.

Giovio, P. *Gli elogi*, trans. L. Domenichi. Florence, 1554.

―――― *Historiarum sui temporis.* Rome: Istituto poligrafico dello stato, 1957.

Landino, C. *Carmina omnia,* ed. A. Perosa. Florence: L. S. Olschki, 1939.

Livy, T. *Ab urbe condita,* trans. B. Foster, F. Moore, et al. 14 vols. Loeb Classical Library. Cambridge, Mass., and London: Harvard University Press, 1925–1951.

Machiavelli, N. *History of Florence,* trans. F. Gilbert. New York: Harper and Row, 1960.

―――― *Opere,* ed. F. Flora and C. Cordié. (The *Istorie fiorentine* are in vol. II.) 2 vols. Milan: Mondadori, 1960.

Malespini, R. *Istoria fiorentina.* Florence, 1718.

Morelli, G. *Ricordi,* ed. V. Branca. Florence: Le Monnier, 1956.

Muratori, L., ed. *Rerum Italicarum scriptores ab anno christi 500–1500.* 25 vols. Milan, 1723–1751.

Naldi, N. *Vita Janotii Manetti.* Vol. XX of *Rerum Italicarum Scriptores,* ed. L. Muratori. Milan, 1731.

Nerli, F. *Commentari dei fatti civili occorsi dentro la città di Firenze dall'anno 1215 al 1537.* Trieste, 1859.

Orosius, P. *Historiarum adversum Paganos libri VII,* in *Corpus Scriptorum eccleseasticorum latinorum.* Vienna, 1882.

Palmieri, M. *Annales.* Vol. XXVI, part 1, of *Rerum Italicarum Scriptores,* ed. G. Scaramella. Città di Castello: Casa editrice S. Lapi, 1906.

―――― *De captivitate Pisarum liber.* Vol. IX, part 1, of *Rerum Italicarum Scriptores,* ed. G. Scaramella. Città di Castello: Casa editrice S. Lapi, 1904.

Patrizzi, F. *Della historia diece dialoghi.* Venice, 1560.

Pitti, B. *Crònica.* Florence, 1720.

Poliziano, A. *Angeli Politiani et aliorum virorum illustrium epistolarum libri XII.* Hanover, 1612.

―――― *Opera.* Basel, 1553.

Polybius. *The Histories,* trans. W. Paton. 6 vols. Loeb Classical Library. Cambridge, Mass., and London: Harvard University Press, 1922–1927.

Pontano, G. *I dialoghi,* ed. C. Previtera. Florence: Sansoni, 1943.

Rerum Italicarum Scriptores. See Bracciolini, Bruni, Capponi, Compagni, Muratori, Naldi, Palmieri, Sozomenus, Stefani.

Sallust. *Bellum Catilinae,* trans. J. Rolfe. Loeb Classical Library. Cambridge, Mass., and London: Harvard University Press, 1931.

―――― *Bellum Jugurthinum,* trans. J. Rolfe. Loeb Classical Library. Cambridge, Mass., and London: Harvard University Press, 1931.

Sannazaro, J. *Opera omnia.* Frankfurt, 1709.

Scala, B. *Historia Florentinorum,* ed. J. Oligero. Rome, 1677.

Sercambi, G. *Chroniche.* Vols. XIX–XXI of *Fonti per la storia d'Italia,* ed. S. Bonghi. Lucca, 1892.

Sozomenus. *Chronicon universale.* Vol. XVI, part 1, of *Rerum Italicarum Scriptores,* ed. G. Zaccagnuri. Città di Castello: Casa editrice S. Lapi, 1907–1908.

Speroni, S. *Dialoghi.* Venice, 1548.

Stefani, Marchionne di Coppo. *Crònica fiorentina.* Vol. XXX, part 1, of *Rerum Italicarum Scriptores,* ed. N. Rodolico. Città di Castello: Casa editrice S. Lapi, 1903.

Tacitus, C. *Ab excessu Divi Augusti annales,* trans. J. Jackson. 3 vols. Loeb

Classical Library. Cambridge, Mass., and London: Harvard University Press, 1931.
—— *Historiarum libri*, trans. C. Moore. 2 vols. Loeb Classical Library. Cambridge, Mass., and London: Harvard University Press, 1925.
Valla, L. *In Poggium Florentinum antidoti libri quatuor*. Cologne, 1527.
—— *Opera*. Basel, 1543.
Verino, U. *De illustratione urbis Florentiae*. Paris, 1583.
Vespasiano da Bisticci. *Vite di uomini illustri*. Milan: U. Hoepli, 1951.
Villani, G. *Cronica*. 4 vols. Florence, 1846.
Villani, M. *Cronica*. 2 vols. Florence, 1846.

SECONDARY WORKS CONSULTED

Anderson, W. "Livy and Machiavelli," *Classical Journal*, 53 (1957–58), 232–235.
Bacci, D. *Cenni biografici e religiosi di Poggio Bracciolini*. Florence: Enrico Ariani, 1963.
—— *Poggio Bracciolini nella luce dei suoi tempi*. Florence, 1959.
Baldwin, C. *Renaissance Literary Theory and Practice*, ed. D. Clark. New York: Columbia University Press, 1939.
Barnes, H. *A History of Historical Writing*. Norman, Okla.: University of Oklahoma Press, 1937.
Baron, H. "Cicero and the Roman Civic Spirit in the Middle Ages and the Early Renaissance," *Bulletin of the John Rylands Library*, 22 (1938), 73–97.
—— *The Crisis of the Early Italian Renaissance*. 2 vols. Princeton: Princeton University Press, 1955 (2nd ed., 1966).
—— "Das Erwachen des Historischen Denkens in Humanismus des Quattrocento," *Historische Zeitschrift*, 147 (1932), 5–21.
—— *Humanistic and Political Literature in Florence and Venice at the Beginning of the Quattrocento*. Cambridge, Mass.: Harvard University Press, 1955.
—— *Leonardo Bruni Aretino: Humanistisch-Philosophische Schriften*. Leipzig: B. G. Teubner, 1928.
—— "Leonardo Bruni: 'Professional Rhetorician' or 'Civic Humanist'?" *Past and Present*, 36 (1967), 21–37.
—— "La rinascita statale romana nell'umanesimo fiorentino del Quattrocento," *Civiltà moderna*, 7 (1935), 21–49.
—— "Lo sfondo storico del Rinascimento fiorentino," *La Rinascita*, 1 (1938), 50–73.
—— "The Social Background of Political Liberty in the Early Italian Renaissance," *Comparative Studies in Society and History*, 2 (1959–60), 440–451.
Baudi di Vesme, C. *Brevi considerazioni sulla storiografia fiorentina e sul pensiero politico nel XV secolo*. Turin: 1953.
Bayley, C. *War and Society in Renaissance Florence*. Toronto: Toronto University Press, 1961.
Beck, F. *Studien zu Leonardo Bruni*. Berlin: Rothschild, 1912.
Benvenuti, G. *Quadri storici fiorentini*. Florence, 1889.
Bertalot, L. "Forschungen über Leonardo Bruni Aretino," *Archivum Romanicum*, 15 (1931), 284–323.
—— "Zur Bibliographie der Übersetzungen des Leonardus Brunus Are-

tinus," *Quellen und Forschungen aus Italienischen Archiven und Bibliotheken*, 27 (1936), 178–195.

———— "Zur Bibliographie des Leonardus Brunus Aretinus," *Quellen und Forschungen aus Italienischen Archiven und Bibliotheken*, 28 (1937), 268–285.

Bezold, F. von. *Aus Mittelalter und Renaissance*. Berlin: R. Oldenbourg, 1918.

Billanovitch, G. "Gli umanisti e le cronache medioevale," *Italia Medioevale e Umanistica*, 1 (1958), 103–138.

Bolgar, R. *The Classical Heritage and its Beneficiaries*. Cambridge, Eng.: Cambridge University Press, 1954.

Brandi, K. *Geschichte der Geschichtswissenschaft*. Bonn: Universitäts Verlag, 1952.

Brown, J. *The 'Methodus ad facilem historiarum cognitionem' of Jean Bodin*. Washington: The Catholic University of America Press, 1939.

Buck, A. *Das Geschichtsdenken der Renaissance*. Vol. IX of *Schriften und Vorträge des Petrarca-Instituts* (Köln). Krefeld: Scherpe-Verlag, 1957.

Burckhardt, J. *The Civilization of the Renaissance in Italy*, trans. S. Middlemore. London: Phaedon Press, 1960.

Capodimonte, C. di. "Poggio Bracciolini autore delle anonime 'Vitae quorundam pontificum,' " *Rivista di storia della chiesa in Italia*, 14 (1960), 27–47.

Capponi, G. *Storia della repubblica di Firenze*. 2 vols. Florence, 1875.

Carbonara, C. *Il secolo XV*. Milan: Fratelli Bocca, 1943.

Chabod, F. "La concezione del mondo di Giovanni Villani," *Nuova rivista storica*, 13 (1929), 336–390.

Christoni, P. "Del tempo in cui P. Bracciolini scrisse le storie fiorentine," *Studi storici*, 6 (1897), 117–122.

Clark, A. "The Literary Discoveries of Poggio," *The Classical Review*, 13 (1899), 119–130.

Clark, D. *Rhetoric and Poetry in the Renaissance*. New York: Columbia University Press, 1952.

Cochrane, E. *Tradition and Enlightenment in the Tuscan Academies: 1690–1800*. Chicago: University of Chicago Press, 1961.

Croce, B. *Teoria e storia della storiografia*. 4th ed. Bari: G. Laterza e figli, 1941.

D'alton, J. *Roman Literary Theory and Criticism*. New York: Russell and Russell, 1962.

Davidsohn, R. *Geschichte von Florence*. 4 vols. Berlin: E. S. Mittler, 1896–1927.

Dini, L. "Bartolommeo Scala," *Miscellanea storica della Valdelsa*, 4 (1896), 60–63.

Ferguson, W. "Interpretation of Italian Humanism: The Contribution of Hans Baron," *Journal of the History of Ideas*, 19 (1958), 14–25.

———— *The Renaissance in Historical Thought*. Boston: Houghton Mifflin, 1948.

Flamini, F. *La lirica toscana del Rinascimento*. Pisa, 1891.

Freudenthal, J. "Leonardo Bruni als Philosoph," *Neue Jahrbücher für das klassiche Altertum*, 27 (1911), 48–66.

Fueter, E. *Geschichte der neueren Historiographie.* Munich and Berlin: R. Oldenbourg, 1911.

Garin, E. "L'ambiente di Poliziano," in *Il Poliziano e il suo tempo.* Atti del IV convegno internazionale di studi sul Rinascimento. Florence: Sansoni, 1954.

—— "I cancellieri umanisti della repubblica fiorentina da Coluccio Salutati a Bartolommeo Scala," *Rivista storica italiana,* 71 (1959), 185–208.

—— *Medioevo e Rinascimento.* Bari: Laterza, 1961.

—— Review of F. Simone's *La coscenza della Rinascita negli umanisti francesi,* in *Rinascimento,* 1 (1950), 93–94.

Gaspary, A. *Geschichte der italienischen Literatur.* 2 vols. Strassburg: K. J. Trübner, 1888.

Gentile, G. *Studi sul Rinascimento.* Florence: Vallechi, 1923.

Gentile, L. "Bartolommeo Scala e i Medici," *Miscellanea storica della Valdelsa,* 10 (1903), 129–138.

Gervinus, G. *Geschichte der Florentinischer Historiografie bis zum sechzehnten Jahrhundert.* Frankfurt, 1833.

Gherardi, A. "Alcune notizie intorno a Leonardo Aretino e alle sue Storie fiorentine," *Archivio storico italiano,* ser. IV, vol. 15 (1885), pp. 416–421.

Gilbert, F. *Machiavelli and Guicciardini.* Princeton: Princeton University Press, 1965.

Gilmore, M. *Humanists and Jurists.* Cambridge, Mass.: Harvard University Press, 1963.

Gmelin, H. "Das Prinzip der Imitatio in den romanischen Literaturen der Renaissance," *Romanische Forschungen* 46 (1932), 83–360.

Gombrich, E. "The Early Medici as Patrons of Art," in *Italian Renaissance Studies,* ed. E. Jacob. London: Faber, 1960.

Gray, H. "History and Rhetoric in Quattrocento Humanism," unpub. diss. Harvard University, 1956.

—— "Renaissance Humanism: the Pursuit of Eloquence," *Journal of the History of Ideas,* 24 (1963), 497–514.

Gundesheimer, W. "The Opportunistic Humanism of Louis le Roy," *Journal of the History of Ideas,* 8 (1964), 324–339.

Gutkind, C. "Poggio Bracciolinis geistige Entwicklung," *Deutsche Vierteljahrschrift,* 10 (1932), 548–597.

Hay, D. "Flavio Biondo and the Middle Ages," *Proceedings of the British Academy* (1959), 97–128.

Hexter, J. H. "Seyssel, Machiavelli, and Polybius VI: The Mystery of the Missing Translation," *Studies in the Renaissance,* 3 (1956), 75–96.

Joachimsen, P. *Geschichtsauffassung und Geschichtschreibung in Deutschland unter dem Einfluss des Humanismus.* Berlin: B. G. Teubner, 1910.

Kaegi, W. *Cronica Mundi: Grundformen der Geschichtschreibung seit dem Mittelalter.* Einsiedeln: Johannes Verlag, 1954.

Kirn, P. *Das Bild des Menschen in der Geschichtschreibung von Polybius bis Ranke.* Göttingen: Vandenhoeck and Ruprecht, 1955.

Kirner, G. *Della Laudatio urbis Florentinae di Leonardo Bruni.* Livorno, 1889.

Kristeller, P. *The Classics and Renaissance Thought.* Cambridge, Mass.: Harvard University Press, 1955.

——— *Studies in Renaissance Thought and Letters*. Rome: Edizioni di storia e letteratura, 1956.

Lami, G. *Lezioni di antichità toscane*. Florence, 1766.

Lamprecht, F. *Zur Theorie der humanistischen Geschichtschreibung*. Zurich: Artemis-Verlag, 1950.

Lazzari, A. *Ugolino e Michele Verino*. Turin, 1897.

Lehnerdt, M. "Zu den Briefen des Leonardo Bruni von Arezzo," *Zeitschrift für Vergleichende Litteraturgeschichte*, 5 (1892), 459–466.

Leyden, W. von. "Antiquity and Authority: A Paradox in the Renaissance Theory of History," *Journal of the History of Ideas*, 19 (1958), 473–492.

Luiso, F. *Commento a una lettera di Leonardo Bruni e cronologia di alcune sue opere*. Florence, 1900.

Manni, D. *Bartholomaei Scalae Collensis vita*. Florence, 1768.

——— *Metodo per istudiare la storia di Firenze*. Florence, 1755.

Mariani, M. "La favola di Roma nell'ambiente fiorentina dei secoli XIII–XV," *Archivio della società romana di storia patria*, 81 (1958), 1–54.

Martines, L. *The Social World of Florentine Humanists: 1390–1460*. Princeton: Princeton University Press, 1963.

Marzi, D. *La cancelleria della repubblica fiorentina*. San Casciano: L. Capelli, 1910.

Marzini, R. "Bartolommeo Scala da Colle di Val d'Elsa," *Miscellanea Storica della Valdelsa*, 32 (1924), 56–62.

Masai, F. *Pléthon et le Platonisme de Mistra*. Paris: Les Belles Lettres, 1956.

Mazzuchelli, G. *Gli scrittori d'Italia*. 2 vols. Brescia, 1753–1763.

McKeon, R. "Rhetoric in the Middle Ages," *Speculum*, 17 (1942), 1–32.

Medin, A. "Documenti su Poggio Bracciolini," *Giornale storico della letteratura italiana*, 12 (1888), 351–367.

Mehl, E. *Die Weltanschauung des Giovanni Villani*. Leipzig: B. G. Teubner, 1927.

Monteleone, G. *Di Leonardo Bruni e delle sue opere studio*. Sora, 1901.

Moreni, D. *Bibliografia storico-ragionata della Toscana*. Florence, 1805.

Morghen, R. "La storiografia fiorentina del Trecento: Ricordano Malespini, Dino Compagni e Giovanni Villani," in *Libera cattedra di storia della civiltà fiorentina*. Florence: Sansoni, 1958.

Negri, P. *Istoria degli scrittori fiorentini*. Ferrara, 1722.

Niceron, J. *Memoires pour servir à l'histoire des hommes illustres*. 42 vols. Paris, 1729–1745.

Nisard, C. *Les gladiateurs de la république des lettres*. Paris, 1860.

Parronchi, A. "The Language of Humanism and of Sculpture," *Journal of the Warburg and Courtauld Institutes*, 27 (1964), 108–136.

Pesenti, G. "Notizie bibliografiche su B. Scala," *Giornale storico della letteratura italiana*, 85 (1925), 264–266.

Petrocchi, G. *La prosa narrativa nel Quattrocento*. Messina: Editrice universitaria, 1958.

Polidori, F. "Due vite di Filippo Scolari," *Archivio storico italiano*, 4 (1843), 151–232.

Radetti, G. "Le origini dell'umanesimo fiorentino nel Quattrocento," *Giornale critico della filosofia italiano*, 38 (1959), 98–122.

Ramat, R. "Classicismo delle 'Istorie fiorentine,'" *Nuova antologia*, 460 (1954), 315–324.

——— *Per la storia dello stile rinascimentale*. Messina: G. d'Anna, 1953.

Recanati, G. *Osservazioni critiche ed apologetiche sopra il libro del sig. Jacopo L'enfant intitolato Poggiana*. Venice, 1721.

Reynolds, B. "Bruni and Perotti Present a Greek Historian," *Bibliothèque d'humanisme et Renaissance*, 16 (1954), 108–118.

——— "Latin Historiography: A Survey, 1400–1600," *Studies in the Renaissance*, 2 (1955), 7–66.

——— "Shifting Currents in Historical Criticism," *Journal of the History of Ideas*, 14 (1953), 471–492.

Roedel, R. "Poggio Bracciolini nel quinto centenario della morte," *Rinascimento*, 11 (1960), 51–68.

Romano, G. *Degli studi sul Medioevo nella storiografia del Rinascimento in Italia*. Pavia, 1892.

Rossi, V. *Il Quattrocento*. Milan: Vallardi, 1933.

Rubinstein, N. "Bartolomeo Scala's Historia Florentinorum," in *Studi di bibliografia e di storia in onore di Tammaro de Marinis*. Verona: Stamperia Valdonega, 1964. IV, 49–59.

——— "The Beginnings of Political Thought in Florence," *Journal of the Warburg and Courtauld Institutes*, 5 (1942), 198–227.

——— "Poggio Bracciolini: Cancelliere e storico di Firenze," *Atti e memorie dell'accademia petrarca di lettere, arti, e scienze di Arezzo*, n.s., vol. XXXVII (1965).

Sabbadini, R. "Bartolommeo della Scala," *Giornale storico della letteratura italiana*, 50 (1907), 34–72.

——— *Il metodo degli umanisti*. Florence: Le Monnier, 1920.

——— "Notizie sulla vita e gli scritti di alcuni dotti umanisti del secolo XV," *Giornale storico della letteratura italiana*, 5 (1885), 148–179.

——— *Storia del ciceronianismo*. Turin, 1885.

——— *Studi sul Panormita e sul Valla*. Florence, 1891.

Saitta, G. *L'educazione dell'umanesimo in Italia*. Venice: La Nuova Italia, 1928.

——— *Il pensiero italiano nell'umanesimo e nel Rinascimento*. 3 vols. Bologna: C. Zuffi, 1949–1951.

Salvemini, G. *Magnati e popolani in Firenze dal 1280–1295*. Florence, 1899.

Santini, E. *Firenze e i suoi oratori nel Quattrocento*. Milan: Sandron, 1922.

——— "La fortuna della storia fiorentina di Leonardo Bruni nel Rinascimento," *Studi Storici*, 20 (1911).

——— *Leonardo Bruni Aretino e i suoi "Historiarum Florentini populi libri xii."* Pisa: Nistri, 1910.

——— "La produzione volgare di Leonardo Bruni Aretino e il suo culto per 'le tre corone fiorentine,'" *Giornale storico della letteratura italiana*, 60 (1912), 289–339.

——— "La protestatio de justitia nella Firenze medicea del secolo XV," *Rinascimento*, 10 (1959), 33–106.

Scaglione, A. "The Humanist as Scholar and Politian's Conception of the Grammaticus," *Studies in the Renaissance*, 8 (1961), 49–70.

Schmeidler, B. *Italienische Geschichtschreiber des XII und XIII Jahrhunderts*. Leipzig: Quelle und Meyer, 1909.

Sciacca, G. "La storia in Salutati," *Annali della facoltà di lettere e filosofia della università degli studi di Palermo*, I (1950).

Seigel, J. "'Civic Humanism' or Ciceronian Rhetoric? The Culture of Petrarch and Bruni," *Past and Present*, 34 (1966), 3–48.

Serie di ritratti d'uomini illustri toscani. Florence, 1776.

Spongano, R. *Un capitolo di storia della nostra prosa d'arte.* Florence: Sansoni, 1941.

Stevens, L. "Humanistic Education and the Hierarchy of Values in the Renaissance," in *Renaissance Papers* (1955).

Syme, R. *Sallust.* Berkeley: University of California Press, 1964.

―――― *Tacitus.* Oxford: Oxford University Press, 1958.

Symonds, J. A. *The Renaissance in Italy,* vol. I, *The Age of Despots.* New York: G. P. Putnam's Sons, 1960.

Tieghen, P. van. "La litterature latine de la Renaissance," *Bibliothèque d'humanisme et Renaissance,* 4 (1944), 177–419.

Toffanin, G. *Machiavelli e il tacitismo.* Padua: A. Draghi, 1921.

Tommasini, O. *La vita e gli scritti di Niccolò Machiavelli.* 2 vols. Rome: E. Loescher, 1911.

Torre, A. della. *Storia dell'Accademia platonica.* Florence: Carnesecchi, 1902.

Trinkaus, C. "A Humanist's Image of Humanism: The Inaugural Oration of Bartolommeo delle Fonte," *Studies in the Renaissance,* 7 (1960), 90–148.

Ullman, B. "Leonardo Bruni and Humanistic Historiography," *Medievalia et Humanistica,* 4 (1946), 45–61.

Valeri, N. *La libertà e la pace.* Turin: Società Subalpina Editrice, 1942.

Vallese, G. "Retorica medievale e retorica umanistica," in *Delta,* n.s., 2 (1952), 39–58.

―――― "Umanisti e frati nella prima metà del '400: Poggio Bracciolini e il contra hypocritas," *Italica,* 23 (1946), 147–151.

Varese, C. *Storia e politica nella prosa del Quattrocento.* Turin: Einaudi, 1961.

Vasoli, C. *Storia e politica nel primo umanesimo fiorentino.* Genoa, 1955.

Venturi, A. *Le orazioni nelle istorie fiorentine di Giovanni Cavalcanti.* Pisa, 1896.

Villari, P. *Niccolò Machiavelli and His Times,* trans. L. Villari. 4 vols. London, 1883.

Voigt, G. *Il risorgimento dell'antichità classica,* trans. D. Valbusa. 2 vols. Florence, 1888–1890.

Vossius, G. *De historicis Latinis.* Lyons, 1651.

Walbank, F. *A Historical Commentary on Polybius.* Oxford: Clarendon Press, 1957.

Walser, E. *Gesammelte Studien zur Geistesgeschichte der Renaissance.* Basel: Benno Schwabe, 1932.

―――― *Poggius Florentinus: Leben und Werke.* Berlin: B. G. Teubner, 1914.

Walsh, P. *Livy: His Historical Aims and Methods.* Cambridge, Eng.: Cambridge University Press, 1961.

Weisinger, H. "Ideas of History during the Renaissance," *Journal of the History of Ideas,* 6 (1945), 417–435.

Weiss, R. "Leonardo Bruni Aretino and Early English Humanism," *Modern Language Review,* 36 (1941), 443–448.

―――― "Lineamenti per una storia degli studi antiquari in Italia," *Rinascimento,* 9 (1958), 141–203.

Whitfield, J. "Machiavelli and Castruccio," *Italian Studies,* 8 (1953), 1–28.

Zeno, A. *Dissertazione Vossiane.* 2 vols. Venice, 1753.

Index

Harvard Historical Studies